For Martin,
with best wishes of friendship,
on the common path
of discovery & joy

Michael Krohnen

Ojai, Feb. 2012

MICHAEL KROHNEN

# The Kitchen Chronicles:

# 1001 Lunches with J. Krishnamurti

EDWIN HOUSE PUBLISHING, OJAI, CALIFORNIA
1997

THE KITCHEN CHRONICLES:
1001 LUNCHES WITH J. KRISHNAMURTI
By Michael Krohnen
Copyright © 1997 by Michael Krohnen

Published by Edwin House Publishing, Inc.
P.O. Box 128, Ojai, California 93024

Designed by Karen Davidson Design
Illustrated by Jennifer Rinaldi
Printed by Tien Wah Press, Singapore
ISBN 0-9649247-1-4
Library of Congress Catalogue Card Number 96-86243

"*Anna dathu*

*sukhi bhava*"

*(May he who gives food be happy)*

– Indian blessing before and after meals

# ACKNOWLEDGMENTS

ALTHOUGH WRITING IS A SOLITARY ACTIVITY, MATCHING THE author and his thoughts with the blank page or screen, it yet involves the cooperation of many people before, during and after publication. As far as this work is concerned, I am deeply indebted to many friends for their kind help and encouragement over the years. And I hope that I may be forgiven if I only mention a few by name.

I must start out by thanking my mother, whose unwavering support was inestimable. Unfortunately, she did not live to see the conclusion of this book but died at the age of 89 in July 1995.

Especially heartfelt thanks also to Mary Zimbalist, who carefully and patiently listened to my readings from the first and second draft manuscripts. She not only encouraged me but also offered great help in getting facts straight and the tone right.

Great thanks to Katherine Han for being a generous and hospitable friend and for sharing the sense of the importance of this work.

It is hard to put into words the help and generosity I received from Friedrich Grohe. It would have been difficult for me to bring the book to a conclusion without his steadfast friendship and inspiration, and his enduring encouragement.

I also would like to thank David Moody and his wife Vivienne for their friendship. Since he was in effect my first reader and editor, offering honest and invaluable advice about all aspects of the work in progress, I cannot think of the book ever having found its final form without his perceptive comments.

Similarly, I am indebted to Ray McCoy who carefully pointed out numerous mistakes and made excellent suggestions in regard to structural changes. I deeply appreciate his friendship, which helped in more ways than one.

My gratitude also goes to Tom Heggestad for his indomitable willingness to lend a helping hand at moments of electronic distress and for his great patience with a computer illiterate friend.

In addition, I would like to express my thanks to Alan and Helen Hooker for ten and more years of cooperation and friendship of the rarest kind, which is at the heart of the endeavor to report about so many luncheons.

Special thanks to Mark, Asha, and Nandini Lee, not only for their help at a crucial moment but also for a lasting relationship of affection and understanding.

It's quite extraordinary to have an editor who is not only skillful and understanding but who also *feels*: my deep appreciation to Stephen and Wendy Smith.

I would not like to neglect mentioning my grateful appreciation for the assistance and friendship of Nikos and Stefania Pilavios, Juan and Maria-Angels Colell, Byron and Alida Allison, Ivan Berkovics, Doug Evans, Sara Cloud, Francis McCann, and Ben Kelley.

And to Rita Zampese I would like to say thanks for the wonderful photos and for kindly letting us use them in this book.

Last but not least, my love and gratitude to Rachel Fernandes.

–Michael Krohnen
Ojai, California, April 1996

# CONTENTS

# DISCLAIMER

THE DIALOGUES WHICH I PRESENT IN THE FOLLOWING PAGES are not, for the most part, verbatim reports of Krishnamurti, even though they seek to represent his thinking. They are predominantly narrative reconstructions based on my recollections and notes from the period described—except for brief quotations from his talks.

Similarly, I have used some poetic license in seeking to recreate the mood and the sense of being in the presence of a great revolutionary thinker and teacher. I wrote the following account because I had seen something of rare and astonishing beauty that I naturally wanted to share with others. I also felt that it was important to bear witness to a life—that of J. Krishnamurti—which has been of vital significance in the course and history of human consciousness. Besides, both friends and strangers have been asking me on many occasions what it had been like to live and work with someone like Krishnamurti. Now, at last, I'm able to provide them with an answer to their questions which I hope will be comprehensive.

Finally, it was also for my own benefit that I gathered my notes and recollections and arranged them in something resembling chronological order. It has helped me gain a clearer perception of a most significant period in my life, the liberating action of which has not ceased to profoundly affect my day-to-day living.

And, although at heart this is a highly subjective account of my impressions of, and interaction with, J. Krishnamurti, the chronology given and the events described are entirely authentic and factual.

—Michael Krohnen

# AUTHOR'S PROLOGUE

FOR FOUR LONG YEARS THE WAR HAD BEEN RAGING around the globe and the tide was gradually beginning to turn against the aggressors when I was born in Arnstein, a small town near Frankfurt/Main in Germany, in the fall of 1943.

Growing up in the aftermath of the war, nature and its beauty assumed a deep meaning for me. Fields of tall golden grass dancing in the sunlight, white clouds across the blue sky, the wind in the trees, and the brilliant stars at night were like discoveries of another, more peaceful dimension, different from the world that man had created. As far back as I can remember, I harbored a burning curiosity for what lay beyond appearances, for ultimate causes, for the sacred. The biblical stories fascinated me, especially the Creation in Genesis. Unfortunately, the Roman Catholic priests were only too willing to inculcate my young, gullible mind with rituals, prayers and dogmas. Before long, I believed I wanted to become a missionary to save ignorant souls from hell.

But, thank God, sin intervened, and I started to experience the power of nature within me, with its accompanying questions and doubts. The female form, girls, suddenly became mysteriously enchanting and seductive. The pleasures and pains of my awakening sexual drive were strange forces that I could neither control nor understand. Traditional explanations didn't shed any light on the matter but only added more to my confusion, with their moral threats, fear and guilt.

At the more intellectual level, history was teaching me a lesson at the same time—the lesson of our recent collective past. It was strange to realize that I and my peers were the offspring of the generation that had embraced Adolf Hitler and his insane schemes. When I saw with my own eyes moving pictures of the horrors of the concentration camps, the shock and the tears penetrated my whole being. The once proud culture and society that I had been growing up in had done this, and my fellow countrymen had been at least silent accomplices. The shame and guilt I felt were inconsolable: pain for Auschwitz, Sobibor and Treblinka, sorrow for humankind that inflicted so much suffering upon itself.

The goals and ideals defined by society, by the culture, by religion were suddenly meaningless to me. Reading books, writing poetry, drawing pictures, playing flute, traveling to distant countries and discovering new cultures—these were activities that still held value for me.

Once I had earned my baccalaureate, I emigrated to 'the land of opportunity and golden dreams', which since childhood had fascinated me with its films, cartoons and Wild West tales. Settling in Southern California and attending college opened the door to a new life, simultaneously kindling my interest in the quest for truth. As I began to explore humanity's various religious expressions, I discovered Zen with its empty space landscapes and sudden awakenings. From Zen it was less than a step to the Buddha and his noble, liberating insights into the universality of suffering. He pointed to the other shore beyond the stream of craving and becoming.

More elusive was the concept of the Tao which, as soon as it was expressed or named, ceased to be the true Tao. Acting without effort, watching without judgment, being undivided from the flow of events was to be in harmony with the hidden law of the universe. The I Ching, the ancient, oracular Book of Changes, expressed the laws of constant change in simple linear symbols. By thus offering a key to decipher the code of heaven and earth, it pointed toward self-knowledge and right action.

From India came the Vedic and Upanishadic wisdom that the individual and the cosmic mind were one and the same. Realization of this fact was liberation from Maya, the universal veil of illusion.

As I went on reading and studying the texts of the human quest for the sacred—the Judaic tradition, the Sufis, the Pharaonic Egyptians, the Christian Mystics, and others—I was intrigued by the similarities between these different expressions. But I was also skeptical. They all appeared to be based on an original insight into the mystery of life, conveying it in the images and language of their respective historical time. Yet at the same time, something essential seemed to be missing. Perhaps it had to do with the passage of time, with the enormous gap of time that separated me, living in the twentieth century, from the Buddha, from Socrates, Pythagoras, Confucius and Meister Eckhardt. Even if in essence they were hinting at the same thing, each one of them had spoken at his own time, from his own cultural setting, in his own tongue, talking to human beings of *his* period. None of them knew anything about World Wars, concentration camps, or moon-landings, nor about telephones, airplanes, cars, television, computers, e-mail and the many other technological devices that define modern life and its enormous complexities.

One fateful morning in San Diego, California, in 1966, I came upon a book not by, but about a man called J. Krishnamurti and his philosophy of the silent mind. Intrigued, I studied it and was less captivated by the interpretation of his philosophy than by the verbatim quotes. His words struck a deep, enduring chord in my mind. Soon I found several books written by him and at once realized that here was a voice of reason, of penetrating insight into the human condition, such as I had never heard before. Without offering a system of belief, a method or an interpretation, he accurately described the global situation of humanity in clear and simple language, demonstrating the destructiveness of religious and national organizations. He urged everyone to find out truth by and for oneself, and he denied any form of spiritual or religious authority, including his own.

Besides providing a new and holistic outlook, he put into precise words what I had been vaguely sensing and wondering about. To come upon his writings was like discovering a precious jewel, and what he said electrified me so completely that I resolved to find out all I could about this man and, if he was still alive, to seek him out and meet him.

I discovered that he was still alive and gave talks in various parts of the world. But it wasn't until December, 1970, that I was able to pinpoint his whereabouts. I had traveled to India to see my old friend Sunyata, who lived within sight of the Himalayan snow peaks in Almora, Uttar Pradesh, near the Tibetan-Nepali border. When I enthusiastically mentioned Krishnamurti, he told me about his own encounter with him, many years earlier in Lahore. My excitement mounted as he produced a notice he had recently received from the Krishnamurti Foundation of India, which specified Krishnamurti's speaking schedule in his native land. When I saw that his next series of talks was going to be in Madras, there was no holding me back. Arriving in New Delhi after a twelve-hour bus ride, I still had a sixty-hour train journey to Madras ahead of me. I only hoped to get there in time to hear him speak.

Upon arrival at Madras on January 14, 1971, I swiftly found my way to Greenways Road, where I had learned that Krishnamurti was speaking. The lady who received me told me with regret that I had just missed the third and last talk the previous day. For a moment I was crushed. Then she quietly suggested that, if I wanted, I could come the following day and participate in a dialogue that Krishnamurti was going to have with a small group of young people. I was elated. My heart soared.

The next morning, I went by auto-rickshaw to the house off Greenways Road, eagerly looking forward to meeting the man who I felt proclaimed the most extraordinary message of freedom for modern-day human beings.

*Part One*

INTRODUCTION TO
A PATHLESS LAND

## Chapter 1
# FIRST STEPS

"*Freedom is pure observation*

*without direction,*

*without fear of punishment*

*and reward.*

*Freedom is without motive;*

*freedom is not at*

*the end of the evolution of man*

*but lies in the first step*

*of his existence.*"

–J. Krishnamurti
*The Core of the Teachings*

HE QUIETLY ENTERED THE HUSHED ROOM. DRESSED IN wide-flowing Indian clothes, he gingerly moved along the wall, careful not to step on anyone sitting on the floor. Although of self-contained and dignified bearing, he appeared unpretentious, almost shy, as he made his way to an unoccupied space in the corner of the large, sun-lit room. Once seated cross-legged on a small carpet, he raised his eyes and fully met the expectant gaze of the forty or fifty young adults, who sat facing him. Most were dressed, as he was, in light-colored, loose-fitting clothes, and appeared intense and respectful.

I felt a calm sense of joy within me: favorable circumstances had led me at last to the man who had inspired my thinking for the past few years. There he was in the flesh, a man in his mid-seventies, a curve of white hair framing his beautiful, sculpted features. He was calmly regarding the group of young men and women in front of him with large mirroring eyes that sparkled with delight. Although I had seen photos of his face, I was surprised by its youthful liveliness and the combination of dignity and openness it displayed.

He didn't seem to be in any hurry to start talking but took the time to gaze at each single face in turn. When our eyes met, I felt a jolt, as if a current of energy had suddenly been switched on between us. Although I was only one among fifty and sat on the outer perimeter of the group, the brief eye contact had an unusually direct impact.

The silence in the room was deepening, becoming almost palpable, even though by the watch it didn't last more than a minute or two. It didn't seem oppressive, though; I experienced it rather as a pleasant stillness in which I became quietly aware of myself, of my body and its movements, of the people around me, of the noises from the street outside, of my constant thought activity. But most of all, I became aware of the man in the corner who was looking at us so earnestly, yet with an element of humor. I was surprised how diminutive and delicate his body was, like a young boy's, and how the subtle power of his presence seemed to communicate itself even without words.

Finally he broke the silence by asking, "What shall we talk about this morning?"

After a moment's hesitation, a young Indian man who was sitting just a few feet from him spoke up, "Sir, you say, 'You are the world, and the world is you'. What is the significance of that statement?"

A Western lady, dressed in a green silk sari, offered another suggestion, "Could we discuss the nature of the religious mind?"

Krishnamurti was attentively listening to the questioners, and, when no one else made any further suggestions, he asked, "Shall we start out by inquiring into the religious mind? Then we'll also get to the other question. Would that be all right?"

There was some eager nodding and a murmur of consent among the group. He started by emphasizing that this was a dialogue, in which everyone was to participate, and that he was not the authority. As the dialogue unfolded, more of the people took part and a lively exchange of views ensued. But he kept probing deeper by putting fundamental, simple questions, "What is religion? What do you mean by 'inquiring into'?" and the like, focusing the inquiry on the original question and insisting that everybody slowly and deliberately move together. All at once, he earnestly entreated us to face the actuality of what we were discussing, "Please listen: we are concerned with understanding the whole of existence, not just one tiny corner of it. You have to find out for yourselves, discover for yourselves, what truth is in your daily life, in your actual everyday existence."

I was struck by the simple immediacy of his approach and its practicality, away from theorizing and abstract conjecturing. No answer seemed to satisfy him, no conclusion was accepted. At one point, drawing attention to the fact that organized religions throughout history had divided humanity and caused untold conflict and suffering, he stopped in mid-sentence, and an impish smile spread over his face.

"May I tell you a joke?" he interjected. "Some of you may have heard it, so don't get bored. The devil and a friend of his are walking the earth. Ahead of them, they see a man bend down and pick up something shiny from the ground. He looks at it with delight, puts it in his pocket and elatedly walks off. The friend asks, 'What did that man find that changed him so much?' The devil answers, 'I know. He found a piece of the truth.' 'By Jove!' exclaims his friend. 'That must be bad business for you.' 'Not at all,' the devil replies with a sly smile, 'I'm going to help him organize it.'"[1]

While recounting the joke, he took on the mien and gestures of a raconteur, relishing the details of the story and readily joining us in the laughter that erupted at the punch line. I thought it extraordinary that a man who insisted on great seriousness and explored the perennial questions of human existence had the freedom to tell jokes and share in a round of liberating laughter.

"I have a lot of jokes, good jokes, not vulgar jokes," he added whimsically as the common mirth quieted down. "Laughter is part of seriousness, isn't it? To be able to really laugh at oneself, to look at ourselves with great clarity and seriousness, and yet with laughter...."

I had been following the animated back-and-forth of the dialogue with growing enthusiasm, marveling at the sense of ease, leisure and depth that communicated itself. Although I was a total newcomer to all this, I felt connected to everyone around, especially to Krishnamurti. Never having participated in a group dialogue of this type, I experienced a thrill at the newness of the situation and the unexpected glimpses of something that might be described as 'wholeness'. The great freedom with which we inquired into our daily lives was exhilarating. Up until this moment, I had not uttered a word, partly from shyness, partly from a feeling of inadequacy, even though I longed to make a memorable contribution to the flow of meaning between the group and the speaker.

Just then Krishnamurti stated, with an emphatic gesture of both hands, "As long as there is suffering and conflict, there cannot be intelligence. So can you live a life completely without conflict? And how are you going to bring this about?"

My brain clicked. I knew the answer and, without further deliberation, blurted out, "Through meditation."

It was a curious sensation to hear myself actively participating in the conversation. For a brief interval I heard the echo of my own voice, saw my words hanging in empty space. Krishnamurti's gaze focused on me. Dressed in Western clothes, my large torso towering above the rest of the group, I was easily identifiable. His sharp glance softened, his head tilted minutely, and a smile played around his features as he said with some forbearance, "No, darling!"

For a moment I thought I hadn't heard him right, then it slowly sank in with certainty: he really had just called me 'darling'. I was in two minds how to take this, then I chose to accept it in a positive and personal sense. That my view had been rejected seemed to matter little. Once I had gained some measure of control over the emotional upsurge that I experienced as a result of the endearment, I focused on the ongoing investigation into the roots of conflict.

"When there is no comparison, no conformity, then conflict comes to an end, and life is intelligence which is neither yours nor mine—it simply *is*," Krishnamurti was saying. "And only a mind without conflict is a religious mind."

As I was listening to his words, to the tone of his voice, everything he said appeared so true, such a precise description of reality—even though he repeatedly pointed out, "The word is not the thing, the description is not the described." It was as if a door in my mind had been opened and I was looking at a breathtakingly beautiful landscape, vast and without limits.

"And when I realize that I am the world, that I am not separate from it, when I can observe my fear and be free of it, then maybe meditation will open a door." His words had taken on a resonance, sounding like a solemn chant.

Everyone had fallen silent. The sunlight was streaming into the room, with a myriad motes dancing in it, and there was a sense of togetherness. For a moment, time and space seemed to become non-specific, as if every place was here and each ticking second was now. Losing track of who and where I was, I found myself looking inwardly, into my own mind, but in a manner different from the habitual turning toward the banks of memory. It was new, extraordinarily new and alive.

When I raised my eyes, I saw Krishnamurti looking at us, taking us all in at the same time, as it were. Then he silently pressed his palms together in the prayer-like *namaste* greeting, the Indian equivalent of 'hello' and 'good-bye'. Everyone in the group reciprocated. But when nobody made to rise, he gestured at those closest to him, asking them in a low voice, "Would you kindly get up?"

While people were rising around me, I looked at my watch with some surprise: our dialogue had lasted almost two hours and yet it seemed like no time at all. I had some difficulty getting to my feet. Despite frequent shifting of position, my legs had thoroughly gone to sleep, and I felt a sharp, tingling sensation as I wobbled to stand straight. But my attention wasn't too much concerned with the body's discomfort: I was still entirely absorbed by Krishnamurti, who was exchanging words with several people. His walk and gestures were graceful; his looks, despite his age, radiant; and he appeared in all respects like an extraordinary human being: a prince.

Two young Indian ladies in colorful silk saris approached him, and after a few words the three of them strode off into an adjoining room, closing the wooden door behind them.

As I put on my shoes by the steps of the house, with people departing left and right, the fragrance of the dialogue lingered with me. It was as if a light had been turned on inside my brain, or perhaps, better, as if my senses had been cleansed and the light could enter. For the remainder of the day I felt an inexplicable lightness and joy, and my perception of the world around me with its bustle and turmoil seemed strangely unencumbered by worries or self-concern.

I KNEW I WANTED MORE. I WANTED TO HEAR MORE of his talks, I wanted to have more personal contact with him. In some sense, it felt like being in love—with Krishnamurti the person, but also with what he said, with his liberating message of freedom and lucidity.

At the house off Greenways Road I had learned that Krishnamurti was going to give a public talk at the Indian Institute of Technology the following afternoon. An hour before the appointed time I hailed one of the small, omnipresent auto-rickshaws to take me to the campus, which was located among pleasant greenery. The open-air amphitheater was teeming with people: there must have been two thousand, most of them students.

When Krishnamurti appeared on the stage, the chattering died down, and everybody turned their attention toward him. He seemed aloof and much more austere than at the small group meeting the previous day. After some rather severe remarks about the chaos people had made of their lives, which he aimed directly at those in front of him, he eased into a more congenial rapport with the audience. Illustrating a situation in which there really was no choice, he injected a dose of humor by joking, "It's like the husband whose pregnant wife is about to give birth. When they arrive at the hospital, the man asks her, 'Are you sure, darling, that you want to go through with this?'"

A wave of laughter ran through the audience. "It's good that we can laugh together," he commented, "It's good to laugh—at a good joke—at ourselves. We have too many tears in our hearts; there is too much misery."

Listening to him speak in front of many people was like watching a consummate artist paint with his words a panoramic picture of the human psyche, showing us the Sistine Chapel of our consciousness. The formality of a larger gathering naturally lessened the warmth and sense of affection that I had experienced during my first direct contact with him, but it didn't diminish the impact of his words. Although he clearly reached out to his listeners, again and again invoking a participatory togetherness, he was not engaging in a dialogue with its back-and-forth mutuality. He very directly presented his insight into the human condition. The simplicity and beauty of this insight made it accessible to anyone who was willing to set aside the accumulated beliefs and doctrines of the past and look anew at his or her actual everyday living.

After the talk I ran into two old friends of mine among the thousands of departing people. I was glad to meet them so unexpectedly and got even more excited when they told me about Krishnamurti's upcoming talks at Rishi Valley, a secondary school which he had founded before the war. Since it was two hundred miles inland from Madras and hard to get to, they offered me a ride in their vehicle, an old English station-wagon.

I felt I had no choice in the matter and gladly accepted. Ever since I had followed my heart from the Himalayas to Madras I thought that things had taken on a momentum of their own, in the right direction. And if I only allowed the configuration of events to unfold without too much interference on my part, I might be hearing a lot more of Krishnamurti. Which was what I wanted.

## Chapter 2
# BEGINNINGS
# OF FRIENDSHIP

"*Love is as real, as strong, as death.*
*It has nothing to do with imagination,*
*or sentiment, or romanticism;*
*and naturally it has nothing to do with*
*power, position, prestige.*
*It is as still as the waters of the sea*
*and as powerful as the sea;*
*it is like the running waters*
*of a rich river flowing endlessly,*
*without a beginning or an end.*"

–J. Krishnamurti
*Krishnamurti To Himself*

RISHI VALLEY IS AN OASIS, A PLACE OF GREEN FERTILITY amidst an arid landscape of barren hills, bizarre rock formations and giant boulders. Centuries-old banyans, mango and tamarind trees shade the campus, and purple and red bougainvillea cascade down the sides of colonial-style cottages. It is an enchanting place.

Shortly after our arrival, Krishnamurti was scheduled to give a talk to the students and teachers of the Rishi Valley School. To my delight, guests, including ourselves, were also invited. There was a festive mood as we joined several hundred students and their solemn-looking teachers in the large auditorium. At one end of the building, which was open on all four sides, there was a low platform draped with colorful carpets. Several potted plants were placed around it, and a microphone-stand on the dais was connected to loudspeakers and to a table with recording equipment.

When Krishnamurti entered, I was again struck by his diminutive physique. The loose clothing he wore accentuated his smallness, which contrasted sharply with the gigantic proportions he was taking on in my mind. Approaching the platform, he turned towards the audience and offered the *namaste* greeting. The excited buzz of the crowd came to an abrupt halt as both teachers and students in unison responded with the same gesture of respect.

Krishnamurti took off his sandals and after slowly and carefully mounting the platform, sat down in a cross-legged position. He faced the audience, a light smile playing around his lips, and again he gave the *namaste* greeting. Again everyone answered silently with the same gesture. His glance swept over the sea of expectant young faces that were turned toward him. He smiled with delight as he started out with the question, "What shall we talk about?" After a brief interval, several of the younger students, both boys and girls, asked some charmingly simple questions, "What is God?" "Why are we being educated?" "Why must I obey my teacher?"

Krishnamurti gently responded to the questions, enjoying the verbal exchange with the young students, whose minds were still fresh and relatively unencumbered by the pressures of earning a livelihood and pursuing a career. There was an atmosphere of unrestrained openness, enlivened by occasional joyful laughter. At one point, laughing exuberantly, he exclaimed, "I haven't had so much fun since my grandmother died." Realizing that the old saying could easily be misunderstood, he quickly corrected himself by saying, "I don't really mean that."

I was sitting on a bench at the very back of the auditorium, observing the man on the platform above a multitude of black-haired heads. I was absorbed not only by what he was saying but also by the tone of his voice. Deep and resonant, it rose at times into higher octaves, with an almost feminine modulation. He tended to clip certain words, giving his speech a distinctly British character.

Although there were about 500 other people present, I felt that he was speaking directly to me, addressing my specific concerns and problems. It was uncanny. While I listened to what he was saying with an open mind and heart, there was a sense of connectedness, of great lightness and joy, unknown and new to me.

Toward the end of the talk, he asked, "Shall we sit still for several minutes of silence?" It was as if he had given a signal: everyone, even the younger students, who were sitting cross-legged on the floor and had been fidgeting throughout the talk, promptly froze. After a minute or two of shared silence, he raised his hands in the *namaste* greeting, which apparently was the sign for the students to jump up and with animated chatter disperse in all directions.

I remained spellbound in my place amidst the sudden movements all around me. As I quietly looked about, I became aware of the bright, colorful day. There were birds with shining plumage flitting about; magnificent flowers were opening out. Nature seemed to be powerfully omnipresent, even within myself.

As I rose from my seat, I noticed that a few people had stayed behind and were crowding around the figure of Krishnamurti. Amiably exchanging a few words with one person, he turned to the next, shaking a Westerner's hand.

I was standing quietly, with a blank mind, wistfully observing the interaction from a distance of about twenty yards. All at once, Krishnamurti caught sight of me, standing by myself. Without a moment's hesitation, he disengaged himself from the person he was talking with, and strode over to where I was. With a friendly smile he held out his hand, and without any words we shook hands.

The impact of this unexpected encounter left me speechless. He did not say anything, either. After what seemed like a long interval of quietness, the urge of social convention to say something got the better of me. I couldn't think of anything poignant to remark; the only words I could gather sprang from a feeling of gratitude toward this unassuming man for affording a view of something radically new.

I stammered, "Thank you, sir. Thank you!"

He smiled brightly, studying me. "Where do you come from?"

I replied, "Well, I'm originally from Germany, but I've been living in the United States for some years now, in California."

"Ah yes, California," he said, "I go there sometimes."

At that moment, I remembered a number of poems written by the young Krishnamurti that I had recently read and that had impressed me. Since I fancied myself a poet, I thought that this might be an opportune moment to address poetry. So I asked him, "I read several of the poems which you wrote many years ago and enjoyed them very much. Do you still write poetry these days?"

It was as if I had touched a nerve or had changed the composition of the field in which we were moving. He seemed to be stepping back from me, and an air of sudden aloofness enveloped him. "I'm sorry, I've forgotten," he replied distantly and walked away after quickly shaking my hand.

Although I wasn't disturbed by his demeanor, I felt slightly mystified by it. The closer I got to this unusual man, the more intrigued I became. It was like looking ever more closely at a rose, which more and more revealed the details of its petals, the depth of its color, and its fragrance.

A FEW DAYS LATER I WAS STROLLING ALONG THE TREE-LINED lanes of the campus, bathed in the glow of the early afternoon sunlight, when I encountered the principal of the school. He was a slim person with balding head and sharp, darting eyes and wore Western clothes. After a friendly greeting, he asked me whether I had inquired about the possibility of a face-to-face meeting with Krishnamurti. I had, in fact, that morning asked one of the school teachers if Krishnamurti still gave private interviews. It had been only a casual inquiry, without any urgency or actual intent on my part. So I was fairly startled to discover that it had been promptly passed on to the top. The principal proceeded to tell me that I could meet Krishnamurti in twenty minutes at his residence. I excitedly dashed back to my room to clean up for such an unexpected event. Remembering two poems I had recently written, I thought that this might be an opportune occasion to present them to Krishnamurti.

I found my way to his house. It was a two-storied building sur-rounded by exotic trees, one of them a flame-tree with brilliant, red flowers. Nobody seemed to be expecting me, and I felt shy and a bit apprehensive, almost like an intruder in a tranquil sanctuary. I knocked on one of the downstairs doors, and an Indian lady with a friendly face opened it. I told her that I had an appointment with Krishnamurti. Hes-itating for a moment, she suggested he might be resting. I gently insisted that the meeting had been arranged by the principal. With a typical Indian gesture, she bade me wait, while she went upstairs to find out about the matter.

As I stood at the foot of the stairs, in the humming stillness of the hot afternoon, I felt suspended in a vacuum, where the normal passage of time seemed absent. A great stillness was enveloping me as my thought processes slowed to a trickle. I asked myself why I was here. What did I expect from meeting Krishnamurti? I didn't have any specific question that I wanted to ask him. He had already amply addressed my concerns in his talks. At the same time, I realized that I harbored a gnawing curiosity about what he was like in his daily life. Perhaps all I wanted was to be in his presence.

A shuffling sound came from above. Looking up, I saw Krishna-murti in bare feet descending the stairs with carefully measured steps. After slipping on a pair of sandals, he turned to face me, and we greeted each other with the *namaste* gesture. He appeared taciturn, almost oth-erworldly, and his finely chiseled face bore an expression of serene, indifferent stillness. He did not utter a word but just stood there waiting for me to make a move, to say something, or perhaps not.

My brain-cells were scrambling to formulate a meaningful state-ment. Clearing my throat, I said haltingly, "Sir, I—I wanted to thank you for, for—everything. I mean, I have read your books, and it's won-derful what you write. I mean, it's true. But now, to see you and hear you live, to actually experience it, is—well, it's beyond words—and...."

He made a soothing gesture, and his voice was calm like a lake at dawn. "It's all right, sir," he said.

I pulled out the sheets of paper from my back-pocket and handed them to him. "Excuse me," I stammered, "these are two poems which I have recently written. I would like to present them to you." A swift smile spread across his face as he took the papers without looking at them. Instead, he simply gazed at me in an unusual, unfocused manner—as if viewing the space around me rather than the form within the space.

I fell silent, and when after a few moments it became apparent that I didn't have any further questions, he simply said, "All right, sir. I will see you tomorrow." With that, he wedged the papers under his arm, offered the *namaste* good-bye and climbed the stairs, after carefully placing his sandals side by side on the landing.

As I pensively strolled off, it occurred to me that I might in fact have interrupted his siesta. Even so, I couldn't but be elated by our brief encounter.

BY NOW, A RESOLUTION HAD FORMED IN MY MIND: I WAS determined to hear Krishnamurti speak wherever I could. It was a great privilege, a case of good luck, to have come upon someone who spoke the truth, without any kind of ulterior motive and without invoking dogma or tradition.

I had noticed that there were a number of people, both Indians and Westerners, who regularly showed up at all of his talks. Some, apparently, were associates and co-workers; others seemed to be 'free agents'—acolytes, *chelas*, disciples, who followed him around. Some of them told me that they had listened to him for many years in different countries around the world, since he followed a regular itinerary, speaking in India, California, New York, Switzerland and England. Each year he gave public talks in the same places at roughly the same time, occasionally speaking at new locations, as he had just done the previous November, when he gave a series of talks and dialogues in Australia.

It seemed to me that following him around confronted one with a contradiction, since he vehemently denied being a spiritual leader and insisted that he didn't have any followers or disciples. In fact, he entirely denied the value of the ancient Hindu tradition that emphasized the quintessential relationship between teacher and disciple. Insisting that there was no such thing as an initiation into, or a transmission of, truth, he maintained that one had to discover truth by and for oneself, and be a light unto oneself. During one of his talks at Rishi Valley, for instance, he poked gentle fun at the attitude of someone who wanted to learn truth from another.

"May I tell you a story?" he started, a mischievous twinkle in his eyes, as he surveyed his young audience. "A young man leaves home to look for truth. He goes to a well-known guru who lives on the banks of a river. 'Please, sir,' he says to the old man, 'allow me to stay with you. I want to learn the truth from you.' And the guru agrees. And so he washes his clothes, cooks for him, and performs all kinds of tasks for the old teacher. After five years, he says to the master, 'I've spent five years with you but I still don't know what truth is and haven't learned a thing. So if you don't mind, I'll leave you. Perhaps I can find another teacher, from whom I can learn more about the truth.' 'I don't mind,' says the old man, 'go right ahead.' So the young chap goes off and finds several other gurus, from whom he learns various magic tricks. After another five years have passed, he remembers his old teacher and goes to visit him. 'So what have you learned?' the old man asks him. And his former student tells him that he can walk on hot coals, levitate and so on. 'Is that all?' the guru asks. The young man points at the river in front of them and says proudly, 'And I can walk on the waters of that river to the opposite shore.' 'And it took you five years to learn that,' the old master exclaims, 'when over there, fifty yards from here, you can take the ferry boat across for twopence!'"

Once I had learned the details of Krishnamurti's worldwide schedule of talks, I arranged my own plans accordingly: follower or not, I wanted to hear him as often as I could reasonably manage. His next public appearance was going to be in Bangalore, a large city a hundred miles west of Rishi Valley, during the following weekend. It wasn't difficult for me to find my way there, since a considerable number of people from Rishi Valley were traveling either by bus or taxi to the capital city of Karnataka State.

The talks were held in a large tent in the Lal Bagh Gardens, a pleasant park, with many trees and blooming flowers. Several thousand people attended the talk, and Krishnamurti was deeply serious, speaking of pleasure and fear, the concepts of karma and reincarnation, and the absurdity of hoping for a better 'next life'. "The other day I saw a cartoon in a magazine," he recounted to the audience. "It's in New York City, at a busy intersection in Times Square. There are two dogs sitting by the curbside, watching the people hurrying by, always busy and in a rush. And one dog says to the other, 'You know, reincarnation gives me the creeps.'"

I was one of the few people who laughed out loud at the joke while the majority of the audience kept quiet, either because they didn't understand it, or because reincarnation was too sacrosanct a subject for them to joke about. I appreciated Krishnamurti's capacity to introduce light-hearted humor into areas of great seriousness and to show that laughter was part of seriousness. The playful, sympathetic observation of the ludicrous in our lives was not only of vital importance—it was intelligence.

THE TALKS IN BOMBAY, A TEEMING, OVERCROWDED metropolis on the Arabian Sea, attracted huge numbers. Between three to four thousand people crammed into a relatively small outdoor space in the center of the city to listen to him speak amidst the unceasing noise of traffic.

I found it fascinating to hear Krishnamurti's talks in different locations. Although his basic message appeared to remain the same, of the utmost simplicity and elegance, certain aspects of it derived from the physical setting and the varying number of participants. Not only that, but one felt that each talk was a living event and not just a mechanical repetition. Therefore, it invariably contained an element of startling newness, of change, of being in time and yet pointing beyond it.

## Chapter 3

# FULL TASTE

"*Truth is not at the top of the ladder; truth is where you are, in what you are doing, thinking, feeling, when you kiss and hug, when you exploit— you must see the truth of all that, not a truth at the end of innumerable cycles of life.*"

—J. Krishnamurti
*The Collected Works of J. Krishnamurti, Vol. V, p. 204*

IN THE SUMMER OF 1971 I VISITED THE SAANEN-GSTAAD region of Switzerland for the first time. It is a magnificent valley of rivers, forests and green meadows, surrounded by snowcapped mountain peaks. For the past ten years, Krishnamurti had been giving a month-long series of talks and discussions here during July and August. A huge tent with a capacity for more than a thousand people had been set up on the banks of the swift-flowing Saane River. Every other morning at eleven o'clock, Krishnamurti spoke for about ninety minutes to the young and old, rich and poor, who had gathered here from around the world to listen to his extraordinary message.

The overwhelming beauty of nature, the clean and orderly towns and roads, the international composition of the audience, and, most of all, the revolutionary exploration of the human mind combined to create an event unique in its clarity and immediacy. I felt enchanted, as if by some magic I had been transported into another, higher dimension. The protagonist at the heart of this exhilarating gathering was, of course, Krishnamurti, who with calm modesty mounted and left the wooden platform from which he spoke. He was impeccably dressed in Western-style clothes. His gestures, spare though they were, had great expressive power, underlining the direct way with which he addressed his listeners.

It was easy to make a mystery of him, perhaps because we have such great need of mysteries, miracles and magic in our ordinary lives. I was certainly not immune to the temptation to create an imposing image of him, especially since data about his personal life was sparse. What I garnered, bit by bit, about his life only strengthened my belief that we were facing an enlightened human being. The more I learned about it, the more his life seemed like a fairy-tale of the most wondrous kind, a legend, a myth.

In 1909 at the age of fourteen, he had been 'discovered' as the Vehicle of the Lord by one of the leaders of the Theosophical Society, a worldwide religious organization. Subsequently adopted by them, he was brought up to be the new Messiah in Europe and America. But in 1929, at a large gathering in Ommen in the Netherlands, he quietly and firmly disbanded the organization of 'The Order of the Star', which had been set up specifically for him, and told his thousands of followers that he didn't want to be their leader. Ever since, he had been traveling the world, speaking to whomsoever came to listen about fear and sorrow, and the need to end them. This, he maintained, could only be done by observing and investigating the ways of the mind.

I had read that the Mahayana Buddhist tradition had a concept which described a person like Krishnamurti—a Bodhisattva, an Awakened Being, someone who out of compassion for the suffering of humankind surrenders all self-concern and points to the truth. By applying this concept to him, I was essentially mystifying him. My curiosity was assailed by other questions: how do illumined beings live? Do they engage in the humdrum activities of everyday life? And, more specifically, what does he, Krishnamurti, do when he isn't giving a talk or a dialogue?

In the treasure house of my imagination, I composed a likely scenario: he would go into *samadhi*, a timeless state of rapture and bliss, until earthly necessities called him back to action.

IT WAS DURING ONE OF THE MANY CONVERSATIONS I HAD AT Saanen about Krishnamurti and his personal life that someone stated that Krishnamurti polished his own shoes. That he enjoyed reading detective stories and watching Westerns on television sounded even more sensational. I was shocked. Could these claims be true? If so, how could they be reconciled with my image of what a Bodhisattva did in his free time?

By coincidence, Krishnamurti touched on this issue during one of the following discussions. "I don't read any books at all, nor have I read any of the so-called sacred books. I really mean it; I only read weekly magazines and detective stories," he declared amidst laughter from the audience. I realized that my information about enlightenment and enlightened beings derived exclusively from sacred books and traditional hearsay. Therefore, my assumptions might be utterly false, and the only thing I could do was discard them and find out for myself. This intensified my curiosity about the person Krishnamurti and his daily life.

THE EXPERIENCE OF BEING WITH A THOUSAND PEOPLE AND listening to this riveting inquiry into the heights and depths of human consciousness created a sense of togetherness between my fellow listeners, myself and the speaker.

When, after a talk, he dashed off with long, determined strides along the narrow road I felt an urge to follow him. Often an eager group of admirers would rush over and cluster around him as he left the tent; he would quickly break away, friendly but determined. At other times, someone might walk alongside him to exchange some words, express their gratitude or simply try to prolong the pleasure of being in his presence. He would good-naturedly tolerate it, although the person might be hard pressed to keep pace with him. A few times I tried to catch up with him only to see him snatched away by the same Mercedes that he arrived in, chauffeured by an elegant lady. While he was swiftly striding along, the car would pull up next to him, he would get in, and they would drive off toward Gstaad.

MAKING DISCREET INQUIRIES, I FOUND THAT KRISHNAMURTI lived in a chalet in the upper part of Gstaad, some distance above the famous Palace Hotel. One sunny afternoon I hiked up wooded lanes to this chic area, that afforded spectacular views of snowy ranges beyond curving green hills. At a sharp turn of the road, I discovered the name 'Tannegg', painted in illuminated letters on the front of a large wooden building.

My heart beat faster with the excitement and joy of discovery. This was where Krishnamurti lived, and every afternoon, I had been told, he went for a walk. If I waited around, I might catch a glimpse of him leaving or entering the chalet. But I felt rather shy about my curiosity and didn't want to be seen conducting this covert surveillance. Therefore, I retreated to the house across the road, which appeared unoccupied at the time and had a good view of the drive-way and doors of Chalet Tannegg. I hid behind one of the large, flowering bushes adorning an oval lawn in front of the house and simply waited. The afternoon sunrays were pleasant on my skin, as I lay on a patch of fragrant grass and looked up into the blue of the sky, watching the movements of a few clouds. Every so often I would survey the road to see if he was coming into view.

After about twenty minutes three people came walking down the road toward the chalet. I ducked low behind the yellow-flowered bush, peering through the foliage. One of the three was indeed Krishnamurti.

The two ladies following him were animatedly conversing with each other. One of them, of delicate build, I recognized as the driver of the Mercedes, while the other woman appeared rather sturdy and tall. I remained out of sight and kept watching Krishnamurti closely. Although my spying activity triggered a guilty pang of conscience, I yet felt a strange thrill watching him.

Suddenly, he reacted, as if he was aware of someone watching him. He appeared startled, looked around quickly and began to walk faster. Keeping his body close to the stone wall of the driveway, as if seeking its protection, he hurried toward the door of the chalet and swiftly entered. After the two ladies had also gone into the chalet, I emerged from behind the bushes and took a walk uphill toward the forest from where they had just come.

A FEW DAYS LATER, ON A BRIGHT MID-MORNING, I WENT TO BUY a copy of the International Herald Tribune at the railway station kiosk in Gstaad. Before crossing the busy street, I looked to my left, then to my right—and all at once he was there, standing right next to me.

With great delight I exclaimed, "Krishnaji, sir! How are you?"

I was not sure whether he remembered any of our previous encounters in Rishi Valley and Madras several months before, nor did it seem to matter at this moment. He smiled as we affectionately shook hands and explained, "I've been giving some talks over in Saanen."

The simplicity and modesty with which he uttered the statement was poignant.

"Yes, sir," I responded enthusiastically, "I've been attending the talks. They are truly magnificent. Thank you, sir."

He carefully scrutinized my face. "You are from California, aren't you?" he asked.

"Well, yes," I answered, falling into step beside him as he crossed to the sidewalk opposite. "I've lived there for quite a few years."

As we were strolling along and conversing, with a lot of pedestrian and car traffic all around, I suddenly wondered what he was doing here by himself. He answered my question as if I had spoken it out loud, "I'm waiting for some friends."

At that moment, a car zoomed by with a loud roar and a dark cloud of exhaust fumes. Krishnamurti shook his head in disapproval, "They are all driving so fast these days."

I concurred, "Yes, it's really dangerous, even in the center of town. And the horrible pollution...."

He abruptly stopped, pointing at a Mercedes which had pulled over on the other side of the road, in front of the terrace of the Hotel Berner Hof. "There they are," he exclaimed. "They have come to pick me up. Good-bye, sir."

He quickly shook my hand, and I could only say, "Good-bye, sir. Thank you very much!"

And he was already crossing the street toward the car. I wistfully watched his energetic walk, with the torso upright and the long arms swinging in a relaxed rhythm.

As I watched the car drive off, I became aware of an unsought sense of joy welling up within me. I found that I frequently experienced this kind of sensation when coming into contact with Krishnamurti, and the very randomness of our encounter just moments ago seemed to enhance its intensity.

THAT FIRST SUMMER IN SAANEN WAS SHEER MAGIC FOR ME, a time of discovering new things, of delving into the complexity of my mental and emotional processes, making new friends, and opening up to nature. But breathing the rare perfume that emanated from our mornings with Krishnamurti in the large tent by the riverside was the crucial element. It was a great, harmonious gathering of human beings willing to question the ways of society and themselves. At the end of the month-long Gathering, one did not feel sadness about its coming to an end, but rather felt enriched beyond measure and open to the living moment.

WHILE AT SAANEN, I LEARNED THAT TWO YEARS EARLIER, in 1969, an international boarding school had been started in England by Krishnamurti. Called Brockwood Park, it was located near the ancient capital of Winchester, in the downland county of Hampshire, about sixty miles from London. At the beginning of September there was going to be a series of four talks and two discussions there. I took little time to make up my mind to visit the south of England for that occasion.

It wasn't far from Switzerland to Germany, where for two weeks I visited my mother, who lived in a city called Krefeld in the northern Rhineland. From there I traveled to England. Apart from the fact that the traffic drove on the left-hand side of the road, I didn't find it too difficult to make my way to Petersfield, whence it was only a few miles to Brockwood Park.

The road off the main highway was bordered on either side by arching copper beeches. It led to an entrance gate, from where a narrow driveway wound between meadows to an 18th-century white mansion. Next to the house was a red-brick water tower adjoined by a large garden and a rose garden. Some distance away from the complex of buildings, an arboretum, called the Grove, was abundant with a great variety of magnificent trees from all over the world, including several giant sequoias. On the back lawn, an imposing, two-hundred-year-old cedar of Lebanon dominated the manicured lawn. Brockwood Park clearly was a tree lover's paradise.

Next to a small apple orchard, a large tent had been set up for the Gathering, which attracted a thousand or more visitors, some of whom camped in the fields adjacent. For about two weeks a festive atmosphere enlivened the grounds.

The talks and discussions at Brockwood Park had a friendly, almost intimate feel about them, with laughter and ease and a natural sense of propriety. On the days of the meetings, lunch would be served after the talk or dialogue in a second tent that was connected to the talk tent. On those occasions it was a lovely surprise to see Krishnamurti mingle with the visitors. Listening to the 'chap on the platform', as he sometimes referred to himself, was a profound experience, but observing him in everyday interaction with others added a special element. Dressed with casual elegance, balancing a paper plate with food in one hand, he could be seen amiably conversing with whoever approached him. It felt as if we had been invited into his home to share in his life.

Since I was helping as a volunteer in the tent and the garden, I was sometimes invited to have lunch in the dining-hall of the main building. More than a hundred staff, students and guests took their meals there. I was thrilled to discover Krishnamurti among them. For some reason, I found it fascinating to watch him in ordinary, daily situations, perhaps because I associated him so much with what we consider lofty pursuits. His manners and gestures, and the way he held himself, were exemplary. At moments when I secretly observed him eat, or converse and laugh with a neighbor, or fall silent, quietly gazing out over the people sitting at the long, wooden dining tables in front of him, I felt a sense of wonder and great gratitude. I thought I had come in contact with goodness, which was manifesting through this man. All at once it was visible all around me.

AFTER THE BROCKWOOD PARK TALKS HAD ENDED, I STAYED ON for another month, working as a volunteer in the vegetable garden. It was a new experience for me to live and work in a communal context at a residential school. What lent it special significance were the regular meetings that Krishnamurti had with staff and students, to which the volunteers were also invited. More intensely than ever I felt that my life was starting anew each morning.

Even so, the time came to say good-bye, and I returned to California in the fall of 1971. I had much to contemplate, and a life in relative solitude appealed to me. All winter long I lived a simple, hermit-like existence in a small cabin in the woods near Mendocino, a hundred miles north of San Francisco. Every so often I would rejoin civilization and visit friends in San Francisco and Berkeley. During one of these outings in the spring of 1972, I went to Los Angeles and learned that Krishnamurti was in California at the time. He was going to give a series of public talks first at the nearby Santa Monica Civic Auditorium and then at the Libbey Bowl in Ojai. It was less than a month hence, and I decided to stay in the area.

One of my friends from Ojai told me that he had attended a small group discussion with Krishnamurti at a house in Malibu a few days earlier. At this news, an overpowering sense of curiosity arose in me, and I excitedly inquired where it was. Although my friend couldn't recall the exact address, he was able to describe various landmarks, which helped me trace the approximate location of the house along the Pacific Coast Highway, where Krishnamurti was apparently residing. By coincidence, I had been staying with friends at Topanga Canyon, which was only a few miles south of there. For reasons that I did not analyze I felt that it would be both wonderful and important to have direct personal contact with Krishnamurti, if possible.

OFF THE BUSY FOUR-LANE HIGHWAY, A DRIVEWAY SLANTED upward to a gate between the caretaker's cottage and a lawn with trees and bushes. A modern, one-story, brick-and-wood building was perched on a promontory, with a dazzling view of the vast Pacific Ocean. When I rang the bell a middle-aged lady with an apron on opened the door of the cottage. "Good afternoon," I said. "Please excuse me, but does Mr. Krishnamurti live here?"

"Wait here for a moment, please," she answered, and without any further questions she scurried off toward the main house.

I looked around, struck by the beauty of the surroundings. After a short while, someone came toward me out of the house. For an instant I took him for a young boy, dressed in blue jeans, long-sleeved, grey cotton shirt, and sandals. A sudden wave of warmth and joy rose within me as I recognized Krishnamurti.

Long strands of white hair were playfully tossed up by a gust of air as he approached. Hesitatingly I took a few steps toward him. And, all at once, we were hugging each other. It seemed quite incredible. I had no idea whether he recalled any of our previous encounters. It was simply a gesture of tremendous affection, and I felt like a huge bear hugging a delicate child. Completely overwhelmed by this spontaneous display of affection, I could only stammer, "It's good to see you, Krishnaji!" Ever since India and Brockwood Park, I had been using this form of address, which everybody seemed to be using. The suffix -ji denotes both respect and endearment. There was a wonderful smile on his face as he gave me a gentle pat on the shoulder and asked, "Where are you coming from now, sir?"

Each time I looked into his face I was struck anew by the sense of affection and bright intelligence that it manifested. "I've been living up in Mendocino County, north of San Francisco, for the past six months. I've come down here to attend your talks in Santa Monica and Ojai. At the moment, I'm staying with friends in Topanga Canyon, just a few miles south of here," I explained.

He calmly regarded me with large, almond-shaped eyes that were like dark mirrors. "How old are you, sir?" he asked as he turned around, leading the way into the house.

"I'm twenty-eight, sir," I responded, following him past the manicured lawn.

"Ah, you're still quite young," he remarked.

While he was opening the sliding glass door, I pulled a folded sheet of paper from my shirt pocket and handed it to him. He regarded it with a puzzled expression as he took it.

"It's a poem, sir," I explained, adding with self-conscious hesitation, "I've written it for you."

"Ah, thank you," he said. "Do you mind if I read it later?"

"Of course not, sir," I responded, "it's yours."

"All right, sir," he said, leading the way into the kitchen.

It was a well-equipped, modern kitchen, sparklingly clean. The lady in the apron who had received me was busy at the sink.

"Would you like any tea or coffee?" Krishnamurti asked.

I hesitated for a moment, surprised at his offer. Then I replied, "Well, yes, thank you. Some coffee would be nice."

He pointed at one of the tall stools by the kitchen counter, indicating I should sit down. "She is going to give you some coffee," he said. With that, he extended his hand and said, "Please excuse me, I have to take care of some things."

Partly glad and partly disappointed that our togetherness had come to such a sudden end, I could only mutter, "Thank you, Krishnaji!"

And very swiftly and quietly he was gone. In a flash, I had a sensation of absence and emptiness.

"Do you take cream and sugar?" the lady asked from the other side of the counter.

"Yes, please," I answered and started to stir the drink she had placed in front of me.

THE TALK AT SANTA MONICA WAS THE FIRST OF Krishnamurti's that I attended in the United States. It also was the first time there was an admission charge for a talk: the previous talks were entirely covered by donations. The cost of renting the Santa Monica Civic Auditorium was apparently quite high and needed to be defrayed directly.

It was a sunny Saturday morning in March, and the large balconied hall was filled with an audience of predominantly Southern Californians. I was surprised to see Krishnamurti dressed in a suit, sitting on a chair in the middle of the stage, with a microphone in front of him. He started out rather sternly and, throughout the talk, maintained a seriousness that contrasted with the casual mood of the audience.

TWO WEEKS LATER, SHORTLY BEFORE THE OJAI TALKS, I AGAIN felt a strong urge to see Krishnamurti at the house in Malibu. I had given much thought to formulating a unique question which might engage him in some sort of dialogue. But it wasn't easy, since in his talks he had already raised, and implicitly answered, all the fundamental questions that I could envision. Even questions that I was barely aware of, that were dormant in some hidden corner of my mind, he appeared to bring out into the open and formulate in very simple, intelligible language.

What I really wanted to ask him about was the man himself and his daily life, but I thought it might be improper to ask questions of a highly personal nature. Besides, any mere verbal answer would hardly have sufficed, either, since my curious brain wanted to see, watch and experience him at firsthand. I wanted a taste of the real thing. And, at the moment, he was the real thing.

IT WAS ANOTHER SUNNY MORNING AS I ARRIVED AT THE LOVELY house off the Pacific Coast Highway and rang the doorbell. Krishnamurti himself opened the door and welcomed me into the living room. As we walked in, I was frantically reviewing the question I had constructed. Wall-sized windows provided a stunning view of the deep-blue ocean, reflecting the brilliant sunlight like a giant mirror. While we were still standing in the middle of the room, I turned toward him and asked, "Krishnaji, may I ask you a question?"

My simple initial question seemed to charge the energy in the field around him: one moment it had been tranquil, the next it was mirror-like and focused.

He faced me fully and said, "Go ahead, sir."

I brought out my question, in which I had mingled a personal concern and a pseudo-scientific conjecture. "For a long time I have been disturbed by the ceaseless chattering of my brain," I said. "There are constant thought activities, worries, fears, desires, plans and dreams going on. But you say that thinking is merely a material process."

His listening was intense, and he was observing me closely while I spoke. "Yes, sir," he said. "What is your question?"

"Couldn't it be that it is the unceasing motion of the electrons in the atoms of the brain that causes this unending chattering?" I asked.

For the briefest of moments I thought I detected a glint of surprise in his eyes on hearing my question. He paused for a moment, as if still listening; then he simply said, "Find out, sir."

That my question bounced off him so easily unnerved me a bit, and I couldn't quite find an angle to pursue my line of reasoning. I was at a loss for words, and he seemed to be aware of my helplessness and eased our conversation toward more mundane matters. He asked me if I had already had lunch. When I answered in the negative, he promptly led me into the kitchen, sitting me down on one of the stools.

"She will give you some food," he said, referring to the lady cook who was washing dishes behind the counter.

I was still profusely thanking him when he gave me a parting handshake. As an afterthought, he added with a smile, "*Auf Wiedersehen!*" Before I knew it he had left the kitchen, and I remained eating a salad. Although at one level I was disappointed that I hadn't succeeded in involving him in a dialogue, I yet felt a lightness and strange sense of elation.

## Chapter 4

# THE SECOND TIME AROUND

> " *T*ime is always repeating its challenge
>
> and its problems; the responses and answers
>
> are concerned with the immediate.
>
> We are taken up with
>
> the immediate challenge
>
> and with the immediate reply to it.
>
> This immediate answer
>
> to the immediate call
>
> is worldliness, with all its
>
> indissoluble problems and agonies...
>
> ...the answer is beyond the immediate. "

–J. Krishnamurti
*Krishnamurti's Notebook*

THE YEAR 1972 SAW ME FOLLOWING, MORE OR LESS, in Krishnamurti's footsteps. After attending the two talks at the Libbey Bowl in Ojai at the beginning of April, I traveled to Europe for the Saanen Gatherings in July and August, followed by the Brockwood Park Talks in September. I stayed on at the School as a volunteer worker for about two months, during which time I was able to participate in the meetings Krishnamurti regularly had with staff and students. They were dialogues of great openness and affection, and here more than at any other place I experienced Krishnamurti as a benevolent patriarch.

Not long after he left for India, I also departed for the Asian subcontinent, in November. After a series of talks in New Delhi, it was south again, to Madras. I found out that Krishnamurti was staying at the same house off Greenways Road where I had first listened to him the previous year. Thanks to a number of small coincidences, his graceful hostess, a business woman, extended her hospitality to me, allowing me to stay for one week in the temporary *pandal* that was being built in the large courtyard of her house. It was a wooden structure with a thatched roof, open on all sides, with a small platform at one end; the grassy area below it was covered with carpets. Krishnamurti was going to give his talks here; and, in addition, several musical performances were going to be staged in his honor. His own room was only forty yards away, on the opposite side of the courtyard. I felt a great thrill, and a sense of privilege, to be able to live so close to him. The tropical night air was pleasant for outdoor sleeping, and the lady of the house not only saw to it that I had the use of a bathroom, but also arranged that her servants served me tea and regular meals in my makeshift habitat.

What I particularly cherished about this temporary situation was that, during the following days and nights, I was able to observe Krishnamurti at close quarters. From my location beneath the *pandal*, I could clearly see him through the latticed window and open door of his room, as he moved about, sat writing at his desk, came and went. It was inspiring for me to watch him inhabit his personal space, which I somehow imagined to be vaster, freer, emptier than mine, although at the same time I saw the futility of indulging in comparisons of that kind.

I tried to keep a respectful distance, anxious not to bother him in any way, although our hostess certainly had informed him of my presence, and he was well aware of it. Every so often, when he stepped out of his room at dawn, or in the afternoon after his siesta, he welcomed me with a friendly wave of his hand. And I would silently respond with a similar gesture from my end of the courtyard. It did not feel as if there was any distance between us, rather a kind of neighborly togetherness.

DURING THE SECOND DAY OF MY STAY AT THE HOUSE, I WAS ON the point of going for an evening stroll through the neighborhood. The light of dusk was already descending, shrouding the earth in that pervasive glow, peculiar to the tropics. Suddenly I encountered Krishnamurti, who was by himself and just leaving the property.

I greeted him in Indian *namaste* fashion, "Good evening, Krishnaji!"

His gaze quietly took me in before there was a brief flash of recognition, and, holding out his hands, he took mine into both of his, shaking them slightly in western fashion. The smooth, cool touch of his fingers was as delicate as silk.

"Ah, good evening, sir," he replied. "You have come. How did you get here?"

Assuming that he did not care for small talk, I replied, "Excuse me, sir, are you just on your way to take an evening walk? Do you mind if I tag along?"

He gave an affectionate smile. "All right sir, come along. I'm only going for a short walk this evening: to the corner and back."

Again I experienced the special sense of being taken into a realm of complete openness and clarity, without barriers and yet sheltered and safe, a sensation I often felt in his company.

For some moments we walked in silence along the dusk-shrouded Greenways Road. Auto-rickshaws and cars passed us on either side of the road, noisily blowing their horns. Bullock carts with huge wheels slowly rolled by. And in front of corner tea-stalls, illumined by oil lamps and naked bulbs, men were squatting and chatting with each other, smoking and sipping tea. Everywhere there seemed to be children, scampering about with shrieks of laughter, or plaintively crying and seeking their mother's comfort.

I started recounting how I had made my way out to India. "Particularly in Europe, I would hitchhike from one city to the next," I said.

"How do you do that?" he asked.

I gave a brief visual demonstration of my hitchhiking technique by stepping into the road and holding up my thumb. This made him laugh.

"Do you go with any old car that stops?" he asked.

"Of course, it has to go where one intends to go, or at least in that direction. And it must also appear safe to go with the people in the vehicle," I explained. As I proceeded to tell him in some detail about the 5,000-mile trek from Central Europe to South India via Greece, Asia Minor, Iran, Afghanistan and Pakistan, he appeared impressed by my account of the adventurous journey. He was curious about some of the countries which he had never visited, like Iran and Afghanistan, asking questions which I had to scramble to answer with any degree of accuracy.

As the nocturnal shadows were growing deeper, lights were coming on along the road and in houses. Halting in front of our common residence, Krishnamurti grabbed my arm with one of his characteristic, affectionate gestures.

"Good night, sir," he said, "see you tomorrow."

And entering the house, he gently closed the door behind him.

"Good night, Krishnaji," I called after him.

BEING SO CLOSE TO HIM NOT ONLY GAVE ME A CHANCE TO observe the course of his daily life; it also imbued my own life with a rhythm of contemplative tranquillity, the like of which I had never known before.

At a certain level, his life seemed to be simplicity itself. He did his morning exercises, yoga and *pranayama*, and took his meals in the house, often in company; he wrote at his desk what I took to be correspondence and diary, since he did not prepare his talks but spoke extemporaneously, from the essence of the situation at hand. In the afternoon, he took an after-lunch siesta. An hour or two before sunset he would go for a walk, often with friends, who took him by car to nearby Adyar beach. Apart from giving public talks and dialogues, he had frequent meetings with his associates. The other visitors he received came to pay obeisance, often with a ceremonial offering of flowers and baskets of fruit. It was part of the ancient Indian tradition to seek *darshan*, the presence of a religious teacher or guru, and be highly devotional toward that person.

I observed an example of this kind of devotion during one of the few musical performances staged in honor of Krishnamurti. One of the most famous South Indian singers, M.S. Subbulakshmi, a woman with an angelic voice, sang devotional songs beneath the *pandal* in front of a large audience, including Krishnamurti. After the enchanting two-hour performance, the lady descended from the stage and paid homage to him by going down on her knees and touching his feet with her finger-tips. Although he did not care for such behavior, he good-naturedly tolerated this public display of devotion, in turn draping a garland of jasmine and plumeria blossoms round her neck.

IT WAS THE DAY AFTER THE MADRAS TALKS. I KNEW THAT Krishnamurti was going to depart for Rishi Valley very early in the morning and had steeled myself to rise for the occasion. It was still dark, and I watched from a distance as the Ambassador car pulled up in front of the small fountain and lotus pool, adorned by an iron statue of Shiva Nataraj. Lights were turned on and servants began loading the car with suitcases. There was a slight chill in the air, and when I looked at the bright stars overhead, I could only detect the most minute indication of dawn, a single streak of light in the east. Suddenly all the servants ceremoniously lined up next to the car, and the chauffeur opened the door on the passenger side. I quickly strode over and stood a few feet behind them. Accompanied by his hostess and one of his associates, Krishna-murti walked up to the car and quietly responded in kind to the solemn *namaste* that we were offering. He looked frail as he got into the car, wrapped in a woolen shawl. As the vehicle pulled out of the courtyard, I felt a strange sense of absence and loss. A week of living in physical proximity to him had enabled me to get glimpses of his simple, radiant life but had also created a form of attachment within me. And now that it was over, I felt both enriched and bereft, even though the next day I was going to follow him to Rishi Valley.

AT RISHI VALLEY, AND SOME WEEKS LATER AT BANGALORE, I saw a lot less of Krishnamurti, except on talk days. At Bombay, the teeming metropolis on the Arabian Sea, he lived in a part of the city called Malabar Hill, near the Towers of Silence, the Zoroastrian burial grounds. After locating the house with some difficulty, I rang the bell in the hope of meeting him. His hostess, a powerful, aristocratic lady, received me cordially, and, after offering me some tea, informed me that he was staying in the house but wasn't seeing anybody. She revealed, however, that in the late afternoons he usually went for a walk in the nearby Hanging Gardens, and that I might possibly see him there.

This sounded intriguing enough for me to find my way to the public park overlooking the crescent bay, crowded with highrise buildings. The Hanging Gardens turned out to be a topiary garden, whose shrubs were clipped into the ornamental shapes of elephants, tigers and other animals. Just before sunset huge crowds, almost without exception dressed in loose, white clothing, thronged the pathways of the gardens. For a moment I wondered whether they had all come to see Krishnamurti. Discarding this notion as unlikely, I asked myself how I might possibly detect him among this densely packed multitude.

Suddenly I saw him. He was walking extremely fast, almost running, around the central lawn of the gardens. Five or six people were frantically trying to keep pace, without ever quite catching up with him. Under the circumstances, it seemed absurd to even want to greet him, so I simply watched him from a distance. I marveled at his stamina, how, without slowing down, he walked round the lawn again and again for about half an hour, before setting off for home, his companions in tow, while the saffron light of dusk suffused everything with a great stillness.

AFTER THE BOMBAY TALKS, I FIRST TRAVELED TO EUROPE AND from there went on to California, since I had learned that Krishnamurti was going to speak in both San Francisco and Ojai. In early March, 1973, he gave four public talks at the Masonic Temple in the City by the Bay. It was a special delight to listen to him in this wonderful metropolis, where I had spent a number of years.

Abundant spring rains had transformed California into a land of lush-green hills and valleys, with carpets of golden poppies and blue lupins along the highways. During the drive south toward Ojai, I thought I had never experienced the earth and its beauty more poignantly.

Turning off the 101 freeway at Ventura, I entered the Ojai Valley on highway 33. The changing colorful panorama in front of me enchanted all my senses. The valley bowl with its undulating contours and geometric patterns of orange groves was bathed in the glow of the setting sun. The crests and folds of the mountains were sharply etched in violet and purple shadows, contrasted by bright patches of yellow and green. An enormous sense of stillness enveloped the earth and the luminous sky. It felt as if I was entering a scene of magic and profound beauty.

On a sun-bright Saturday morning in April, Krishnamurti was giving the first of four talks at the Libbey Bowl in Ojai. A breeze was rustling the sycamore leaves, as a side-door opened and the slender, diminutive figure stepped into the limelight of the amphitheater, the ranks of which were filled with a thousand people or more. He was dressed with modest elegance in dark-grey, sharp-creased trousers, highly-polished, red-brown cordovans, and a long-sleeved knit shirt. I noted that the Bordeaux-red of his shirt matched the color of the one I was wearing. As he stepped forward, I marveled at how complete he appeared in himself and the sense of focused stillness that enveloped him.

Once seated on the chair in the middle of the large stage, a small microphone stand in front of him, he gazed with imperturbable calm at the many faces that were watching him.

When finally he began to speak, he seemed to be addressing each person singly and everyone collectively at the same time. He spoke of thought and the fragmentation it had caused on all levels of existence; he spoke of pleasure and fear, of the beauty of nature, of death, love and meditation, unraveling the whole spectrum of human life. Then, after a concluding interval of silence, he gestured to people to get up, as he found it impolite to get up before they did.

Suddenly I remembered a poem which I had recently written and intended to give to him. I was sitting in the third row and noticed a passageway from the stage to the road, screened off by a wooden enclosure with a door. I quickly walked over there and found the door unlocked. Nobody but myself—in contrast to Saanen and India—appeared to be rushing to seek post-talk contact with the speaker. I quietly slipped through the door and, turning around, found myself face to face with Krishnamurti.

My first sensation was silent shock and a thunderous heartbeat of recognition. Then I instinctively pulled back, afraid that I had intruded into his sphere of privacy. He was by himself, leaning with one arm on a table, as if catching his breath after a marathon run. There was a faint flush across his face, and his eyes had an unusual glow. Yet he seemed neither surprised nor disturbed by my unexpected appearance, but only watched me with quiet detachment.

I had never seen him like that: tremulously fragile and utterly vulnerable. I felt embarrassed by my own massiveness. My gesture of handing him a piece of paper with a poem on it appeared ludicrous in the context of the moment. But I did it anyhow, stammering, "Thank you, sir. Thank you."

He accepted the sheet of paper with trembling hands and looked at it, puzzled, as if unable to decipher it.

"It's a poem I've written for you, sir," I explained with a voice that sounded rather alien to me.

"All right, sir. I'll read it later, if you don't mind."

I didn't know what else to say. After an interval of silence that seemed endless he shook my hand, saying, "Thank you, sir. Good-bye."

I felt immense gratitude and friendship toward him as he turned and walked out to the road.

THAT SAME YEAR, I WAS DRAWN AGAIN TO THE SUMMER TALKS at Saanen. I helped with the setting-up of the tent by the riverside. One afternoon, several of us were busy finishing off the job, since the talks were to start the following day. I was digging a ditch around the tent overhang. Just then, a Mercedes sedan drove up and rolled to a stop at the side exit. A jolt of excitement shot through me when I recognized Krishnamurti stepping out of the car. The lady who accompanied him, of almost equal height and stature, was dressed with elegant but subdued sophistication. As they walked around the tent, carefully studying the inside and outside details, Krishnamurti greeted each person they encountered. I was inside the tent when they entered the large geodesic space. Both of them recognized me from our previous encounters, and I felt a wave of joy when Krishnamurti addressed me by my first name. I stammered, "It's wonderful to see you again, sir. We're almost finished with getting the tent ready for tomorrow."

"It's quite a bit of work, isn't it?" he remarked.

After exchanging a few words with his companion, he asked me,

"Would you mind, sir, going up on that platform and sitting on the chair for a moment?"

"Of course not, sir," I replied, briefly bewildered by the request. As I walked onto the stage, I felt a little awkward, and conflicting thought signals crossed my mind as to the purpose of the exercise.

"Yes, please, sir, sit down on the chair," he repeated, when he noticed my slight hesitation.

Lowering myself onto the wooden chair, I was for a moment tempted to assume one of Krishnamurti's characteristic poses: holding the edge of the seat with both hands and sitting on them. Krishnamurti and the lady walked up the aisle to the far end of the tent, checking the angles of visibility, while I sat there in immobile silence, looking out over the empty ranks of wooden benches.

"Could you please move the chair a bit to the left?" Krishnamurti called out from the back row.

Moving the chair, I watched quietly as they consulted with one another. As I was sitting there on the platform, in the speaker's place, it occurred to me how inherently contradictory it was to imitate him, or anyone else. Simultaneously, I realized that I did want to be like him, or whatever I imagined him to be like. I wanted to lead a life without conflict, to have a silent mind of compassion and serenity, and yet full of extraordinary energy and liveliness.

While these thoughts were crossing my mind, Krishnamurti waved from the back, calling across the rows of empty benches, "Thank you, sir."

"You're welcome, sir," I answered and walked off the stage to continue with the preparatory work.

*Part Two*

# LUNCHES WITH KRISHNAMURTI

## Chapter 5

# IN THE VALLEY OF THE MOON

### Starters

*Tossed green salad with a choice of
vinaigrette or yogurt dressing.
A selection of raw vegetables: sliced tomatoes,
sliced cucumbers, cubed celery and
grated carrots with lemon and honey.
Lentil soup with peppers, onions, celery,
carrots, tomatoes and parsley.*

### Main Dishes

*Steamed whole brown rice
with slivered almonds.
Ratatouille, containing garlic, onions,
mushrooms. bell peppers, zucchini,
tomatoes and eggplant, served with
freshly grated Gruyère cheese.*

### Dessert

*Tropical fruit salad, with pineapple,
papaya, bananas, tangerines and peaches,
garnished with slices of fresh coconut.*

AFTER ATTENDING THE TALKS AT BROCKWOOD PARK and those at New Delhi in November, I toured Southeast Asia for a year, eventually arriving at the Land of the Rising Sun during the *ume*-blossom season of 1975. While teaching at a private school in Kyoto, I went through an intense period, examining the course and the texture of my life. The introduction to Krishnamurti's work had radically altered my outlook on life, and the sporadic personal contact with him over the past four years had opened a door to what I thought was another dimension of consciousness. But it was only a glimpse of the promised land, something that I seemed far from realizing in my own life. My mind-set of searching for the sacred was fully operative, and living in cultures with a Buddhist tradition, like Nepal, Laos, Thailand and Japan, provided me with a compelling insight into the fact that any religious undertaking, once organized and institutionalized, would result in predominantly empty forms, superstitions, dogmas, and rituals, away from the living essence of the truth.

Seeing this, I wondered whether it might not be possible to work together with like-minded people in a context without power hierarchies, conflict, competition and pressure, and without falling into the traps that all, or most, institutions fall into. I longed to work at something meaningful, beyond the narrow perimeters of self-interest that I observed all around me and within myself, something which might carry the potential of transforming human consciousness.

Just then, I received a letter from a friend in Ojai, informing me that a new Krishnamurti School was going to start there in September. There were still some job openings—for a gardener, cook and maintenance man—that I could apply for if I was interested. This was like a message from heaven, exactly answering my questions and longings. I got on the phone and called my friend in Ojai to confirm that I was indeed interested in working at the school, in whatever capacity.

I had met Alan Hooker and his wife Helen at Rishi Valley in 1972, and we had struck up a correspondence. They were the owners of the famous Ranch House Restaurant, popular with a great many film and stage celebrities. He suggested that I stop over at Saanen for the Talks there, before coming on to California. That sounded like an excellent plan, and we agreed to meet in Switzerland in July.

LISTENING TO KRISHNAMURTI IN SAANEN THAT YEAR WAS AN
entirely new experience for me—like listening to him for the first time.
Of course, I had heard the words before, had read them, pondered
them. But what he managed to convey in the tent by the riverside had
a quality of revolutionary newness. The prospect of working with him
on the new educational project in Ojai filled me with a sense of being
involved in an enterprise of vital importance for humanity.

WHEN I ARRIVED AT OJAI IN MID-AUGUST, I FOUND MYSELF
in a completely new situation. The first surprise was the beauty of the
valley at the height of summer, hot and dry, with that peculiar starkness
of the desert region, the strong scent of sumac and sage, and a night sky
of brilliant stars. The property where I lived and worked was at the east
end of the valley; it was a large ranch-style building constructed in the
early part of the century and surrounded by a dozen acres of orange and
avocado groves. It was appropriately called Arya Vihara, A.V. for short,
the Sanskrit words for 'noble abode', and Krishnamurti, his brother, and
other figures associated with him, had lived here since 1922. Apart from
the orchards, there was an abundance of vegetation: eucalyptus,
cypress, pine, fig, persimmon and many other varieties of trees, as well
as different kinds of flowering bushes, such as oleander, rose, and jasmine. This lovely estate was not only to be the residence of the school
staff, but also was to contain the classrooms, at least until the time when
the new school buildings at the other end of the valley, next to the Oak
Grove, would be ready for use.

The greatest surprise for me was when I learned that I was to be the
school cook. For a moment I was utterly speechless, since I had naively
imagined that I would have a choice in the matter. I had, in fact, fancied myself as the gardener and groundsman, although my experience
of gardens was virtually nil. But it didn't take me long to adjust internally to this radically different situation. There was great freedom in
starting from scratch, from absolute zero. I realized that I didn't know a
thing and, therefore, was free to discover and find out for myself. I did
not harbor any pretense about my ability and importance and felt like a
child, free to roam and explore. This state of mind also allowed me to
delve deeply into culinary matters. One circumstance which helped me

immensely in slowly acquiring the art of cooking was the proximity of the Hookers, who for starters presented me with one of the vegetarian cookbooks[2] that Alan had written.

For the next few months I studied it from cover to cover, learning about herbs and spices, measuring, chopping, stirring and testing. It became a culinary bible, of sorts, and it turned out to be extremely convenient that the author was present to answer questions and to teach me hands-on the tricks of the trade. In fact, both Alan and Helen were magnificent teachers, never asserting themselves, never imposing anything or pulling rank, but only offering to help: the true way of the teacher— to allow the student, even if he is an ignoramus, to do it his way, and only lending a helping hand when necessary.

Another factor which helped me ease into my new role of marshaling the art of vegetarian cuisine was the circumstance that the combined number of students and staff seldom exceeded ten, at least during my first few months at A.V. Even so, I was not at all immune from that curious psychological malady that afflicts so many people caught in balancing career and private life, namely: tension, stress, or simply time pressure. In my case, of course, it was to a large degree caused by the hands of the kitchen clock, that inexorably dictated the lunch or dinner hour.

When the director specified my responsibilities as the School chef as well as the Foundation's, he made clear that preparing meals for Krishnamurti during his visits to Ojai was part of the job. This was another great surprise, which shocked, concerned and delighted me. I was still very much in need of broadening my culinary expertise and, therefore, felt underqualified for a task of that order. Besides, I saw cooking for Krishnamurti as a tremendous responsibility. What if something went wrong?

But, at another level, I felt elated by this unexpected aspect of my position. It certainly was a privilege and honor to cook for someone whom one admired and cherished, and, in addition to acquiring new techniques and recipes, I tried to find out as much as possible about Krishnamurti's likes and dislikes in food. Again, it was primarily Alan who was able to fill me in on the basic essentials of cooking for K. He had not only cooked for him on many occasions during the past twenty-five years, but had also been instrumental in setting up the kitchen at the Brockwood Park School.

Within a basic vegetarian diet Krishnamurti's dietary restrictions were few: no rich food, which meant minimal use of fats and oils and of dairy products; avoidance of butter and cream altogether, as well as of refined flour and sugar products, and other processed food. No sharp, hot spices, like cayenne peppers. Use of the freshest produce available, of organic origin, if possible.

Since Krishnamurti usually arrived in California toward the end of February, I had almost half a year to refine my cooking skills and become adept at preparing food to his liking.

SUDDENLY, IN LATE OCTOBER, 1975, SOMETHING LIKE A STATE of emergency was declared in my mind. It was cause for both alarm and joy: Krishnamurti had canceled his usual three-month trip to India and was going to come to California instead. The reason for this dramatic change was that, earlier in the year, the Indian prime minister Indira Gandhi had declared a state of emergency, which mandated prior censorship of all publications, media transmissions, and public presentations. Talks like Krishnamurti's fell into the latter category, and, since he was unwilling to operate under such restraints, he had canceled his visit to India outright. There was some irony in this, since the prime minister frequently sought his spiritual and perhaps even practical counsel. But, even if special exemption from the emergency regulations were offered him, he clearly would not accept such favors. Thus, he came to California.

At first he stayed in Malibu but eventually, we assumed, he would come to visit the new school in Ojai.

It was an unusually warm, sunny morning in November and the news had spread fast that Krishnamurti was going to visit us at A.V. and stay for lunch. I immediately saw this as my first great test, demonstrating what I had learned in the field of the culinary arts during the past three months. It was a challenge which both stimulated and scared me.

It was a blessing that Alan and Helen appeared two hours before lunch-time to help with the preparation of the meal and the setting of the table. Despite the auspicious occasion, I wasn't in any mood for extravagant or experimental cuisine but simply wanted to play it safe. The luncheon for fourteen started with a tossed green salad, with a choice of vinaigrette or yogurt dressing, accompanied by a selection of raw vegetables: sliced tomatoes, sliced cucumbers, cubed celery and grated carrots, the latter touched up with lemon and honey. This was followed by a lentil soup which contained peppers, onions, celery, carrots, tomatoes, and parsley, all finely cut. The main dishes were steamed: whole brown rice, adorned with slivered almonds, and a fragrant stew of ratatouille, containing garlic and onions, mushrooms and bell peppers, zucchini and tomatoes, and eggplant, cut in fairly large chunks and initially cooked separately with their respective herbs, before being combined in one pot and simmered slowly to what one hoped was perfection. Some freshly grated Gruyère cheese was offered on the side.

I was just in the middle of preparing the dessert, a tropical fruit salad, consisting of pineapple, papaya, bananas, tangerines, and peaches, embellished with slivers of fresh coconut, when the director came hurrying into the kitchen. He told me that Krishnamurti was on his way over from Pine Cottage, his home in Ojai since the early twenties, separated from the A.V. buildings by about fifty yards of orange grove. He was going to meet the school staff in the sitting room in a few minutes.

Meeting Krishnamurti always was an exciting event that I could never entirely get accustomed to, and seeing him now in my new capacity of *chef de cuisine* made it especially thrilling. After turning off the gas-burners on the range, I removed my apron and went into my quarters, that adjoined the kitchen. I quietly washed and, checking in the mirror that I looked somewhat presentable, combed my hair and dabbed on a splash of cologne before walking through the kitchen and dining-room into the library.

Trustees, staff and volunteers, a dozen people altogether, were standing around in small groups, conversing with one another in respectful tones. It looked a bit like a scene from a drama, in which the actors were compulsively entertaining one another, keeping each other in check, as it were, while the actual protagonist, the focus of attention, was off by himself, involved in his own internal monologue. So it was here: Krishnamurti, dressed with simple elegance, was standing by himself in front of the bookcase that covered one wall, studying the book-spines, every once in a while taking out a volume and, after briefly perusing it, placing it back on the shelf.

Although I knew everyone in the room, I felt rather shy and a bit nervous and, standing by myself, watched Krishnamurti for a moment, before the director, a tall man with startlingly blue eyes, noticed my pensive helplessness and gestured for me to approach, so that he could introduce me to Krishnamurti.

"Excuse me, Krishnaji," he said to Krishnamurti, who turned around to face us, a book in his hands.

Replacing the book, he acknowledged, "Yes, sir."

"Sir, this is Michael Krohnen, our new cook."

"How are you, sir?" Krishnamurti asked me as we shook hands.

"Thank you, sir. It's wonderful to be here and work at the new school. But I still have a lot to learn," I ceremoniously remarked.

Neither of us referred to our previous encounters, nor was I sure that he had any recollection of them. It did not seem to matter, since we were in a new configuration of events, as if meeting for the first time. While I was still groping for more to say, overpowered by a surge of elation, Krishnamurti turned to resume the study of the book titles. Suddenly I noticed on top of the bookcase, just above him, an alabaster sculpture of the Buddha's head in the Gandhara style, combining Indic and Hellenic features, and somehow resembling Krishnamurti's face.

As I returned to the kitchen, it occurred to me that I was not only a spectator and a witness but also an actor in a play that was spontaneously unfolding, the form and outlines of which I could not yet fathom.

After I had put the finishing touches to the lunch preparations, we carried the dishes to the serving table on the back patio just outside the kitchen. It was still pleasantly warm and sunny, and the two rustic redwood tables with long benches on either side of them were set with table-mats, cutlery and glasses, with bread and butter, and pitchers with water, milk and juice. Everybody lined up to serve themselves, and I noticed that Krishnamurti was the last in line. After I had brought a semblance of order to the kitchen, I took a plate for myself and stepped behind him; he had just started putting some food on his plate. He must have felt my presence because he turned around, regarding me with friendly eyes.

"Ah, Michael," he said. Stepping aside to let me pass, he urged me politely, "Please, sir, go ahead."

"No, please, sir," I apologized with some firmness, "it wouldn't be proper that I precede you: the person who prepares the food should go last. I mean, it's always like that—in the home, at banquets, and so on."

There was a swift sparkle of delight in his eyes as he listened to my argument, watching me closely. "All right, sir," he admitted with a laugh, giving his words a playfully formal emphasis, "you'll be the last in line."

Of the two places left at the tables, he chose the one in the shade. I sat a few seats away from him, but almost involuntarily my glance would wander in his direction. Chewing his food, he was quietly following the low-key conversation that flowed between us. He seemed rather shy and, when asked a question, he answered briefly but politely. It was only when the talk turned to cars, speed limits, and traffic regulations in different countries, that his interest perked up. "I was going ninety miles an hour on the Swiss autoroute earlier this summer," he recounted enthusiastically, and, noting the shocked surprise among some of the guests, added, "It's not against the law there. And it was quite safe, I was driving a Mercedes."

Some of us laughed, as we envisioned him racing along.

"I must tell you this joke," he started, but then asked somewhat puckishly, "There aren't any Christians here?"

"We're all Christians, Krishnaji," one lady responded jokingly, "or most of us were — until we heard you." More laughter.

"All right, then you won't mind if I tell you this joke about heaven," he continued. "A man dies, Mr. Smith, a used-car salesman, and goes to heaven. St. Peter receives him at the Pearly Gates and, going over his daily list, says to him, 'All right, Mr. Smith, you've led a fairly decent life, didn't commit too many sins, you can enter heaven. Any wish you have, we will fulfill.' The man immediately says, 'Ah, I've always wanted to have a brand-new Ferrari convertible.' St. Peter replies, 'That's no problem at all. We've got any model, color, year you could dream of. Just follow me.' And he takes him to an immense parking lot above the clouds, filled with rows upon rows of the most wonderful cars. 'Pick any model you want,' St. Peter says to the man. So he picks one to his liking, new and highly polished. And St. Peter says to him, 'But I have to tell you that we have a speed limit up here — it's a celestial law: you can't go over thirty-five miles per hour. Everybody has to obey this law; and if you transgress, that'll be the end of that. I hope you understand this.' And Mr. Smith agrees to it. And so he happily drives around, always staying within the speed limit. Then one day, a car zooms past him at a hundred miles an hour. He's quite upset by this and drives over to St. Peter. 'A car just passed me at a hundred miles an hour,' he complains, 'and I have always kept...' St. Peter interrupts him. 'What type of car was it?' he asks. 'Well, I think it was a red convertible, a Porsche,' Mr. Smith answers. 'And did you see the driver? Did he have a beard and long hair?' St. Peter inquires. The man is surprised and says, 'That's right. How did you know?' 'Well,' says St. Peter with a sigh and a dismissive shrug, 'there's nothing we can do — that's the boss's son.'"

We all broke out laughing, not only about the joke itself, but also about the amusing way Krishnamurti told it, with animated gestures and comical facial expressions. It was apparent that he took great delight in recounting it.

WHILE CLASSES FOR THE INITIAL THREE STUDENTS OF THE OAK Grove School, as it had recently been named, were going on at A.V., the first school building, the Pavilion, was being constructed about seven miles to the west, at the other end of the valley. Krishnamurti and Mrs. Mary Zimbalist, his hostess and secretary, came driving up from Malibu almost every weekend. They would take lunch with the resident staff at A.V., and I would carry their dinner over to Pine Cottage, where they stayed overnight. On sunny days, we'd be serving lunch outdoors on the back patio.

These lunch encounters with Krishnamurti had a certain touch of magic for me. There was an ambiance of refinement and an ease of exploration that were quite unique. Moreover, it was a great opportunity to observe and interact with him. But in the beginning I felt too self-conscious to try to engage him in any type of conversation other than ordinary small talk, especially in the presence of other people. Every so often, however, we would have an unexpected encounter and converse about all sorts of unlikely matters. One Saturday, as I was carrying dishes from the kitchen to the serving table outside, I suddenly found him standing in front of the so-called 'freedom machine' that we had fixed to the patio wall a few days earlier. He was carefully studying the contraption, that emitted a bluish radiance, accompanied by a steady humming noise.

"What is this, sir?" he asked me.

"Well, Krishnaji," I said respectfully, "it's an electrical machine designed to attract bugs, flies and other flying insects and to, to — eliminate them."

None of the reactions, like revulsion or disgust, which I had anticipated he might have at the sight of the destructive apparatus, were forthcoming. He showed only a type of cool scientific interest, without any
emotional or moral judgment.

"How does it attract them?" he inquired.

"I think somehow this bluish light excites them, particularly at
night," I conjectured.

"And how does it kill them?" he continued unceremoniously, using
the word I had tried to avoid. I was starting to feel nervous and slightly
uncomfortable, since it was I who had suggested the installation of the
device to get rid of the many bugs which bred in the decaying fruit on
the ground of the orange grove and were a considerable nuisance during our lunches *al fresco*.

"You see this wire grating in front of the light tubes? It's electrically
charged. When an insect flies toward the light, it touches it with its
wings and gets electrocuted," I explained.

Just then, as if to illustrate my explanation, a fly flew toward the
seductive glow, and, as its fluttering wings struck against a filament,
there was a tiny explosion of sparks accompanied by a sharp, brief hiss.
I skeptically looked at him as he watched the deadly action of the
machine. A stillness had come over him, and his eyes had the bright
alertness of observation. He quickly stepped back at the sizzling sound
but continued to watch the process intensely, until the abrupt activity
had died down. Turning toward me, he stated matter-of-factly, "It's
quite deadly, isn't it?"

I was surprised that he so non-judgmentally regarded both the
insect-zapping machine and the fact that we used it here, since in his
talks and dialogues he emphatically condemned any killing of animals
by man, calling the killing of one human being by another the greatest
of evils. Naturally I concluded that this, like a dogma, inevitably covered everything. But dogma in any shape or form had obviously nothing
to do with it. His intelligence perceived the whole context, unencumbered by ideals or beliefs and guided only by actual facts; thus capable
of operating in any field—even the smallest, and seemingly trivial.

I nodded in response to his remark and pointed at a small plaque
attached to the appliance. "You see, sir, what they call it?"

He looked closely and read, "'Freedom Machine'. By Jove!"

I laughed out loud at this expression and at the paradoxical irony of the name. Krishnamurti briefly joined in with my laughter, before turning serious again.

"But it smells bad," he remarked.

I shrugged apologetically. "Perhaps we should turn it off while we're having lunch," I suggested.

"That's a good idea, sir," he said and turned to enter the kitchen through the screen door.

*Chapter 6*

# GATHERINGS WITH KRISHNAJI

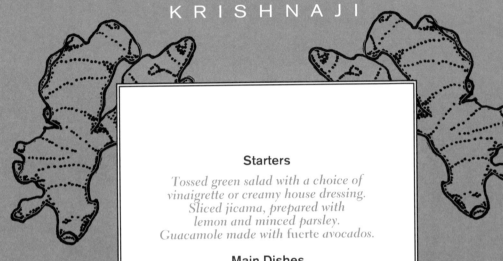

### Starters

*Tossed green salad with a choice of*
*vinaigrette or creamy house dressing.*
*Sliced jicama, prepared with*
*lemon and minced parsley.*
*Guacamole made with fuerte avocados.*

### Main Dishes

*Steamed corn-on-the-cob.*
*Pinto beans cooked in a sauce of*
*tomato & chili sauce.*
*Chili rellenos: mild green chili peppers.*
*stuffed with Monterey Jack cheese and baked*
*in a light mixture of eggs, milk and flour.*

### Dessert

*Giant sequoia strawberries, served with a*
*sauce of sour cream and sweet ginger.*

THE NEWS I RECEIVED IN MID-FEBRUARY WAS BOTH intimidating and electrifying. Within less than a month, in March, 1976, a six-day conference with Krishnamurti and more than twenty scientists and academics from all over North America was going to be taking place at A.V. It had been organized by Dr. David Bohm, a close associate of Krishnamurti, under the theme, "In a disintegrating society, what is the correct action for survival in freedom?"

It was going to affect me in more ways than one, since I was to take care of all catering matters for this meeting. Altogether, there would be between forty-five and fifty lunch guests, including conferees, spouses and staff. Barely six months into acquiring a basic *modus operandi* with vegetarian cuisine, I, the novice, was to compose and prepare the lunch and dinner menus for the week-long event. It seemed a daunting task, but fortunately Alan and Helen came, both to assist and to lend their expertise. In addition, several able volunteers materialized, who were willing to give a helping hand.

While the meals were served at A.V., the conference itself took place at the nearby home of Theo and Erna Lilliefelt, trustees of the Foundation and long-time friends of Krishnamurti. After each morning session, the doctors and professors and their spouses would arrive at A.V. in the early afternoon, still animated by the recent deliberations, and would continue discussing the topics during lunch. Amidst the academics, absorbed by their reasonings, Krishnamurti seemed rather pensive, almost reticent. It was fascinating to observe his interaction with the academic world, which, on the one hand, intrigued him and which, on the other, he did not hesitate to lambaste. He, who had repeatedly failed entrance examinations for well-known English universities and didn't have a degree or title to his name, was challenging the assembled scientists and professors in a fundamental way.

On the first day of the meetings, he exploded a psychological bomb in their very midst by declaring that "all thought leads to sorrow." The absoluteness of the simple statement not only questioned the foundations of knowledge on which the livelihood and careers of most of those present depended, it also implicitly negated their personal and collective value structures. It wasn't surprising therefore, that the uproar that followed did not die down until after the conference was over.

The presence of several flamboyant participants added to the heightened sense of drama, which prevailed throughout the seminar. Early on, a professor from a Canadian university exhibited somewhat eccentric behavior. When he found to his frustration that he wouldn't have an opportunity to present his lengthy dissertation on the self, he became rude and loud. After some abusive shouting, he departed prematurely on the third day. One scholar from Southern California wore a broad-brimmed cowboy hat with a feather in it, even when he sat down to eat. He referred to it as his 'power hat', a concept adopted from the writings of Carlos Castaneda, who at that time had started to become famous. The professor endeavored to draw parallels between the teachings of the books' central character, Don Juan, and the teachings of Krishnamurti. An attractive woman in her late twenties arrived incognito but blew her own cover the following day, perhaps out of frustration that nobody recognized her. She turned out to be the well-known spouse of a national leader with considerable celebrity status.

Amidst all these hectic goings-on, Krishnamurti remained calm, quietly observing what was happening around him. During one lunch conversation that dealt with the conflict between the two superpowers, the U.S. and the Soviet Union, he all at once joined the conversation, asking, "May I tell you a joke? Late at night, a drunk staggers across Red Square in front of the Kremlin, singing at the top of his voice, 'Brezhnev is an idiot! Brezhnev is an idiot!' Immediately, several KGB agents close in on him and haul him off to jail. The following morning he appears before the judge, who declares his sentence, 'Twenty years and two days of hard labor in Siberia.' The man cries out in disbelief, 'Twenty years and two days!? But why? I was only drunk in public.' And the judge responds, 'Two days are for being drunk in public. Twenty years for betraying a state secret.'"

There was a round of laughter at the table, and a few of the professors promptly recounted jokes of their own. Krishnamurti listened with rapt attention to their stories, laughing with whole-hearted abandon about some of them, until there was a brief lapse of silence. Then he told another joke from his repertoire. "You may remember the time when the Russians put the first cosmonauts into space. Upon their return, they were feted at a marvelous banquet at the Kremlin. All the party leadership was there, including Chairman Brezhnev. As he was pinning some medals to their chests, he said to them in a low voice, 'Please come and see me in my quarters later on.' They obediently agreed and went to see him. And he asked them, 'When you were up there in cosmic space above the earth, did you perhaps see a very old man with a long white beard and a halo around his head?' The cosmonauts answered, 'Well, yes, Comrade Chairman, we did indeed see someone like that up there.' Brezhnev nodded his head, 'That's what I thought. But listen here, comrades. Not a word of this to anyone! It's a state secret. If you tell anyone of this, it'll be Siberia and the Gulag for you. Is that understood?' The cosmonauts gave a smart salute, 'Yes, Comrade Chairman.' Next, they went on a tour of all the Communist countries of Eastern Europe and also visited Italy, which had a large Communist party. The Pope heard of this and invited them to a splendid banquet at the Vatican. Afterwards, they were led to him for a special blessing, and he asked them *sotto voce*, 'Please come and see me in my chambers.' The cosmonauts marveled at the private papal quarters, which surpassed the Chairman's in splendor and antiquity. And the Pope asked them, 'When you were up there in outer space, did you perhaps see an old man with a long white beard and a halo around his head?' The cosmonauts looked at each other in surprise, then shook their heads, 'No, Comrade Pope, we didn't see anyone like that up there.' The Pope pensively stroked his chin, 'Well, that's what I thought. But, please, don't tell a soul about it.'"

At that, the whole table broke out in exuberant laughter.

At the end of the six-day seminar, there were questions as to its success. Krishnamurti, with his rigorous skepticism, doubted that it had accomplished what it set out to do: to examine the role of thought and knowledge in a fundamentally new way. From the narrow kitchen angle, however, the conference was a success. Not even those guests who normally ate meat complained about the exclusively vegetarian fare we offered. In fact, there were a number of compliments, and the occasional request for a recipe. I felt it had been a culinary baptism by fire.

AT THE BEGINNING OF APRIL THERE WERE TWO WEEKS OF public talks at the Oak Grove. They attracted several thousand people from all over the country, even from overseas, who gathered on the grass and sat on chairs beneath a canopy of live-oaks. It was a secluded area of virgin nature that had never been built on or used for commercial purposes. On the northern side of the Grove a platform had been erected among the trees, from which Krishnamurti, sitting on a simple wooden chair, would be talking to the assembled people. They were a friendly crowd, easy-going and casual in the Southern Californian way, and sometimes eccentric: a good cross-section of humanity, with various races, ethnicities, classes and ages.

In a society where entertainment not only played an important role but also occupied a place in the sun, Krishnamurti was most emphatic in pointing out that this gathering was not an entertainment, nor a lecture, nor any kind of propaganda or preaching. For him, it was inquiring together into the many problems of existence; it was constant questioning, doubting, and examining together the way we live our lives. The key word was 'together'. Unless there was this movement of togetherness between him, the speaker, and us, the listeners, at the very same moment, the creative spark would be lost. The blue mountains in the background, the play of light and shade through the ever-green live-oaks, and the intense listening of the audience to the words amplified through loudspeakers all combined to create in my mind the impression of an exalted event.

AFTER THE OJAI TALKS, KRISHNAMURTI FLEW TO NEW YORK AND from there to Europe and India. This time, however, my continuing responsibilities at the Oak Grove School kept me from attending any of these gatherings, and it wasn't until the following February that we met again in Ojai.

A conference in March, 1977, scheduled to last for three weeks, was to bring together the trustees of the five international Krishnamurti Foundations. These nationally chartered institutions arranged his public talks in their respective countries, managed publications and translations, oversaw the administration of the various schools bearing his name, and collected the donations that supported these activities. About twenty trustees from the United States, Canada, England, India and Latin America had come to Ojai and several of them were staying at A.V. for the duration of the conference. It was my responsibility to cook for them during that time.

It was fascinating for me to see Krishnamurti's daily interaction with his close associates and friends of many years. On the one hand, he was completely democratic and egalitarian in the way he treated those around him. From the simple volunteer, gardener and cook to the successful businessman and well-to-do aristocrat, they all seemed to be the same to him; he treated everyone with equal respect and consideration. It wasn't only that he addressed everyone as 'sir' or 'madam', one could actually see his deeply observant, affectionate concern about every human being. Animals, flowers, trees and the things of daily life were not excluded from that gentle care and respect. I had never seen a person who was so well-mannered, in fact chivalrous, without its being in any way affected or mechanical.

On the other hand, I couldn't help the impression of being at a sovereign's court, with all sorts of subtle and not-so-subtle hierarchical distinctions. The uncontested focus of attention, to which everyone naturally paid deference, was Krishnamurti. He was the object of affection, with whom practically everyone was in love, and proximity to and distance from him appeared to bestow a subtle ranking. But it was primarily us who created these psychological distinctions, with their implicit comparisons and divisive barriers.

Even so, the lunches were delightful affairs, and with Krishnamurti in our midst, we felt like one large family, for whom comparison, envy and jealousy may not have been entirely absent, but where generally speaking, goodwill prevailed. Although I did not take part in the deliberations at the Lilliefelts' home, I was able to glean enough information from the lunch-time conversations that followed, and from the general mood and demeanor of the guests, to gain an impression of the meetings and their overall trend.

Clearly, he was taking them to task; their serious miens upon arrival for lunch at A.V. attested to that. They didn't appear gloomy or depressed, but rather thoughtful and turned inward—as if someone had shown them a jewel, the radiance of which emanated from their own hearts. Usually, during his meetings with the staff or the public, he took us to task, without any personal scolding or nagging, but rather mirroring what we were at that moment, outlining, so to speak, both the contours and the essence of our lives. But here, among his friends and co-workers, he apparently went beyond that, questioning everything, including their contribution to his work, as well as touching upon the future event of his death and how it might affect them and the Foundations. His concern was not about their financial survival, nor about the preservation of his recorded work, but rather about its living quality: whether the flame could be kept alive beyond his personal death. Would they who had worked with him for many years be able to convey the sense and feeling of what it had been like to live with him to a person who had never met him, he asked his trustees. "What will you tell the man from Seattle who comes here to find out about K, who doesn't know a thing about any of this? How will you convey it to him?" he asked with great urgency. Subsequently, the fictitious man from Seattle became a bit of a legend.

And, as if to fathom the strength of their commitment, he rhetorically posited the case of a disciple surviving the Buddha, and asked whether they would not travel to the ends of the earth to meet such a person in order to find out from him what it had been like to live with the Buddha.

WHILE ALL THIS WAS GOING ON, I WAS IN THE KITCHEN, preparing lunch for about thirty-five. The meal that day had a Mexican theme, consisting of green salad with sliced jicama, guacamole made with fuerte avocados from our orchard, and steamed corn on the cob. In addition, there were pinto beans cooked in a chili sauce and, as the main dish, chili rellenos, green chili peppers stuffed with cheese and, rather than deep-fried, baked in a light mixture of eggs, milk and flour. The dessert consisted of giant sequoia strawberries from the nearby Oxnard fields, served with a sauce of sour cream and sweet ginger.

The trustees and other lunch guests had already arrived and were in the sitting room, animatedly conversing with one another while waiting for Krishnamurti's arrival. Fifteen minutes later, he entered the kitchen from the patio with a, "Good morning, Michael," although it was past one o'clock in the afternoon. I stopped what I was doing and turned my full attention toward him. "Good morning, Krishnaji," I responded.

He wore blue jeans and a blue wool cardigan over a grey, checkered cotton shirt. He looked cheerful and carefree and as I looked at him with affection, there was a sudden feeling of being fully in the present moment, a sense of vibrant newness that I often experienced in his presence.

"What's for lunch, sir?" he asked, stepping up to the range to look into the pots. I gave a synopsis of the menu. When I mentioned the chili rellenos, he said, "Are they spicy?"

"They may have a little zing," I answered, "but I removed the seeds and membranes to make them less hot."

"Then I have to be careful and only take a small portion," he remarked. While I busied myself taking a ceramic baking dish out of the oven, he suddenly broke into joyful laughter. He responded to my curious look by pointing at the small rubber sticker that I had pinned to the refrigerator.

"'I'm not greedy, I just want the whole thing'," he read out loud, laughing delightedly, "That's very good; where did you get it?"

"Alan gave it to me," I explained. "I thought it had an appropriate ring."

Wiping tears from his eyes, he asked with a twinkle, "Is everything ready, sir? Can I tell them that lunch is being served?"

"Yes, please, Krishnaji. All that's left to do is to take the cooked food to the serving table."

"Can I carry something?" he offered.

I hesitated for a brief moment and then pointed at the dish piled high with steaming corn-on-the-cob. "If you don't mind, sir, you can carry this dish." I handed him two cloth potholders and held the automatic screen-door open for him as he carefully balanced the dish, placing it on the serving table in the patio, before proceeding to the sitting-room to inform the guests that lunch was ready.

I happened to be sitting with him at the same table, together with eight other guests, most of whom were trustees from India and the U.S. At some point the conversation turned to the traditional Indian belief that truth is transmitted from master to disciple, emphasizing the value of being in the presence of an enlightened person or spiritual teacher, which the Hindus call *darshan*. Probably everyone at the table was aware that Krishnamurti deeply questioned this concept. While listening to the discussion, it occurred to me that most of us here, in one way or another, were paradoxically in the situation of listening to the master, though in attenuated circumstances.

Krishnamurti had been following the conversation closely, occasionally contributing some words of his own, when all at once a smile spread over his face and he announced, "I have to tell you a story." Everyone at the table fell silent and turned toward him. "A young man wanting to find truth goes to see a famous guru. 'Master, can you teach me meditation and truth?' he asks. The guru agrees, and the disciple immediately assumes the lotus posture, closing his eyes and breathing rhythmically to show what he knows. The master doesn't say anything but picks up two stones from the ground and starts rubbing them against each other. Hearing the strange noise, the disciple opens his eyes and asks, 'Master, what are you doing?' The guru answers, 'I'm rubbing these two stones against each other to polish them into a mirror so I can look at myself.' The disciple laughs, 'But master, if you don't mind my telling you: you'll never be able to make a mirror of these stones by rubbing them against each other. You can do that forever, and it won't work.' 'Similarly, my friend,' the master says, 'You can sit like that forever, but you'll never be meditating or understanding truth.'"

Appreciative laughter erupted around the table, as he concluded the story with its multifaceted applications.

AFTER THE INTERNATIONAL TRUSTEES' CONFERENCE AT A.V., he gave ten public talks and discussions in the Oak Grove, before traveling to New York City for a weekend seminar with psychiatrists and psychologists. But instead of going on to Europe, as he usually did, he returned to California to undergo a prostate operation at a Los Angeles hospital. After recuperating for two weeks in Malibu, he visited Ojai a few times. After the first postoperative luncheon at A.V., he asked me to get some cranberry juice for him and to serve it during meals, which I promptly did. Just before lunch the following day, I ran into him on the terraced back lawn and, curious about his juice preference, asked him about it. It was on the recommendation of his doctors, he explained, that he was taking this particular fruit juice, since it cleansed the kidneys and urinary system. Then, to my astonishment, he proceeded to provide me with a brief but detailed description of the ailment that had afflicted him and the type of surgery he had just undergone. He was quite ingenuous about it, with an innocence that moved me deeply.

In the late afternoon, I carried a tray with his dinner to Pine Cottage. On my ringing the bell, he opened the door and I immediately felt a quality of unreserved friendliness, of being in the presence of a person who erected no psychological barriers. After I had placed the tray on the dining table, he said to me, "Michael, could you perhaps cook that soup for me?"

"Of course, Krishnaji," I consented. "Which soup are you thinking of?"

"You have sometimes cooked a soup with beans in it, several different kinds of beans," he explained. "What do you call it?"

After going through my internal index of soup ingredients and recipes for some seconds, I retrieved a likely name, "Do you mean the nine-bean soup?"

He laughed. "Yes, that's it. You prepared it the other day. Mrs. Zimbalist will be gone for a few days, and I'll be by myself in Malibu. So perhaps you could cook a large amount of it and put it in gallon glass jars, so that we can easily transport and freeze it."

"You don't mind eating the same food for several days in a row—and frozen at that?"

"It's a hearty and nourishing soup, isn't it? Practically a meal in itself. And all I have to do is heat it up. I don't know much about cooking but I can do that."

"Have you never cooked for yourself, Krishnaji?"

"When my brother and I first came to live here, we often prepared our meals. So we had to learn how to make toast, fry eggs, cook rice and so on," he recounted, the recollection of those youthful days half a century ago causing a smile to spread over his face.

"And how did it turn out?"

"We'd often burn things, or they tasted simply awful," he went on and started to laugh. "Once I spent some time in the mountains, in the High Sierras with the magnificent sequoias. I lived by myself in a cabin and prepared my own food. I threw everything into one pot and kept stirring it until it was one mush." He was laughing exuberantly now, his eyes sparkling, and his delight so infectious that I could not but share in his mirth. He was mimicking the gestures of throwing many things into one pot and stirring them vigorously. Our laughter created a momentary bond of joy between us as his words evoked the image of the young, inexperienced Krishnamurti in the mountain hut stirring his stew.

"And," I inquired, "was it edible?"

He kept laughing, tears rolling down his cheeks. "I had no choice. There wasn't anything else to eat."

Another delicious wave of liberating laughter swept over both of us. Calming down, we looked at each other with affection and without embarrassment.

"How many jars of the bean soup would you like, Krishnaji? You know that a gallon is quite a bit."

Wiping his moist eyes with a handkerchief, he agreed, "All right, sir. I think two of them should be enough."

When he returned to Ojai the following weekend, he told me privately after lunch, "Thank you very much for the soup, sir. It was really quite delicious. We still have half a jar of it. I didn't realize it was that much." And he rolled his expressive eyes in comical surprise, hastening to assure me, "And we won't throw it away, sir. It will keep for some time when frozen, won't it?"

"If you keep it frozen it should stay edible for about a month or so," I ventured.

At the end of June, he left for Europe, following his annual round of talks and discussions in Switzerland, England and India, while I remained in Ojai attending to the culinary needs of the staff.

### Starters

*Mixed green salad with a variety of
fresh garden greens, with a choice of
vinaigrette or sesame-tahini dressing.
Alfalfa sprouts and radishes.
Cherry tomatoes and sliced avocados
touched with lemon.*

### Main Dishes

*Baked yams.
Nine-bean soup, made with
nine different beans and legumes,
with onions, bell peppers,
celery and carrots, parsley and chives.
Fresh spinach leaves quickly stir-fried
with a touch of olive oil & garlic.*

### Dessert

*Apple crumble prepared with
grated apples, raisins and walnuts,
sweetened with honey and cinnamon,
a touch of lemon juice; baked in the oven
and covered with a topping made from
oats, flour, sugar and butter,
served with whipped cream on the side.
Fresh, seasonal fruit.*

IT WAS 1978 AND FOR THE PAST FEW MONTHS A SERIES OF rainstorms had been sweeping into California from the Pacific Ocean, lashing the coastal region with destructive force. Farther inland, the barrancas, dry riverbeds, had been turned into raging torrents, uprooting trees and sweeping away cars, houses and people.

But this particular afternoon in late March was calm, with an extraordinarily clear atmosphere, washed clean of pollutants and revealing the beauty of the valley in resplendent colors. A small group of staff and trustees were gathered beneath the old pepper-tree in front of Pine Cottage, awaiting the arrival of Krishnamurti. The tree had a massive trunk with large, bulging protuberances, and its arching branches reached wide into space, creating a dome of lacy leaves filtering the sunrays. There were hundreds of bees buzzing amidst the tiny white blossoms, dangling in long strands from the branches. The whole scene was a pastoral image of peace.

There were ten of us waiting beneath the tree, in front of the two-car garage, from where a flagstone path led to Pine Cottage. The house where Krishnamurti had lived since 1922, named after the pine trees that had once surrounded it, had been thoroughly rebuilt during the past year. It was an elegant structure built from adobe bricks, whitewashed, with many large windows, and since Mary Z. was giving up her house in Malibu, Krishnamurti was going to make Pine Cottage his home again. By a fitting coincidence, he had also just been granted permanent residency in the United States, thereby becoming a 'resident alien' and holder of a 'green card'.

Some of us were sitting on the low stone wall which protectively surrounded the pepper-tree, while others stood or paced about on the asphalt turning-circle between tree and garage. The warm afternoon seemed to be full of leisure, and an easy, amiable conversation was flowing between us.

I was sauntering back and forth along the driveway, some distance away from the others. I felt an odd mixture of joyful stimulation and great calm within me, not only because of seeing Krishnamurti again, but also because of the entirely new and thrilling prospect of having him live in our midst for three whole months of the year. It promised to be a great change for me and possibly for all of us at the School and Foundation. It implied especially meeting him every day during the three spring months, since I was to prepare daily luncheons for him and his guests at A.V. For that period, I would temporarily give up my other duties at the school.

The sunrays were already slanting at a low angle through the trees when I heard a car approaching. A moment later, the grey Mercedes sedan appeared on the long driveway through the orchard. Everyone stopped talking at the sight of the car. Those who had been sitting down got up, and it seemed that we instinctively arranged ourselves into an orderly line, like a guard of honor. After the sedan had rolled to a stop in front of the garage, the passenger door swung open—and there he was, looking rather frail and thin, in an elegant outfit of suit and tie. I felt a strong impulse to hold the door and help him out of the car, but I knew that he was adamant in refusing help in most matters relating to his person.

He slowly put his feet on the ground, pushing himself out of the seat as he held on to the door to steady himself. His gaze fell on the small, welcoming group standing at attention. There was an infinitesimal space of stillness, a moment of direct perception between us. Then a sudden burst of laughter shattered the silence. Krishnamurti tickled at the absurdity of the situation, was laughing out loud, "Why are you all standing there so solemnly?"

As if awakened from a moment's day-dream, we joined in with his laughter, as he swiftly approached us to shake hands with everyone in turn, exchanging a few friendly words of welcome and even gallantly kissing the hand of one lady. Finally he stepped over to me, the last person in the reception line. He carefully looked me up and down, as if to evaluate the state of my physical and mental well-being. Shaking my hand, he asked, "How are you, Michael?"

At that simple question, a wave of affection rose within me, tightening my vocal chords. I sensed a care and honesty coming from him such as one only encounters among the best of friends. That he had addressed me by my first name intensified this feeling of friendship.

"Thank you, Krishnaji," I responded, "we've been very busy here, preparing for your arrival. It's wonderful to see you again and to have you staying here now."

"All right, sir," he said, shaking my hand again. As he turned away from us, he looked appreciatively at the different kinds of flowers that adorned the walkway, remarking, "And now that all of this welcoming has been taken care of...", implying that the somewhat formal ceremony was over and we could all resume our normal activities.

But, in fact, the opposite was true: his entry into the situation was already altering the configuration of our daily lives and, like a catalyst of change, affecting the field of our experience.

As he now walked over the flagstone path toward the house, he took in the scenery around him with the excited eyes of a child.

"What a country this is!" he exclaimed with joyful awe, lingering to admire the tall rosebushes in front of the roofed porch. Red, yellow and pink roses were flowering profusely, and he gently held one open, the crimson blossom in his hands, and breathed in its perfume.

While one of the teachers and I carried the heavy suitcases from the car to Krishnamurti's room or into the vestibule of the house, he tarried in the small courtyard in front of the mandarin-red door. There were several flower beds, with violets, pansies and forget-me-nots. He looked at them with undisguised, tender joy, as if at that moment he was communicating with them.

Descending the wide stone steps from the house, I saw him standing in front of the violets, quietly immersed in their beauty. I stopped next to him and remarked after a moment's contemplation, "They are really lovely, aren't they?"

He turned sideways toward me, giving me a full, appraising look, almost as if he was seeing me for the first time. Then he gently and affectionately patted my slightly protruding belly with one hand, stating matter-of-factly, "You have got fat, haven't you?"

I was usually very self-conscious about my body-weight and, for an instant, felt acutely embarrassed by his frank observation. I was still at a loss for words when he admonished me in a caring and non-reproachful tone, "You really have to watch your weight, Michael."

I stammered apologetically, "Well, it's true—I have recently gained some weight."

This elicited a peal of unabashed, comradely laughter from him. He gave me an affectionate pat on my well-rounded shoulder. "Gained some weight!" he laughed.

Mary Z., who was coming up the path and had evidently overheard our exchange, also started to laugh. Overcoming my embarrassment, I finally could not help but join in the merriment. A wonderful lightness communicated itself as we shared a good, liberating laugh.

HAVING KRISHNAMURTI IN OUR MIDST FOR AN EXTENDED period very much changed the rhythm and quality of our lives at A.V., where daily luncheons were prepared and served. The number of participants changed from day to day, averaging twelve during the week and rising to twenty or more at weekends. At certain times, I also prepared dinners, especially when Dr. Bohm and his wife Saral were visiting. Krishnamurti and Mary Z., however, usually had their evening meal at Pine Cottage.

From the outset of my engagement as chef at A.V., I was convinced that I was a witness to and a participant in the apotheosis and germination of a new global culture. Primarily, people came to A.V. to have lunch together. But, more than the sharing of a meal, it was Krishnamurti's philosophy and presence that drew so many minds, both ordinary and illustrious, to the lunch table. The beauty of the setting, the food, and a good conversation among like-minded people all combined to create a special ambiance.

Invariably, the conversations spanned the whole spectrum of the human condition, freely but without frivolity or superficiality. Everybody was at liberty to say what they wanted, express their views, ask questions. There wasn't any agenda or expectation, nor any taboo, except outright vulgarity. Krishnamurti easily and without intent became the focus of attention. The unsought effect of his presence was like a natural phenomenon: as the wind blowing from one direction bends the tall grass of summer in the opposite direction, so was the affect of his personality on us.

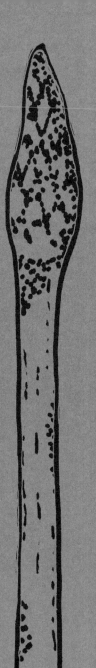

Chapter 8
# LUNCHING WITH KRISHNAJI

### Starters

*Crisp, green salad with a choice of
vinaigrette and creamy Roquefort dressing.
Tomato salad, with chopped olives,
minced garlic, garnished with capers.
Tabouli made with bulgur wheat,
finely-chopped fresh parsley
& mint, green onions and tomatoes,
flavored with olive oil and lemon juice.*

### Main Dishes

*Minestrone soup served with croutons
and grated Parmesan cheese.
Freshly-made Capelli di Angeli
served with a pesto sauce of
fresh basil leaves, olive oil, pine nuts,
Parmesan cheese, garlic, and salt & pepper.
Green asparagus spears, quickly steamed and
touched with herbs, olive oil, and lemon juice.*

### Dessert

*Chocolate mousse and oatmeal cookies.
Fresh, seasonal fruit.*

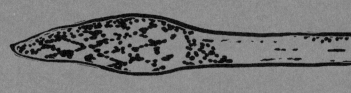

I WAS BY MYSELF IN THE KITCHEN. IT WAS A LITTLE PAST EIGHT o'clock on a bright Saturday morning, and I was getting ready to start the lunch preparations. I had done the shopping the previous afternoon in Santa Barbara and Ojai—at several stores I knew had good, fresh produce. I tended to plan a meal around the availability of fresh, seasonal vegetables and fruit, organic if possible. This morning I was going to prepare three salads. One of the them was an Arabic dish called tabouli, the second was a tomato salad with chopped olives, some minced garlic and fresh basil, embellished with capers; the third dish made with raw vegetables—I usually aimed to offer an equal part of raw and cooked food—was a simple green salad, with two side dressings.

Next on the list was minestrone soup, served with croutons and grated Parmesan cheese. I regularly prepared soups, since Krishnamurti had a fondness for them. In addition, I was going to make fresh pasta, *capelli di angeli*, on the pasta machine somebody had recently donated to the kitchen, and serve it with a pesto sauce of fresh basil, olive oil, pine nuts, Parmesan cheese, a little garlic, and salt and pepper. This was to be complemented with some of the delicious asparagus just coming into season, quickly steamed and touched with a sprinkling of herbs, olive oil and lemon juice. I had given up serving it with *sauce hollandaise*, which was simply too rich in fat and cholesterol. For dessert, there would be chocolate mousse which, of course, could not be described as light or low in calories.

I enjoyed working quietly by myself in the kitchen. It had a lot of light and plenty of space, and the tools and appliances were easily accessible. After working in silence for an hour or two, I turned on the classical music station. (Every so often, I switched to the all-news station to follow the latest developments in the global situation.) I envisioned my cooking activity as a form of dance, a choreographed series of movements, centering around the cutting-board table in the middle of the kitchen. From there it radiated to sink, stove, refrigerator, and storage shelves, bringing together the various ingredients and utensils, blending them to the strains of the music. When slicing, chopping or cubing vegetables, however, a contemplative mood would arise, and it appeared as if everything was moving of its own accord, and all I had to do was watch things unfold and flavors blend.

At around eleven or eleven-thirty, Alan and Helen arrived at A.V. They usually gave a hand by setting the table, preparing a dish, and helping in many other ways. Simultaneously, I used the opportunity to learn more of Alan's expertise. He was one of the great innovators of Southern California cuisine, willing to answer any of my questions and offering excellent practical advice, without ever assuming a superior attitude.

Even though it was a Saturday, only fourteen people had notified me that they were coming for lunch. By one o'clock, everything was ready. Alan and Helen had gone to the sitting room to join the other guests, while I swept the floor, cleaned the utensils, and wiped and cleared the counters, trying to make the kitchen space appear as empty and unused as possible. Having everything ready to serve was a special moment for me. I felt a pleasant sense of leisure and an upsurge of energy. At some mental and emotional level, I was looking forward to and readying myself for what I referred to as 'the entrance', Krishnamurti's arrival for lunch. It was the high point of the day and usually occurred around 1:30 in the afternoon.

During the first few years, when I still lived in the small room adjoining the kitchen, I would use the interval between clean-up and the serving of the meal to retire into the quiet semi-dark of the room's large walk-in closet. Sitting cross-legged on a pillow for a few moments, breathing deeply and deliberately, I would aim to empty my mind of the pressures and worries accumulated over the past few hours. After I had thus internally prepared myself for the upcoming encounter with Krishnamurti and the other guests, I'd go into the bathroom next door to freshen up. After moving to the small cottage just a few steps outside the kitchen, I only rarely got around to immersing myself in pre-lunch tranquillity, since it was difficult to monitor his arrival from there and keep an eye on whatever was simmering on the stove. Now I quickly went to comb my hair and splash on some cologne. Standing in front of the mirror, I carefully studied my appearance and decided to change my shirt.

Although we met several times a day, I experienced each time as something special. Somehow, it was a challenge to come into contact with him, heightening my level of energy and acuteness of perception. Being completely in the moment, as he was, there was always a subtle newness about him which was as surprising as the beginning of a new day. And nothing seemed quite able to prepare one for the actuality of the event.

Re-entering the kitchen, I checked the temperature controls at the stove. Everything appeared to be in order. I walked over to the radio, turned it off and stowed it beneath the counter. Official lunch time was one o'clock, but it was seldom that Krishnamurti and Mary Z. appeared before 1:30. And, although most guests tended to be on time, no one seemed to mind waiting for them.

As I was taking the salads out of the refrigerator, I heard Krishnamurti and Mary Z. in front of the screen door. Looking up at the clock above the refrigerator, I noticed it was 1:15. They were a bit earlier than usual. Stepping up to the door, I saw him balancing a pile of neatly folded clothes in one hand and, with the other, struggling to pull open the screen door. Mary Z. stood behind him with two empty plastic water bottles in her hands. She was pleading with him, "Please, sir, let me open the door for you."

He didn't seem to pay any heed to her entreaties but was watching his own movements with intense attention. Because of the door's automatic spring, it required a strong pull to get it open. As he tried to do this, he insisted, "No, no, Maria. I can do it. You have your hands full."

"Good morning, Krishnaji. Good morning, Mary," I said, carefully pushing the door open from the inside.

Krishnamurti looked at me briefly and responded, "Good morning, Michael," and smoothly maneuvered past me.

"Good afternoon," said Mary Z., correcting our time assessment. For a reason that wasn't quite clear to me, I usually greeted him with "Good morning", even though it was clearly past noon, and he tended to answer in like manner.

"Shall I take these, if you don't mind?" I asked Mary Z.

"Yes, thank you," she replied with a smile. After handing me the two one-gallon containers, she walked over to enter the sitting room through the patio's French door.

While I was putting the empty water bottles on the table next to the five-gallon dispenser, he was placing the stack of clothes on the long counter, making sure it was clean.

"Here are some shirts, sir. They are clean. See if any of them fit you. If not, give them to someone else." He made a slightly dismissive gesture. I considered it an honor to be offered garments which he had worn. They were almost like new, immaculately clean and freshly pressed, most likely by Mary Z. She took care of most of his laundry while they resided at Pine Cottage.

Thanking him sincerely, I examined the shirts to see if any of them might fit me. He quietly stood beside me, watching me. It was a miracle that I might wear any of his shirts at all, given the considerable difference in our sizes. But many of his garments tailored in India tended to be cut generously wide and sometimes were large enough for me.

Apart from the shirts, there was a sleeveless, buttonless Indian *bundi* vest that was beautifully tailored and had a lovely feel to it. Trying it on, I remarked excitedly, "This fits me well, sir. It's really wonderful. What is it made of?"

"It's raw silk."

"Thank you, Krishnaji."

"That's all right," he calmly replied, placing his hand on two paperbacks, which were also among the things on the counter. "Here are some thrillers, sir. Maybe you haven't read them yet."

While I was studying the titles and captions of the books, he strolled over to the other side of the kitchen and started to fill one of the empty bottles from the water dispenser. As he stood in front of the large plastic container, his slim, narrow back turned toward me, he appeared strangely vulnerable. He was paying close attention to what he was doing, one hand holding the bottle to the spout, the other one depressing the lever. He stood very close to the dispenser, intently gazing down as the water flowed from the larger to the smaller container, accompanied by loud gurgling noises. I had been pondering a question, which now popped into my mind, and I stepped up to his right, intent on asking him. But, since I did not want to divert his attention, I quietly stood there watching him.

As he pulled the full bottle away from the spigot, he misjudged the timing by a fraction of a second, flicking back the lever a bit too late. Some water spilled onto the floor. He jumped back with lightning speed, avoiding the spray and at the same time exclaiming, "Oh, I'm sorry. I spilled some water. I'm so sorry, sir, I'll wipe it up."

He seemed not only chagrined by his brief inattention but also annoyed at himself for causing the spillage. I hastened over to the other side, tearing off a few paper towels from the roll dispenser, and assured him, "I'll get it, Krishnaji. I can clean it up."

He insisted however, "I'll clean it up, sir."

But by then I was already bent down, wiping up the drops from the floor, "I'm doing it, sir. It's already taken care of."

Only then did he resign himself to watching me mop up the last few droplets. "All right, sir," he said. "Thank you."

After he had succeeded in filling the second bottle with much care, and without spilling a drop, I started to put my question to him, "Krishnaji, may I ask you a question?"

As I had noticed on previous occasions, his demeanor and the field of energy around him changed dramatically when he was asked a serious question. One moment he had been relaxed and easy-going—despite the small mishap—the next moment he appeared completely collected within himself, with a focused attention remarkable to behold. His eyes took on a bright sparkle and fixed on me with passive alertness, ready for the most brilliant inquiry. Alas, my question, as so often, was more personal than investigative and in no way matched his quiet vibrancy.

"Go ahead, sir."

"Krishnaji, yesterday when you came for lunch I asked you if you were hungry. And you answered that you were never hungry—I'm not sure if you recall."

"Yes, that's right."

"Do you mean by that that you simply don't experience the sensation of hunger?"

He seemed to be downshifting the torque of his brain, which for a moment had been geared to top speed. Gently resting one hand on top of the maple kitchen table, he lowered his eyelids halfway, before answering, "The body simply doesn't feel hungry. We experimented with it. For a whole week we didn't eat anything. Only some water, of course."

"And there was no hunger at all, not even at the beginning?"

"There was no sense of hunger at all. But one felt how the body was getting weaker and weaker. Eventually we had to have some food, otherwise...." He completed the sentence with a dismissive gesture, indicating how the body would simply have faded away. He said it with a peculiar childlike earnestness. "You know, sir," he went on, lightly touching my elbow with a characteristic gesture of his, "we have experimented with all these things: went around blindfolded for a week, or didn't speak a word to anyone for days on end, absolute silence."

"But why would you do that?"

He laughed. "I just wanted to know what it was like, you know: not to be able to speak—silent, only listening. Just for fun, to see what it feels like. Or to see what it was like to be blind."

"And what did it feel like?"

"All the other senses became extraordinarily sensitive. Both touch and hearing became very keen. One could hear the finest sound. From an inch away, one could sense an object, a wall or a chair." He held up his finely pointed fingertips, slightly tremulous, to illustrate the heightened sensitivity of touch. "But all of this was many years ago."

Just then a scraping noise could be heard, coming from the screen door.

"What is that, sir?" Krishnamurti asked.

Walking over to the door, I exclaimed. "Look, Krishnaji, it's the cat."

He came up to me and together we watched the spectacle in front of us. A grey-striped tomcat was standing on his hind legs, arching his furry body against the screen and, with unsheathed claws, scratching the fine mesh. This caused a dissonant noise, sharply twanging on one's nerves. At the same time, the cat maneuvered his whiskered head sideways across his front legs, staring straight at us out of wide, bright-green eyes and meowing plaintively. Krishnamurti smiled at the comical sight. "It's the cat," he said, "she wants to get in."

It was, in fact, Alexander the Grey, the A.V. house cat. Shortly after school had started at A.V. in 1975, this full-grown, neutered tomcat had shown up at the kitchen door and refused to be shooed away. None of the neighbors knew where he belonged but he appeared thoroughly domesticated, exhibiting a fearless affection toward people, which was mingled, in equal parts, with assertiveness. He fondly allowed himself to be picked up by each and everyone, reacting to any petting with immediate arched back and twitching curved tail, purring. One of the first students of the Oak Grove School had named him Alexander, which was later expanded by one of the trustees to Alexander the Grey. His pet name, however, to which he instantly responded, was "kitty-kitty-kitty", preferably pronounced in a high pitched voice. His unusual fondness for human company was matched, by contrast, by his abhorrence of other cats, whom he sought either to terrorize or to avoid. On several occasions we saw him chasing dogs considerably larger than himself. At other times, he showed uncanny behavioral skills and comprehension. He would raise himself on his hind legs and paw at the doorknob when he wanted to go outside. Or he'd push against the swing-door until it moved back and forth, allowing him to pass quickly from the kitchen to the sitting room, where he liked to curl up on a soft armchair. But ever since he had got his tail caught between the closing door and the jamb, he was rather apprehensive about performing this maneuver.

Krishnamurti had a great fondness for and fascination with animals, wild or domesticated. Every so often he enjoyed telling us a story of encounters with animals in the wilderness.

Now he demanded, "Let her in. She wants food."

I pushed the screen door open a little, and the cat quickly came in. His curious tail curved vertically upright and around, touching his back. He pranced up to Krishnamurti and, rubbing against his leg, looked up at him with his knowing eyes, uttering low, solicitous cat sounds.

"She's hungry," Krishnamurti diagnosed, as he bent down to stroke the cat's back with his fingertips. It induced immediate purring.

"Krishnaji, he's a tom-cat," I pointed out, as I had done several times before. "I've already fed him this morning. There's quite a bit of food left in his dish." But I knew, of course, that Alexander loved to be fed tidbits by humans, as if wanting to have a personal relationship.

Krishnamurti ignored my comment, "Give him some food, sir."

It was one of Krishnamurti's idiosyncrasies that his relationship with animals seemed momentarily to eclipse the human realm. I took a piece of cheese out of the refrigerator and broke it into several smaller portions, placing them on the table next to Krishnamurti. "Perhaps you would like to feed him some of this cheese. He's quite fond of it."

He took some of the cheese and held it down toward the cat, intoning, "Here, kitty-kitty."

The cat raised himself halfway on his haunches, gingerly grasping the piece of cheese between his paws and teeth, careful not to hurt the proffered hand. We quietly observed the cat squatting down, mashing the cheese in feline fashion. Having devoured it, he brushed his whiskers a few times, licked his chops and, struck by the sudden recollection of the pleasure, looked up at us, evidently ready for some more cheese.

"He wants more," Krishnamurti said, and he took the remaining pieces of cheese and placed them on the floor in front of the cat.

While he continued to observe the cat, I became aware of the great stillness which enveloped him: as if watching the cat was the only thing in the world. I also became very quiet, and for a brief interval there was only the sound of the cat chewing away. For that moment the fact that a dozen guests were gathered next door, waiting to be fed, entirely slipped my mind.

Another careful pawing of the whiskers, a big satisfied cat yawn, and, with his curved tail twitching, Alexander the Grey proudly pranced off to the water and food bowls beneath the sink.

"What a curious tail he's got," Krishnamurti exclaimed.

Following the cat, I waited for him to take a sip of water from his bowl before letting him out the door.

Meanwhile, Krishnamurti had stepped closer to the range to take a look at what was cooking.

"What is this, Michael?" he asked, reaching out with one hand to lift the lid of the soup pot.

"Careful, Krishnaji," I warned, "it may be quite hot."

His hand slowed in mid-motion, and he tapped the knob of the lid very lightly with his fingertips, hurriedly pulling them back. He turned toward me. His elongated dark eyes, shaded by long eyelashes, had become round with quizzical playfulness, twinkling with sparks of childlike surprise.

"By Jove!" he exclaimed. "It *is* hot."

Taking two potholders from beside the spice rack next to the stove, I offered them to Krishnamurti. "Here, sir. Please use these."

With the help of the potholders he delicately lifted the top and peeked into the pot, carefully keeping his head away from the cloud of rising steam.

"Soup," he stated, replacing the lid. "What kind of soup is it, sir?"

"It's minestrone soup, Krishnaji,"

"Ah, minestre," he said with an Italian intonation. He was fond of Italy, its cuisine and culture. He had spent a fair amount of time there and was well-versed in the Italian language.

"And what else are we having for lunch?" he inquired.

"Well, sir," I began, "apart from the soup and the salads, there will be pasta, *capelli di angeli*, with *pesto di genoa*, and also steamed asparagus."

"*Capelli di angeli*," he repeated with gusto, letting the Italian sounds roll off his tongue.

While I was placing a stick of butter on a porcelain butter dish, he sauntered over to the wall by the screen door. A monthly picture calendar was posted there, next to a board with small hooks for keys to tool-shed and garage, while next to that was a large poster which somebody had donated to A.V.; subsequently I had attached it with thumb-tacks to the only free portion of wall. A large headline proclaimed the title: 'Murphy's Law'. A subtitle provided the definition: 'Everything that can go wrong will go wrong'. A central black and white photo graphically illustrated the statement. A vintage Ford T was stuck deeply in a field of mud. Every conceivable part was broken or had fallen off the vehicle. The driver, dressed in old-fashioned automotive gear, stood knee-deep in mud next to his car, helplessly contemplating the disaster and scratching his head. The remaining portion of the poster consisted of about fifty comical sayings—a cross between insight, joke and absurdity—the ironies of life honed to a fine point. The poster had been there for some time, and Krishnamurti regularly paused in front of it, finding it amusing even after repeated reading.

Now he broke into loud laughter about one of the aphorisms, and I curiously went over to stand next to him.

"Which one is funny, Krishnaji?" I asked him.

"'Everything I like is either fattening or immoral'," he read out, still laughing and brushing tears from his eyes. "That's very clever."

I joined in with his laughter. It was a heart-warming delight to share with him a good laugh about the human tragicomedy.

"Or what about this one, Krishnaji?"

He carefully read it and gave an amused chuckle before pointing at another he found particularly hilarious.

So we carried on for a while in front of the poster, laughing at the ironies and absurdities of life, and perhaps implicitly also at ourselves. At moments like this, the sense of unreserved friendship had an unforgettable poignancy.

"Is everything ready, sir?" Krishnamurti asked.

"I think so, sir," I replied, checking the asparagus. It took only a very little time to steam it, and one had to be careful not to overcook it. I took the bunch out of the pot with a pair of tongs and, after untying the string that held them together, placed the single stalks side by side in a ceramic serving dish.

"Can I carry anything?"

"Yes, if you don't mind, Krishnaji. You could perhaps take the soup pot."

With great care he took the handles of the stainless-steel pot and balanced it through the swing-door, which I held open to let him pass. Today we were having lunch indoors. (Since he preferred taking the meal in the dining room rather than on the patio, we now ate mostly inside.) He gently placed the pot next to the stack of soup bowls on the solid round table in the small serving area that adjoined the dining room. "Is this where it goes?" he asked.

"Yes, thank you, sir," I answered and went to fetch the few remaining items from the kitchen, while he quietly surveyed the lunch scene.

"There are not so many of us today," he observed. "Is it all out now? Shall I tell them?"

"Yes, please, Krishnaji," I said. "If you don't mind."

For the first year or two, I used to ring a small brass bell to call the guests to table. It was originally an ornament with which an Indian elephant was adorned for a festive parade. Somehow it had disappeared and I had assumed the role of butler, walking up to the guests in the sitting room and proclaiming in stentorian tones that lunch was served. My announcement was usually greeted with stunned silence by the chatting crowd, and after a minuscule pause they carried on with their conversations as if nothing had happened. I often felt frustrated that a second verbal invitation had to be issued and more gentle coaxing was necessary to bring the guests in line for the self-service buffet. It was much more effective when Krishnamurti made the announcement that lunch was ready.

I remained near the swing-door, watching how he quietly, almost shyly walked the length of the dining room and approached the guests, who were lounging on the sofa or standing around in groups. The noise level immediately quieted down, as the guests became aware of him. There was an interval of silence before he politely bowed to several of the ladies and announced with calm dignity, "*Madame est servie.*" It was superb role-playing, that even a first-class butler couldn't have topped. Everybody promptly got up to comply with the invitation to table. But another bottleneck was looming ahead in the narrow aisles around the lunch table. With persistent politeness each person insisted that the other precede him or her, until after some back-and-forth Krishnamurti suggested with a quiet laugh, "Ladies first." But, once the ladies had grouped themselves, none wanted to bear the onus of being the first to serve herself. After some embarrassed protestations, a lady trustee successfully invited a special guest to make the first step.

In the meantime, I had edged my way to the end of the line, behind Krishnamurti. He was grasping the arm of the school director, who with a delighted smile was saying to him, "Please, Krishnaji, you first." There was a light-hearted playfulness in Krishnamurti's voice as he insisted with just enough firmness to convince the other, "No, sir. You go ahead."

The director yielded, as he knew quite well that Krishnamurti was adamant in having others precede him, even the occasional latecomer. As far as I knew, Krishnamurti behaved like this only in Ojai, perhaps because here he was mostly among a smaller, more intimate group of friends than at the other places where he stayed.

I was quietly watching as the director and he exchanged some information about the Oak Grove School, when all at once he became aware of my presence behind him. Pivoting around, he grabbed my arm and earnestly entreated me, "Please, sir, go ahead."

I looked at him with a tender feeling in my heart, because I realized this was not just a conventional gesture of his: it was his natural modesty to think of others first.

I objected with an embarrassed laugh, "I'm sorry, Krishnaji—I have to go last. After all, I prepared the food. And the cook should allow all others to first help themselves before he takes food for himself. That's practically a culinary tradition."

He studied me with his peculiar, skeptical half-smile.

"It's the same in a home, isn't it?" I emphatically continued. "It seems to be quite logical and sane."

Finally he yielded to the force of my argument, conceding, "All right, sir. You go last."

We had been playing this little game, going more or less through the same argumentation, dozens of times for the past few years. A curious blend of seriousness and fine humor underlay our playful interaction. Oddly enough it never felt repetitive but had an endearing quality to it. It reminded me of Saint-Exupery's story of the Little Prince taming the little fox. Of course, I saw myself as the fox.

By now everyone was seated, while Krishnamurti and I were the last to walk around the serving table. I was striding behind him, ready to provide the culinary information he frequently requested. He was balancing his plate in both hands, resting it next to each dish, as he bent down to have a closer look at the contents before serving himself with some of it.

"What is this, sir?" he inquired.

"It's called *tabouli*, Krishnaji," I explained. "It's made with bulgur wheat, a precooked cracked wheat. It's mixed with lots of finely-chopped fresh parsley and mint, some green onions and tomatoes, and flavored with olive oil and lemon juice."

He had straightened himself as I recited the recipe, listening attentively to what I was saying. As I trailed off, he rounded his eyes in playful admiration and amusedly remarked, "I'll try some of that, sir."

After placing two large spoonfuls on his plate, he proceeded to take small portions of the other dishes. Looking at what was left—a little pasta, several stalks of asparagus, and some soup—he hesitated and turned to me. "There is hardly anything left, Michael."

Feeling somewhat defensive, I observed, "But, Krishnaji, we are the last ones in line. Don't you think this is enough for the two of us?"

"Well, sir," he insisted, "you are cutting it awfully close."

"Krishnaji," I protested, "I'm trying to prepare just enough for everyone, so that there won't be too many leftovers and waste."

"All right, sir, but you are certainly measuring it very finely."

Placing a few stalks of asparagus on his plate, he added with a soothing smile, "You are some cook."

He usually avoided personal praise and never flattered anyone, as far as I observed. Feeling a bit ambiguous as how to take his last remark, I inquisitively gazed at him and concluded that no irony was intended.

Halting before a small side-table, where fruit and dessert were on display, he asked, "What is this, Michael?"

"That's the dessert, Krishnaji. It's chocolate mousse."

At the mention of the word 'chocolate', his face took on a startled expression of dislike. "Oh, I won't take any of that," he declared.

I had previously noticed that he avoided chocolate and anything containing chocolate but had never understood the reasons for his distaste.

"Why is it, sir, that you don't like chocolate?"

A swift shadow of aversion crossed his benign features. "It's a drug, a stimulant, you know, sir. And it's too rich: oils, sugar, and so on."

I was quite a chocolate fan myself and was surprised to hear it described as a drug. I had, however, read about its stimulating properties, which were said to activate a hormonal secretion like the one the brain produced when a person fell in love. Without disowning the sweet, rich substance right there and then, I said guardedly, "I see."

Foreseeing his antipathy, I had prepared another dessert. "But I also baked some oatmeal cookies—biscuits." I corrected myself, adopting the British term he usually employed.

His face lit up with childlike delight. "Good. I'll take some later."

Placing his plate next to the soup pot, he ladled some soup into a bowl, announcing with zest, "*Minestre.*" Sprinkling some Parmesan on top of it, he fondly added, "*Con parmigiano.*"

In my best Italian, I intoned, "*C'è bene.*"

"*C'è buono,*" he corrected me.

"Ah, yes," I said, "*buono*—adjective."

"I'll come back for that," he said, nodding at the soup bowl, as he turned to carry his plate to the table, where the other guests had already started to eat.

"I'll bring it, sir."

It gave me a secret sense satisfaction to do things for him. Even to perform a minuscule service—asked for or not—was a source of great joy. I carried the soup bowl and placed it before him. He calmly looked up at me, "Thank you, sir."

It was a lively luncheon, and the conversation touched on the current political situation worldwide and the different cultural attitudes toward the man-woman relationship. Sometimes, it seemed Krishnamurti held rather Victorian views, although it was also clear that, far from condemning sex, he disapproved only of its display and exploitation.

We were talking about the cross-cultural custom of some priests, nuns and monks to eschew any intimate contact with the opposite sex by taking vows of chastity. Krishnamurti questioned the significance of this tradition. "I wonder, sir, if celibacy has anything to do with the truly religious life," he remarked to the trustee who was sitting across from him. "Taking a vow of chastity...but inside they are burning with frustration and desire, boiling with it. Suppress, suppress, don't ever look at a woman, at a beautiful face! That has nothing to do with the religious mind." He paused after delivering this last statement, rather emphatically and with much passion. "I must tell you a lovely story about this. There are two monks in India, walking from one village to the next, begging for alms. One day they come upon a young girl who's crying to herself near the banks of a river. One of the monks approaches her and asks, 'Sister, what are you crying for?' She says, 'You see that house on the other side of the river? That's where I live, and early this morning I waded across the river without any problem. But now the water has risen, and I can't get back and there is no boat anywhere near to take me across.' 'Don't worry,' the monk says, 'I'll help you.' And he picks her up and carries her on his back safely across the waters to the other shore. And the two monks continue towards the next village. They walk in silence for several hours, when suddenly the second monk speaks up and says, 'Brother, you have committed a terrible sin. We have taken a vow of chastity, never to touch a woman. Didn't you feel pleasure and a strong sensation when you touched that woman?' The first monk replies, 'I left her behind two hours ago—but you, apparently, are still carrying her with you.' You understand this story, sir?"

We burst out laughing at the story, but Krishnamurti regarded us with serious eyes.

*Chapter 9*

# "WHAT'S THE NEWS, SIR?"

### Starters

*Mixed salad of lettuce, shredded red cabbage,
sprouts and cherry tomatoes with a choice of
oil & vinegar or tahini dressing.
Grated zucchini salad and grated beets,
prepared with a touch of orange juice
and zest of orange.*

### Main Dishes

*Baked cumin potatoes.
Swiss cheese pie made with a crust of crackers,
mustard, green onions, parsley, grated
Emmenthal cheese, eggs and sour cream.
Steamed cauliflower, carrots & green peas
garnished with minced parsley and sliced olives.*

### Dessert

*Apricot cream made of sun-dried apricots
softened in water and blended with
cream and vanilla.
Fresh, seasonal fruit.*

DURING THE FOLLOWING WEEKS AND MONTHS OF SPRING, 1978, we were invited to frequent dialogue meetings with Krishnamurti at Pine Cottage. These meetings usually included the trustees, the Oak Grove School staff, and a few parents and volunteers. They took place in the large living room of the new Pine Cottage. It seemed a fitting venue for serious dialogue, a large open space with a lot of light: a row of skylights just under the ridge of the high, gabled ceiling, plus several large windows and a French window allowed the brightness of the day to stream into the room. The walls, ceiling and fan-shaped rafters dissecting the upper portion of the room were painted white. The white Italian floor tiles had a delicate floral design. A large fireplace with a natural rock hearth was the focal point around which were arranged sofas, armchairs, and low tables with lamps and vases. Open bookshelves and a number of subdued modern paintings adorned the walls, all in a light color. There was a pair of gilded baroque cherubs holding up lampshades, and several potted plants and a tall ornamental ficus tree enlivened the room. It was a place of simple, yet sophisticated elegance, airy and bright, and even the presence of fifty people did not crowd its spaciousness. Here, Krishnamurti would meet with us to explore the most serious questions pertaining to our daily lives, to the way we perceived, thought and acted, and to the way we educated the young people entrusted to us.

During these dialogues, he would often mention *Mind in the Waters*, a phrase that caught my attention. It took me a while to figure out that he was referring to the great variety of mammalian life-forms that existed in the oceans of the earth. It was, in fact, the title of a book,[3] which he had recently been reading. He was fascinated by the vivid descriptions of the cetaceans' intelligence, that apparently was so akin to our own. It was as if he had all at once discovered an entirely new realm of life, and television reports, photos and other accounts of dolphins and whales endlessly delighted him. By the same token, he was appalled by the cruel destruction that humans inflicted on harp-seal pups, whales and other aquatic creatures. Whenever he lashed out against these atrocities, his voice would become laden with genuine sorrow and pain, and his face mirrored the enormous suffering humankind had inflicted on its fellow creatures, on its natural environment, and on itself.

Besides *Mind in the Waters*, there were plenty of other media-generated topics that informed our conversations at the A.V. lunch table. For a while it was Jacob Bronowski's documentary "The Ascent of Man" that inspired frequent comments by Krishnamurti. Although he was impressed by the style and presentation of the television series, he strongly disputed its contention that humanity had evolved through its increasing knowledge. On the contrary, he proposed that men and women today were psychologically as primitive as their Stone Age ancestors—oppressed by fear and superstition, selfish, cruel and violent—despite the enormous progress in science and technology. News programs like "60 Minutes" and "The McNeil-Lehrer News Hour" provided a lot of the raw material for our daily review of the current world situation. The main actors on the global scene in the late 70's were the two superpowers, the U.S. and the U.S.S.R., who were still competing against each other, even though the 'Cold War' had officially been replaced by 'détente'. A few months earlier, Jimmy Carter had been sworn in as President of the United States, and everyone at the lunch table seemed to like him. While we were discussing how the new American president might get along with the Soviet leader, Leonid Brezhnev, Krishnamurti said, "I must tell you this joke, if I may." And he politely looked around the table. Everyone fell silent and turned toward him, eager to hear his story. "This happens to be the time when Nixon was still President," he explained with a smile. "Brezhnev calls Nixon over the hotline telephone and says, 'Hello, Mr. President, how are you? I've heard that you have the most incredible super-computer in the whole world.' Nixon replies, 'Well, Mr. Chairman, I don't know how you obtained this information, because it's top-secret. But I can tell you that it's the fastest computer in the world and can foretell events up to thirty years ahead.' Brezhnev is impressed. 'Thirty years: that is truly astonishing. Not even here in the Soviet Union do we have anything like that. In fact, I would like to ask you a favor, if you don't mind.' Nixon answers, 'Anything you like, in the name of détente, as long as it isn't a state secret or against the interests of the United States.' Brezhnev replies, 'I wouldn't dream of anything like that. But could you please ask your computer who will be in the Communist Party politburo here in the year 2000?' The President answers, 'No problem, Leonid. Just give me a minute.' And the telephone line goes silent while he is consulting the computer. Brezhnev presses his ear to the receiver but hears only Moscow static as the minutes tick by. Finally he asks, 'Are you still there,

Richard?' (They're on first name terms by now.) 'Well, yes, Leonid,' Nixon replies, 'but I can't figure it out.' 'But what does it say?' Brezhnev asks impatiently. And Nixon says, 'That's just it. I can't read what it says—it's all in Chinese.'"

Everyone joined in a round of hearty laughter. I was sitting across from Krishnamurti and saw how much he enjoyed telling the joke. Tilting back his head, he laughed with abandon. Although I was seldom able to remember jokes, I invariably recalled the ones that he recounted, perhaps because I so highly cherished his sense of humor and the joy it engendered. When the laughter had quieted down, I asked him, "Do you know another one, sir?"

"Another joke?" he asked, raising his eyebrows.

"Yes, please, sir."

He looked around the table at the expectant faces, then at me, and, taking a breath, said, "All right, sir, I know another joke, also about Brezhnev. He has ruled as General Secretary of the Communist Party and President of the U.S.S.R. for some years, and the country is at the height of its powers. Every other Sunday, his old mother comes from the country to visit him in the Kremlin. This time she brings him some of his favorite dumplings. Before leaving, she tells him how worried she is. Brezhnev tries to calm her down, 'Look, Mama, there is really nothing to worry about. I have enough to eat here in the Kremlin and my room is warm.' But she keeps on, 'No, no, my son, I'm worried about you and the country.' Two weeks later she visits him again and brings him warm gloves and a muffler. He thanks her and tells her how splendid things are, but she insists, 'No, no, my dear Leonid, all is not well. I'm really worried about you and how things are going. Who knows what all could happen?' 'But, dear mother,' he says, 'I really live a very good and secure life here. There are guards at the door to protect me, and I'm in control, telling everyone what to do.' 'No, no,' she mumbles as she is leaving, 'all is not well.' Two weeks later she comes again, bringing him a bottle of his favorite home-made vodka. After a while she again expresses her deep worries to him. Brezhnev tries to calm her down once and for all. 'Dear mother,' he says, 'I've got everything anybody could ever want—even the most expensive sports cars from the decadent West. I'm wearing fine clothes and eat the best food. In fact, I'm the most powerful man in the whole country, maybe the whole world. So can you please tell me why you keep on worrying?' 'Leonid, my son,' she says to him, 'Don't you know? The Communists might take over.'"

At that, everyone at the table burst out in almost raucous laughter. The way he had told the joke was quite inimitable, with illustrative gestures and mime-like facial expressions, and a youthful *élan*.

APART FROM KRISHNAMURTI AND MARY Z., THERE WAS A CORE group of about six to eight trustees and staff who regularly participated in the daily luncheons at A.V. All of them were quite interested in current political and cultural affairs and regularly followed the news on television and in the newspapers. I also happened to be a fan of world news and usually endeavored to read the newspaper from front to back.

Evidently, Krishnamurti was also very interested in what was happening in the world and seemed surprisingly well informed about recent developments. While I subscribed to the Christian Science Monitor, Mary Z. received the *Los Angeles Times*. After they were through with their copy, I would either pick it up in the late afternoon or Krishnamurti would bring it over at lunch.

This particular afternoon he entered the kitchen as he usually did, through the patio screen door. Greeting me in his friendly way, he strolled over to the window and placed a copy of the *Los Angeles Times* on the counter. "There it is, sir," he said, "so much paper."

"Thank you, Krishnaji. Do you actually read it?"

"No, sir," he replied. "There's simply too much to read. Day after day, all these long articles. And they are always writing the same stuff— repeat, repeat, repeat. Sometimes I look at the headlines, that's all."

"Oh," I said, somewhat disappointed by his skeptical attitude, which ran contrary to my own enthusiastic studies. "But what about the comics, sir? Do you look at those at all?"

"The cartoons? I like the ones in the *New Yorker* magazine, they are often very clever. Or the little boy, what is his name?"

"Charlie Brown in the 'Peanuts' comic strip?"

"No," he said. "This boy is always getting into some sort of trouble. He's a bit mischievous."

Reviewing my memory file of cartoon characters, I quickly came upon a likely candidate, "Is it Dennis the Menace, Krishnaji?"

"Yes, that's him—full of mischief, but very charming."

That afternoon there were only a few of us for lunch—the inner circle, as it were. Often when we were *en famille*, we would have very lively discussions, but this time everyone was rather subdued, and the conversation was sporadic. I was sitting across from Krishnamurti, and every so often my gaze would wander over to him. He was chewing slowly and carefully with his eyes half closed. His long, narrow, left hand lay on top of the white paper napkin by his plate. He appeared completely self-contained and calm, exhibiting no trace of nervousness or discomfort because of the silence around the table. When we made eye-contact, I felt a bit shy and self-conscious but did not discern any reaction on his part. There was only a mirror-like quality in his eyes.

Perturbed by our continuing reticence, I felt a sudden urge to entertain him with something. I leaned forward and asked in a low voice, "Excuse me, Krishnaji. Have you heard what is going on in China?" He looked at me very directly but gave no hint of curiosity: I could only detect the same mirror-like tranquillity. There was a brief interval, which felt like a balancing act on a high wire, as I returned his gaze, waiting for his reply. Then an amused sparkle entered his eyes, and he said, "No, I haven't. What has been happening in China, sir?"

I went into a fairly lengthy discourse on the most recent developments in China and Southeast Asia, backtracking a bit here, elaborating a bit there, and generally fleshing out the details of an article I had read the previous day. At the beginning of my account, I felt unsure of myself, but once I had given up any wish to be encouraged, and stopped looking for signs of interest in my listener, my brief dissertation took on its own momentum. I warmed to the subject as I went along, sketching an outline of recent and ancient Chinese history, with diverse pieces of information that came to me from God knows where. I started to enjoy myself as I went on about Confucian customs and psychological attitudes. Krishnamurti listened with increasing intensity, asking a number of questions, which added weight to my discourse. Eventually the other people at the table fell in, contributing to an animated conversation about the survival of traditions in revolutionary societies.

Suddenly Krishnamurti raised his hand, "That reminds me of a joke I heard recently. This happens to be the Kremlin in Moscow, the seat of supreme power. Every morning the captain of the guard enters the bedroom of Chairman Brezhnev, carrying his breakfast on a tray, with a copy of the *Pravda* newspaper. He pulls back the curtains from the large window overlooking Red Square, gives a smart salute and briefs the Chairman on the latest developments in the world. At the end of it, Brezhnev says, 'All right, comrade, is that all?' The adjutant hesitates, 'Well, Comrade Chairman, there is one other thing: there is a large crowd outside in Red Square, and they seem to be picnicking.' Brezhnev responds magnanimously, 'It's a lovely morning, and the sun is shining; let the workers enjoy themselves for once.' The adjutant salutes and leaves." Each time he mentioned the adjutant, Krishnamurti raised his hand to his forehead, imitating the officer's snappy salute. "The next morning it's the same routine: breakfast, newspaper, curtains back, salute, report on the latest events, and so on. And Brezhnev asks, 'Is there anything else I should know?' The captain says, 'Yes, Comrade Chairman, there is an even larger crowd out there in Red Square, perhaps a hundred thousand of them, and they seem to be picnicking.' 'Let them, let them,' replies the Chairman. 'On a sunny morning like this, the proletarian masses should enjoy themselves a bit.' The adjutant gives his salute and trots off. The next morning, the same thing again. 'Is there anything else?' Brezhnev asks at the end of it. And when the chap starts, pointing down at Red Square, the Chairman laughingly raises his hand and stops him, 'All right comrade, I think I know exactly what you are going to tell me: on this lovely morning there is a large crowd of a million people down there in Red Square, and they are having a picnic. Am I right?' 'Yes, you are right, Comrade Chairman,' answers the adjutant. 'But there is one other thing: they are all eating with chopsticks.'"

After we had been laughing for a while, Krishnamurti turned to me and asked, with a twinkle in his eye and a touch of irony in his voice, "Is there any other important news that I should know about?" This inflamed our laughter anew, and it also poured oil on my fire. I remembered a short notice in the science section of the Times that described the recent discovery of a celestial body, called a quasar, in the vicinity of our galaxy. This quasar was said to have prodigious energy. Krishnamurti was quite captivated by my account of the cosmic discovery, listening with great attention.

Inspired by this impromptu performance, I would, in the following days and weeks, give an account of the most salient world events to Krishnamurti, especially when there was a lull in the conversation. But

I would only do so when we were in a small circle and when I happened to be sitting close to Krishnamurti, since it was primarily to him that I was reporting. Telling him the world news gradually became a new role of mine. His playful attitude toward my lunch-table anchoring had a lot to do with it. He clearly enjoyed my brief informative reviews of global events and, before long, began to encourage me, particularly when I forgot to make my daily news announcement, by asking me quite seriously, "What's the news, sir?"

It became an endearing little game between us, that, although amusing at a certain level, allowed a new form of seriousness. It was a special bond that had come about quite naturally, practically of its own accord, without motive or plan on either side. His generous humor and genuine curiosity about what was happening in the world kept it alive. There also was a playfulness about it, and I was glad to have a specific medium of communication with him, although this was by no means exclusive, since anyone could tune in at any time.

At the beginning of our game, I reported the news on the spur of the moment off the top of my head, without any prior thought or rehearsal. But as "What's the news, sir?" became a regular question, an almost daily occurrence, it also became a challenge. I rarely found myself unable to pull a newsworthy item out of the media-hat. But sometimes the facts I presented, or the particular angle of my presentation, would be challenged by a well-informed lunch participant. So I had to get my facts straight, in order not to be on the defensive about them. Simultaneously, I felt a great urge to be both accurate and excellent in the entertainment I provided. The challenge was primarily inspired by Krishnamurti, who without effort or intention seemed to bring out a person's higher aspirations.

My initial off-the-cuff news-anchoring gradually became more sophisticated and stylized, but also less repetitive. At the outset, I simply quoted headlines and provided a synopsis of the most outstanding events of the day. Krishnamurti was probably familiar with most of what I was talking about. Even so, he listened attentively to my recapitulation of the day's top stories, and it was seldom that he interrupted me with, "I know, sir, I know." Therefore, I tended to focus more and more on less publicized events. Before long I found that I was dedicating considerable amounts of time and energy to researching the often convoluted happenings in the political arena. My mainstay, however, remained the small beat-up desk-top radio that I kept tuned to the all-news station.

When there were many guests or someone special was invited for lunch, we would suspend the game of "What's the news, sir?" On these occasions, Krishnamurti would seldom forget to query me in the kitchen, or, like an afterthought, he would walk up to me after the meal and inquire, "What's the news, sir," just between the two of us. Our news game went on for months and years, starting anew each season when Krishnamurti came to Ojai. Each time, it took on a slightly different form, as "What's the news, sir?" became something of an institution at A.V.

But, of course, ours wasn't the only game in town: I discovered that Krishnamurti was fond of playing these small personal games with several of his friends. One of them, Mr. Lilliefelt, a retired U.N. diplomat from Sweden, had a rain-measuring device in his garden. He would ask him, "How many inches, sir?"

"We had one inch of rain this morning, Krishnaji."

And they proceeded to express their delighted satisfaction at the abundant watering of the valley and engage in a brief exchange about seasonal and average rainfall.

ANOTHER GAME REVOLVED AROUND KRISHNAMURTI'S precious Patek-Philippe pocket-watch. Here the question was, "How many seconds, sir?" When he discovered that his timepiece was several seconds slow, he was eager to have it fine-tuned. The maintenance man with whom he had compared the time offered to check and adjust it for him. He had it cleaned and set it to Universal Standard Time, then returned the watch to Krishnamurti. Whenever he came for lunch, Krishnamurti would walk up to him and hand him his watch, asking upon its return, "How many seconds, sir?" and the other man would answer, "It's still half a second slow, sir." This went on for some weeks, until at last the answer was: "It's accurate to the second, sir."

Although these endearing games and jokes brought a light-hearted element to our lunch gatherings at A.V., they did not deflect from the sense of profound seriousness that Krishnamurti manifested among us. His seriousness was like a rock, and nothing could move it. It was rooted in the actuality of the moment, in the living source of energy, but it did not exclude humor and laughter.

### Starters

*Tossed green salad with choice of*
*vinaigrette or parsley dressing.*
*Wild rice salad prepared with currants, capers,*
*pine nuts and marinated, sun-dried tomatoes.*
*Grated carrots, touched with lemon and honey.*

### Main Dishes

*Steamed millet garnished*
*with toasted almond slivers.*
*Garbanzo bean stew, cooked in its*
*own sauce with tahini and lemon juice,*
*finely chopped onions, celery and parsley.*
*Swiss chard, steamed and dressed with olive oil,*
*garlic, lemon juice and a round of*
*freshly grated nutmeg.*

### Dessert

*Yam soufflé, made of baked yams,*
*maple syrup, butter, eggs and zest of orange.*
*Fresh, seasonal fruit.*

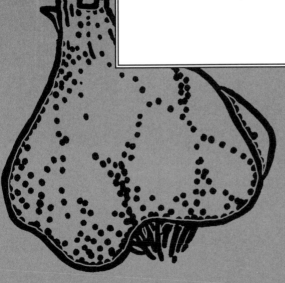

1978 WAS A YEAR OF PRODIGIOUS RAINFALL IN SOUTHERN California, with dramatic flooding, especially in mountainous regions like the Ojai Valley. For days on end, it kept pouring down from dark-grey, cloud-covered skies. The dry barranca of Thacher Creek, which intersected McAndrew Road underneath a bridge just a hundred yards up from A.V., was almost overflowing with dark-brown, swirling water.

While we were gathered around the lunch table, we could hear not only the intense drumming of the rain on the roof, but also the roar of Thacher Creek and the loud knock of giant boulders smashing against one another. We were discussing what would happen with the Public Talks, which were scheduled to start next week, at the beginning of April. A lady trustee outlined a contingency plan. It was clear, she said, that the Talks could not take place as planned in the Oak Grove, even if the rains had stopped by then, since the parking lot was a field of mud. For most of the weekend talks, arrangements had been made for Krishnamurti to speak in the Nordhoff High School gymnasium. The Tuesday and Thursday question-and-answer meetings were to be held at the Libbey Bowl, weather permitting. It was an animated discussion and everybody chipped in, while Krishnamurti leaned back in his chair and listened quietly but intensely to what was being said. At first, it seemed odd to me that, in a matter of vital concern to him, he would remain rather taciturn. Only on reflection did it occur to me that this simply was his style: he had delegated the responsibility for the organization of the talks to the trustees, and they were taking care of it. Naturally, they consulted with him and would not do anything against his wishes, but basically he let them do their job without undue interference on his part.

The continuing downpour and our common concern about the forthcoming Talks created a strong sense of togetherness among us, as we huddled around the table. While the other ten guests were involved in a lively conversation about dates, locations and alternative possibilities, I was watching Krishnamurti. His facial expression was neutral, as he intently followed the goings-on. Just then his hand reached for his empty glass, as if he wanted to take a drink, so I quickly grasped the water pitcher next to me and made to pour some water into the glass. Surprised at my quick reaction, he raised his eyes toward me.

"Just pour me a little, sir," he said.

I had poured less than half an inch into his glass when he said, "Thank you, sir. That's enough."

I was always surprised at the small amount of liquid he consumed during meals. Sometimes, when I had poured him some water, he would point out to me at the end of the meal carefully that he hadn't touched it. I, in turn, would assure him that it wouldn't go to waste and pour it into the kettle for the next cup of tea. He would smile, satisfied with my frugality.

Now he took a small sip from the glass and turned his attention to the ongoing discussion. After some minutes, most of the details seemed to have been clarified, and one of the lady trustees turned toward Krishnamurti and asked, "How does that sound, Krishnaji? Do you think we can do it like this?"

He gave her a bright smile and replied, "Yes, it appears all right. Only, what shall we do if it rains on a day of dialogue?"

The lady sighed. "Well, Krishnaji, then we either have to cancel it, or we might rent the Art Center auditorium. What do you think?" she asked the director.

"That's a possibility," he answered. "Only the capacity there is rather limited: one hundred and fifty or seventy-five maximum, I think. And the Fire Marshall is quite strict about it."

Just then a squall of rain created a loud staccato noise, and everyone fell silent. After a while Krishnamurti said, "You'll work it out." With a quick look around, he continued, "This rain reminds me of a lovely story. You may have heard it before. Narada is a yogi so accomplished that one day the god Vishnu appears to him and says, 'Narada, I grant you any wish you may have. Just tell me and I'll make it happen.' So Narada says to Vishnu, 'All I want is to understand Maya, the power of illusion.' And Vishnu sighs, 'That is very difficult to do. Is there nothing else you want, money or power, or some divine pleasure?' But Narada insists, 'That's all I want.' Vishnu says, 'All right, then. But it's a lovely day, so let's take a walk while I explain this to you.' They are walking among the hills like two friends, looking at the magnificent snow-capped mountains in the distance. The sun is shining very strongly, and Vishnu stops beneath a shady tree and says to Narada, "By Jove, it's hot and I'm very thirsty. So before we go into this, could you perhaps fetch me a glass of water from that cottage down there? I'll wait here.' Narada says, 'But of course, Lord. I'll be right back.' And he trots off and knocks on the door of the cottage. The door is opened by a girl of the most enchanting beauty. He's quite entranced as she asks him into the house.

He meets her family and they invite him to have lunch with them, and before he knows it he's fallen in love with the young girl. They invite him to stay for the night, and eventually he marries the girl. They have children and lead a happy and prosperous life. One year, though, the monsoons are stronger than ever. It keeps on raining day after day, flooding the fields and sweeping away houses. As the waters keep rising, Narada takes his wife and children by the hand, the youngest on his shoulders, and together they try to save their lives by climbing on top of the roof. But the children, one after the other, are swept away by the raging waters. And just as he attempts to pull his wife onto the roof, she also is engulfed by the flood. Narada feels utterly devastated by this total loss of everything he cherished. He is barely hanging on to dear life and, in his despair, he fervently starts to pray, 'Please, Lord, help me in this misery.' And through the roar of the water comes Lord Vishnu's voice, 'And where is my glass of water?'"

Amidst the noise of the descending rain, we burst out laughing. Hearing Krishnamurti tell an anecdote or joke was always a great enjoyment for me. It never ceased to amaze me that a man who lived and formulated a teaching of unique insight and sublimity would at the same time enjoy telling jokes. Of course, they were good jokes. In this case, I recognized the story as an abbreviated version of the ancient Hindu myth of Narada and Vishnu, which is also retold in the final chapter of Hermann Hesse's *The Glass-Bead Game*.

SUBSEQUENTLY, THE 1978 PUBLIC TALKS WERE HELD AT THE Nordhoff High School gymnasium and the Libbey Bowl. Rain forced one of the dialogue meetings to be moved to the Ojai Arts Center at the last moment. The hall was completely packed, and an additional hundred and fifty people were waiting to get in. Since there was no more room, several loudspeakers were quickly installed outside, so that those standing in the rain could follow the dialogue protected by umbrellas and rain gear.

Indoors, it appeared rather claustrophobic, with people crammed against one another. Even Krishnamurti on the small stage couldn't escape from being wedged in by people who had no other place to sit or stand. Several of the school staff, including myself, formed a kind of protective circle around him, so that he might at least have some minimum of elbow room. Besides, the acoustics of the hall, combined with the sound of the rain streaming down, made it difficult for him to hear what was being said. Consequently, he asked one of the teachers who was sitting next to him to repeat each question and statement from the audience. Despite this somewhat awkward arrangement, it turned out to be a very lively and invigorating question-and-answer meeting. Its special quality of togetherness might have been created, in part, by our physical closeness and the adversity of the elements.

IT HAD BECOME MORE AND MORE EVIDENT THAT Krishnamurti sometimes had difficulty hearing, especially when there was a great deal of background noise, or when several people were speaking at once. During staff discussions at Pine Cottage and at public dialogues it was often necessary to repeat a question several times before he understood it. Some of the staff became concerned about his increasing deafness. Talking it over with him and Mary Z., they proposed that he make use of a hearing aid. After lengthy deliberations and initial hesitation, he agreed to try it out. After wearing the device a number of times, he couldn't get accustomed to adjusting the sound level, which produced a penetrating high-pitch whine. Nor did he seem to like the sensation of having something jammed behind his earlobes. Consequently, we had to continue repeating the questions.

THE FINAL TALK OF THE 1978 OJAI SERIES TOOK PLACE AT A rather unlikely location, the Nordhoff High School sports grounds. A small stage had been set up on the football field in front of the bleachers. It was a sparklingly clear morning, and a cold wind was chasing white clouds across the deep-blue sky. It seemed an odd set-up—the steeply tiered benches on one side filled with people huddled in coats and blankets, and, on the other side, one single man speaking from a platform in an otherwise empty field. The wind created whirring sound effects on the loudspeaker system, while, on the left, cars were busily passing by along the Maricopa Highway. But on this beautiful morning Krishnamurti appeared unfazed by these unusual circumstances. Unperturbed and almost stern, he talked about meditation, death, love and the sacred.

A FEW DAYS AFTER THE CONCLUSION OF THE TALKS, HE AND Mary Z. went to visit the new Wolf Lake School on Vancouver Island in British Columbia. After his return to Ojai, he only stayed another week before embarking on his annual journey, which led him to Brockwood Park at the beginning of May, then to Saanen, back to Brockwood Park, and on to India in October.

I STAYED IN CALIFORNIA AND WAS BUSY AT THE OAK GROVE School, but I missed attending the talks in the various locations. In September, 1978 we started receiving circular letters from him. These were later published as *Letters to the Schools*. In pointed and succinct style, they focused the attention of both teachers and students on the serious questions of life. They averaged between one and two pages in length, encapsulating the essence of his teaching and the meaning of education as he envisioned it. In them, he often employed rather startling phrases, such as 'ideals corrupt the mind'; 'leisure implies a mind that has infinite time to observe'; 'earning a livelihood is the denial of living'; 'God is disorder'; 'we live by words and words become our prison'; and so on. Although they were written in an impersonal tone and addressed to the hundreds of staff and thousands of students at the schools in Ojai, Canada, England and India, I felt they were speaking to me personally. As we received them for several years, they became the basis for many animated staff discussions about the significance of education and our role in it.

KRISHNAMURTI RETURNED TO OJAI IN FEBRUARY, 1979. THERE were about sixteen guests at the Saturday luncheon following his arrival. Everyone was glad to see him again, and it felt like one big family, a gathering of friends who welcomed back the person who had brought them all together in the first place. I was sitting diagonally across from

Krishnamurti and noticed that he was rather pensive and reticent. Although he followed the lively conversation, he rarely participated in any of it. Since he had only recently arrived from India, with a brief stopover at Brockwood Park, some people asked him about the schools there, but received only perfunctory answers. Something else was occupying his mind.

Most of the guests had started to enjoy their chocolate mousse, when Krishnamurti all at once abandoned his remoteness and addressed the two people next to him. As was often the case, his question was deceptively simple in style, and yet it had the impact of a perspective entirely different from that of other brains. And it seemed to be directly related to the situation at hand. Out of the blue he asked, "What is the American mind?"

The people around the table reacted in silent unison as they absorbed the question: everyone stopped chewing, lowered forks or spoons, and turned their heads toward the source of the question. It reminded me of a television commercial: when Krishnaji spoke, people listened. I also vaguely recalled that Krishnamurti had raised the identical question several years earlier on his arrival in California. Maybe he asked it because the immediate impressions of American culture and society were still fresh in his mind.

No immediate response was forthcoming. He repeated it urgently into the silence that was created by a dozen brains pondering his words: "What is the American mind?" I could almost hear the mental wheels turning and creaking in each individual skull, because it wasn't a flippant or casual question but one that touched the cultural roots of most of those present. Only a few of us, like Krishnamurti and myself, were resident aliens.

After some time, several people began voicing their opinions. An older lady volunteered, "Well, material and commercial concerns certainly are important features of the American mind. Money, property, and material standard of living are probably cherished more than anything else."

"Of course, it's the American Dream," someone concurred.

"What is the American Dream?" I asked, having a rather vague notion of what was implied by this often-heard term.

"It's having your own house, your own car, and also the expectation and belief that everything will always become better," Alan explained.

"No, no," Krishnamurti said with a dismissive gesture, "that doesn't really answer the question. After all, most of the Western world, perhaps even the whole world, is highly materialistic and commercialized. That's not a uniquely American characteristic. No. What is the American mind—in its essence? What makes it different from the French, the English, the Chinese mind?"

One of the trustees opined, "The American mind is highly individualistic. Personal initiative and enterprise are highly valued...."

Another disapproving headshake by Krishnamurti, who kept a tight rein on the course of the discussion, holding it within the parameters of his question. "No, no...."

"There is a naiveté there, an innocence of mind, a childlike quality, which is curious about everything—playful, but also very generous," another lady suggested.

This intrigued Krishnamurti and was at length examined by him and several others, who concurred with it as a characterization of the American mind. In several respects it corresponded with some of Krishnamurti's earliest impressions of America, when he and his brother Nitya had come to California for the first time in 1922. He had written an essay about this initial contact with the New World, in which he enthusiastically described the beauty of the land and the open, unprejudiced mentality of the people, with their youthful zest for life. Encountering a more tolerant attitude than he had found in Britain and other parts of the world, where his dark complexion sometimes caused public derision, had clearly had a positive impact on the young Krishnamurti's mind. But, of course, a great many things had changed in America and elsewhere during the intervening six decades. Not only had the U.S. grown enormously in population and in military and economic power, there were also unmistakable indications of social decadence.

He partly concurred with the view offered, but he also dissented. I don't think he had already arrived at a specific answer to his question and was waiting for us to ferret it out, but he had a specific, and probably very holistic perception of the quality of the American mind. This mind was now, through amiably shared investigation, to be explored in actual operation.

He carefully concealed his response by saying, "Yes, there is something to that. There is a certain naiveté and innocence, but it doesn't quite capture the unique quality of that mind."

Another person attempted to phrase her sentiments about the quintessence of the American psyche. "But sir, isn't it freedom which is the great accomplishment of the American mind? Social freedom, freedom to choose, equal opportunities for all?"

Her suggestion caused laughter, in which Krishnamurti joined, because so much of what he proposed in his teaching pivoted around freedom as a psychological actuality. Thus, he used the word 'freedom' in a very subtle and pure sense. It wasn't 'freedom from' or 'freedom to' that he was talking about, nor popular conceptualizations like 'freedom of choice' or 'freedom to do what one likes'. None of these touched the intrinsic beauty of the primal quality of existence that he was hinting at. The closest verbal formulation that I could think of was 'freedom of observation'.

Another guest now suggested, "One could indeed propose that, in this society, an actual basic equality exists for everyone. It's exemplified by the judicial system, to which everyone has access."

A lively discussion, pro and con, ensued, during which the virtues and vices of the U.S. legal system were appraised. A teacher argued, "Well, it's true, isn't it, that everyone has equal access to the law. That really means everyone can sue anyone else for any old reason. There is, of course, a measure of justice in that but...."

One of the trustees interrupted him, "But see what happens: we have the most litigious society in the world. Nobody's word means anything any more; any kind of agreement or deal has to be put in documents, sealed, confirmed, and signed by judges and lawyers."

A lady concurred, "Quite right: there are now over 700,000 lawyers in this country, thousands more being added each year—more than anywhere else in the world. But is there any real concern about justice? Every attorney just wants to win his or her case, regardless of the actual facts of the matter."

"But how else would you propose that an open justice system function?" interjected a lawyer.

"Please," Krishnamurti calmed the choppy waves, only to trigger a *tsunami* of his own, "let's face the simple fact: there is no justice in the world. Not here, nor anywhere else. That's an indisputable fact. Justice doesn't exist. Face it, sirs!"

For a moment I felt thunderstruck by his simple assessment. It was not so much that I had never before heard or entertained a notion like that, but, as was often the case, his observations, expressed in simple, precise words, had a tremendous force and seemed to affect the very depth of my consciousness. I felt I was directly perceiving the truth of what he was saying, with its multifarious implications. It was as if in an instant I was viewing the whole network of illusion, which had been created by the concept 'justice', and the underlying assumption that it existed or might be realized by human endeavor. Simultaneously, it was clear to me that this insight did not negate the desirability, indeed the necessity, for any human social structure to strive for balance, fairness, and equality before the law. But understanding the fact that justice did not exist and was nothing but a construct of thought was the precondition for making it possible at all.

Everybody at the table seemed as shocked as myself and listened attentively, as Krishnamurti continued to expound his view. "What justice is there in this: you are born here, in this country—good education, rich family and so on. The other chap is born in Africa, or some dreadfully poor country—poor family, starving, no education. What justice is there in that? Or you get into trouble," he said with a chuckle, perhaps at the absurdity of it all, "you get into trouble with the law. You have got the money to hire a good lawyer, and you walk away from it. The other chap—poor, uneducated, and all that—he is put in jail for the same offense, right? You know all that, don't you? No, justice does not exist."

There was a long interval of silence after this statement. I looked around and saw everybody following their own thoughts, or listening inwardly as the startling revelation sank in.

It was not uncommon at all that moments of clear silence occurred around the lunch table, settling gently like snow on a hilly landscape. One could feel the beating of one's heart and the rhythm of breath, and we were quiet together.

"No, no, no," Krishnamurti said. "What is the American mind? Answer my question, sir. What is its fundamental quality?"

A lady trustee raised a sudden objection. "But, Krishnaji, is this the right question? What do you mean by 'American mind'? That's an enormous generalization, isn't it? And isn't this what creates prejudices about different nationalities and cultures?"

Krishnamurti listened to her with a smile, then looked at the teacher sitting across from him, who hadn't uttered a word throughout the whole conversation. Without directly responding to the lady's argument, he addressed him, "Listen, sir. Of course it's a tremendous generalization. But there is something like the American mind—that's clear, isn't it? The American mind differs from the Indian mind, which is very clever, superstitious, sloppy, believes in hierarchy, authority, tradition, and so on. Or the French mind—highly individualistic, selfish, analytical, very sharp, linguistic. Or the English mind—which is insular, isolated, snobbish and all that."

The theme of national characteristics was eagerly picked up and everybody voiced their observations and opinions, until eventually Krishnamurti reined in the discussion by quietly persisting, "What is the American mind?"

Since nobody said anything, he proceeded to answer his own question by combining a number of previous suggestions, "All right. The American mind is gullible, superficial, vulgar. It's very changeable and believes in all sorts of specialists for every aspect of life. There is a specialist for religion, for sex, how to behave, live, how to sit, and how to comb your hair. It's enthralled by entertainment, is highly commercial and so on. But it's also very generous, naive, open, curious and active."

The teacher who sat across from Krishnamurti and hadn't said very much until now offered his assessment of the American mind by deliberately uttering one word: "Pluralism." Krishnamurti seemed intrigued by this slightly mystifying evaluation. Some of the people at the other end of the table asked, "What did he say?"

The teacher willingly repeated and expanded his notion. "Pluralism. It implies that the American mind and society allow for many different views, life styles, values and groupings. Ethnic, cultural, political or religious groups can freely exercise their respective activities, can organize themselves and propagate their views. The rights of minorities are protected by the Constitution and the law of the land."

His concise outline fascinated Krishnamurti, maybe because it came closer than anything previously mentioned to what he felt was the essence of the American mind. His elaboration reminded me of the motto 'E pluribus unum' written on all U.S. coins and the one-dollar bill, which expressed the idea of unity and pluralism.

"Right, sir," Krishnamurti confirmed. "The American mind is pluralistic. That means, doesn't it, that there actually may not be such a thing as an American mind, because it lacks tradition; it's still young, moving, changing. But it probably is also tremendously broken up, fragmented and confused."

"Like most of us," quipped one of the lady trustees.

This fittingly captured what could be said about the existence or non-existence of the American mind. Most people were nodding in silent agreement. By now, however, it was almost three o'clock, and several people reluctantly got up and apologized for having to leave because of a commitment.

The conversation meandered idly from one subject to another: last night's splendid piano concerto, the recent political upheaval in Iran, some school issues, and so on. At one point, a lady asked him, "Krishnaji, when you give a public talk, as in the Oak Grove, can you tell whether anyone in the audience really understands what you are saying?" His answer was curt and seemed to indicate that he wasn't interested in pursuing the subject: "No, madam. I have no idea."

THE FOLLOWING MONTH, AT THE END OF MARCH, A week-long conference with young artists, scientists and philosophers was scheduled to take place at Pine Cottage. A German professor of physics who, with his Danish-born wife, had joined the school two years earlier was organizing the event. The meetings brought together a group of people from disparate cultural backgrounds. There was a rabbi, several South American radicals, and even a couple from the Persian Gulf. It rarely happened that people from an Islamic background were interested in Krishnamurti's teaching. It was, therefore, a surprise to see two young Arabs from Kuwait and Bahrain, both students at the University of California at Santa Barbara, come to participate in the conference. Throughout the meetings, the young man kept assertively repeating his views, which weren't really shared by anyone else present, except perhaps by his girlfriend, who kept quiet. His insistence disturbed the flow of the dialogue. At the same time, he was perturbed by the opposition he encountered.

After the second lunch, which was served on the back patio, Krishnamurti went to sit with him. They conversed animatedly about some of the troubling issues. The young Arab, with curly hair and handsome, dark features, was passionate in the defense of his beliefs. Krishnamurti was also passionate, but in a calm manner. Since it wasn't a private conversation, a small group of us remained sitting at the redwood tables, eagerly listening to the conversation. The student was heatedly stating his point of view, delivering it with explosive, guttural emphasis. He vehemently objected to the suggestion that 'God' might only be a concept created by human thought, and that psychological evolution did not exist. But Krishnamurti was hinting at something different. He was concerned with the totality of human life in its everyday manifestation, with generational patterns that accumulated into ever-increasing cultural conditioning, so that bit by bit, the vast beauty of life was narrowed into one small corner of specialization and routine.

At one point, Krishnamurti vigorously pressed his long, elegant index finger on the maroon surface of the table. I was fascinated by the flexibility with which the top two fingerjoints bent at an almost ninety-degree angle. He categorically stated, "Born." He paused to look at the other person for an indication that he had grasped his meaning. But, clearly, the Arab was not the only one who looked puzzled: most of us felt somewhat mystified.

Krishnamurti slid his bent finger ten inches toward the right and said, "Die." And again he looked around for a sign of understanding before delivering the punch line, "Is that all?"

There was no response. I felt rather perplexed, even confused, about what he was saying. For several moments, I was so absorbed by his finger movement across the table edge that I thought he was talking about the table itself. Then it dawned on me that he was illustrating the brevity and limitation of the individual life span. He repeated the same motion, this time more quickly, using the same words to describe the movement's polar points: "Born—die. Is that all?"

His gesture and words started to take on the power of a Zen koan. The young Arab was getting impatient and was on the point of evading the issue by bringing in his own ideas. Before he had even opened his mouth, Krishnamurti anticipated the other's move with lightning speed and grasped the man's hand. Again, he repeated the digital motion across the table, stating emphatically, "Born—die. Is that all?"

One of the listeners, a lady trustee, came to the young man's rescue by querying, "Well, what else is there, Krishnaji? One is born, one lives and one dies."

He glanced at her with mock surprise, as if astonished by her simple-mindedness. Then he shrugged, throwing up his hands in a gesture of resignation, "If that is all—born and die—then...."

He dramatically left the sentence unfinished, allowing everyone's imagination to fill in the gap.

The Kuwaiti did not follow the argument and returned to his assertion that God had a hand in it all. Each time he made his point, Krishnamurti would calmly take the young man's hand in his, placing their clasped hands on the table between them. I saw it as a gesture of impersonal friendship: that, despite diverging points of view, there was no division between them. Whenever the Arab spoke, he half-consciously freed his hand from the older man's grip, and as soon as it was Krishnamurti's turn he again took hold of the other's hand. This happened several times, to the subdued amusement of the onlookers, while the young man in his agitated state appeared unaware of the recurring gesture of affection. Finally, Krishnamurti deliberately grasped the other's hand and lifted it high for everyone to see, as a referee raises the victor's arm in the boxing ring. We started to laugh out loud. At this point the young man became conscious of the hand-holding, hand-releasing pattern, and gave an embarrassed smile, before finally sharing in the common mirth. Krishnamurti, raising their joined hands once more, laughed, "I just won't let you go like that."

Several weeks later, the Kuwaiti appeared at A.V. with a large woven basket of dates, dried fruit and sweets that he wanted to present to Krishnamurti. Two years after that, I encountered him again at the talks in the Oak Grove. His Bahraini girlfriend, now his wife, was with him, and they told me that before long they were going to return to their homeland in the Persian Gulf.

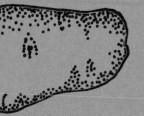

*Chapter 11*

# A MAN WITH A RELIGIOUS MIND

### Starters

*Cantaloupe slices touched with lemon juice.*
*Tossed green salad with choice of*
*vinaigrette or 1000 island dressing.*
*Marinated spinach roots.*
*Grated carrots.*
*Green cabbage coleslaw.*

### Main Dishes

*Green split pea soup, made with onions,*
*bell peppers, celery, and cubed carrots*
*with plenty of parsley.*
*Baked potatoes with sour cream.*
*Steamed cauliflower, served with*
*sauce olivos — olives, capers and*
*'smoked' yeast in olive oil.*

### Dessert

*Rice pudding, prepared with white basmati rice,*
*raisins, almonds, sugar, vanilla,*
*cinnamon, eggs, and milk.*
*Fresh, seasonal fruit.*

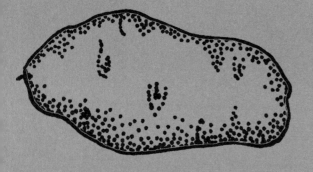

AFTER THE CONCLUSION OF THE CONFERENCE IT WAS ONLY a week until the beginning of the public talks on April 7, 1979. On the intervening Wednesday we were *en famille* around the lunch table. It was a simple luncheon for fourteen people, starting with cantaloupe and tossed green salad, marinated spinach roots, grated carrots and coleslaw. The hot food was green split pea soup, baked potatoes with sour cream, and steamed cauliflower with *sauce olivos*. The dessert was rice pudding.

Everybody was relaxed, and the easy-going conversation centered around poetry. Several of us were talking about our favorite poets. In response to a question, I said, "I really like Rilke, but also Lorca, Neruda, and some of the French poets, like Villon, Rimbaud and Baudelaire." Noting that Krishnamurti hadn't as yet revealed his poetic preferences, I addressed him (he was sitting diagonally across from me), "Are there any poets that you are fond of, Krishnaji?"

Everyone's attention shifted toward him, as he leaned back in his chair and with a fond smile said, "Ah, the poetry of Keats is very special. What is it called, *Ode..?*"

"*Ode to a Nightingale?*" I suggested.

"No, the other one," he said, suddenly remembering it, "*Ode on a Grecian Urn*: 'Thou still unravish'd bride of quietness', that's how it starts, and it ends with 'Beauty is truth, truth beauty—that is all / Ye know on earth, and all ye need to know.'" While he was reciting the lines he closed his eyes, and his voice assumed a dramatic tone. One could tell that he loved the poetry. Opening his eyes again, he took a deep breath, shaking his head a little as if to dispel an overwhelming impression and, with a delighted smile, said, "I used to be able to recite the whole poem but I've forgotten most of it—also some of the other Romantic poets we used to read: Shelley, Lord Byron, Coleridge, and Wordsworth."

A young female teacher asked, "Is it true, sir, that you used to read the Bible?"

To our surprise he answered with a quick laugh, "Yes, but only the old part, what is it called, the Old Testament in the King James translation."

"Why would you read the Scriptures, Krishnaji? I thought you said you never read any of the so-called Holy Books?"

"I love the language, the poetry of it," he responded. "I'm not interested in the fairy tales about an angry god and all that rubbish. I don't read it because I believe it contains a particular message of truth, or is some sort of divine revelation. That is such utter nonsense. No book can contain the truth. Truth is a living thing. It is..." He raised his hand passionately with fanned-out fingers, straining for a word to describe the indescribable. He left the sentence dangling in the air, its incompleteness extending into charged silence. Suddenly he turned to the questioner and declaimed, "'My beloved spake, and said unto me, rise up, my love, my fair one, and come away, for, lo, the winter is past, the rain is over and gone; the flowers appear on the earth; the time of the singing of birds is come, and the voice of the turtle dove is heard in our land; arise my love, my fair one, and come away.'"

The way he intoned the verses was enchanting, and the passion embedded in them became alive for an instant. "Do you see the beauty of these words?" he asked after a vibrant pause. "They are over three-thousand years old. The Song of Songs or Solomon's Song—it's really quite remarkable, isn't it?" An older trustee concurred, "And think of the poetry of the Psalms, or the Book of Job—they are literary masterpieces."

A young lady who had recently taken on the job of secretary at the Foundation office was sitting across from Krishnamurti. She was probably the only one at the table who wasn't especially interested in the teachings, since her prime reason for being here was to be with her boyfriend, who worked at the school. Hence her image of Krishnamurti, in stark contrast to the rest of us, was probably minimal; she saw him as a charming old gentleman, 'cute', as she once told me. She had been quietly following the conversation and now turned to Krishnamurti, "What about whodunits, sir? Do you ever read any of those?"

He didn't respond immediately to her question but looked at her with a puzzled expression. She quickly rephrased it, "You know—mysteries, detective stories?"

A delighted sparkle entered his eyes. "Yes, thrillers," he replied. "I enjoy reading them. What about them?"

"So do I! I adore mysteries. So who is your favorite author, Krishnaji?"

"I've read plenty of Agatha Christie. And I enjoy the stories by Rex Stout. What is his name, the fat detective?"

"Nero Wolfe."

"And his assistant, a sort of bungling..."

"Archie," she said. "What about Raymond Chandler, did you ever read any of his stories?"

"Who is he?"

"He invented Philip Marlow, the tough private eye, who lives in Los Angeles in the 40's and 50's."

"Ah, yes, I think I've read all of those."

"And are you familiar with John D. MacDonald? He is one of my favorites."

"John D. —?"

"The hero is Travis McGee, and the title of each book has a different color in it. And it usually takes place in Florida..."

"And he lives on a boat and drives a blue Rolls-Royce — is that him?"

"Right. And there's always a lot of philosophizing in it. But then there is also a lot of romantic stuff, when the hero gets involved with a lady. I mean it's a bit sexy, don't you think?"

This she asked with a quick sideways glance at the other people around the table.

Krishnamurti responded without any sign of embarrassment, "Ah, I always skip those parts. I find them rather boring, so I just pass over them very quickly."

She was laughing exuberantly at his facial expression, which resembled that of a child displeased at having to witness the love life of the grown-ups. The others at the table were also laughing now. Krishnamurti became aware of his dismissive reaction and joined in the common merriment.

"But what do you do, Krishnaji," she continued, "when you watch a movie or a TV-show, and they kiss and embrace?"

"I simply close my eyes," he declared, covering his eyes with his hands, then opening the fingers and peeking through. "And when it's all over, I look again."

Laughter spread like wildfire round the table.

When, after lunch, I went to clean the serving table, I found Krishnamurti standing in front of the bookcase which occupied half the wall of the corner servery. It was packed with paperbacks, mostly thrillers and spy stories. I stopped what I was doing and went up to him, to see which mystery he would choose.

"Tell me which one is a really good thriller," he said. "You know: good plot and well-written, not all that sentimental stuff."

I hesitated for a moment. "Well, Krishnaji, you've probably read most of the books here. I recently read some spy thrillers by Eric

Ambler, which were quite fascinating." I removed a paperback from a shelf and showed it to him. "Here is one of them."

"*The Mask of Dimitrios*," he read out loud and briefly skimmed over the front and back cover. "I think I've read that," he remarked and placed it back on the shelf.

"Or what about Ross Macdonald," I suggested, pointing at a row of bookspines bearing his name. "He's really a good writer and lives over in Santa Barbara where most of his stories take place."

"All right, sir, give me the two best ones."

I picked two titles which I thought were captivating. He studied the synopses on the back covers for a moment and then remarked pensively, "I may have read these before, but I can't remember. It doesn't matter, it's just a pastime. Nothing is retained."

He gave me a quick, friendly pat on the shoulder, clamped the paperbacks under his arm and turned to leave. "Good-bye, sir," he said. "Thank you."

"Thank you, Krishnaji," I answered.

A FEW DAYS LATER, AN INDIAN ACTOR AND ACTRESS CAME TO see Krishnamurti and were invited to take lunch with us. She was fairly tall, with stunning, classical Indian features and lustrous dark hair falling below her shoulders. Dressed in an exquisite sari, with gold threads running through the azure silk, she moved with elegant poise. A crimson *bindi* dot between her eyes embellished their exotic beauty. Her companion was athletically built and handsome in a rugged, masculine way.

During lunch the lady, a beauty queen turned movie star, said that both of them were on their way to Hollywood—she to make her U.S. debut in a major science fiction film, he to play the hero in an adventure film for television. She went on to tell us that her role required her to shave off her luxuriant hair. Seeing it cascading down to her shoulders, it was hard for me to imagine that she would actually go through with it and for a moment I thought she was just telling a tall story.

As the conversation idly flowed around films, acting, and actors, Krishnamurti remarked quite generally, "Actors are terribly vain." At this, the actress stopped chewing her food and her dark eyes flashed, perhaps because she took his remark as being directed against her.

Composing herself, she retorted without anger but with a somewhat cool intonation, "But, Krishnaji, aren't you also a little vain? After all, you comb your hair to conceal the bald spot on your forehead."

Her matter-of-fact, calm delivery softened the forthright statement and resulted in a minuscule silence around the table. I, for one, was taken by surprise, both by her acute observation and by the fact that until then I simply hadn't noticed that he did have a large bald spot which was covered by an adventurous sweep of hair.

Krishnamurti didn't react at all. For a breathless second he quietly looked at her, not batting an eyelid, nor uttering a word. With a tiny smile around his lips, he brought the fork to his mouth to take food. The conversation continued amiably. After lunch, Krishnamurti took the couple on a walk through the Oak Grove, lush-green after recent rains.

Months later, toward the end of the year, I went to see the film in which the lady starred, *Star Trek One*. At first I had some difficulty recognizing her with a shaved head. Despite baldness, or perhaps because of it, she came across as stunningly beautiful.

THE RAINS HAD BEEN PLENTIFUL DURING THE PAST FEW WEEKS, and we waited with bated breath to see if they would stop in time for the Talks at the Oak Grove, or whether we would have to run all over town again, as we had the previous year. In the end, it turned out that the ground was just dry enough for us to go ahead as planned. Everything was green and blossoming, and appeared to be ready for an event, that for me evoked a feeling of festivity—as if Christmas, Easter and New Year were happening on the same day.

Thousands of people from all over the world had been gathering in the valley to hear Krishnamurti speak. Undoubtedly, it was a cultural event of the first order, exploring and laying the basis for a new consciousness, perhaps even heralding a new culture. During the first few talks, he went into what he considered the source of a new culture— goodness. "A good society—the ancient Indians, Greeks and Egyptians already dreamt of this," he declared.

In many respects, he seemed to embody the essence of this new culture in his own person, because culture was a living thing to him, not something recorded, dead and fossilized. To see him arrive for a talk, climb onto the platform, and conduct a conversation with several thousand people was to see a human being of great culture and refinement. There wasn't anything pompous or frivolous about him. He was rooted in intelligence, in awareness of the moment at hand, and in genuine compassion for all living things. He seemed to manifest what the word 'culture' implied: a profound respect and care for the earth, for its animals, trees and flowers, and, more than anything else, respect and care for human beings—all human beings, regardless of their status, social class or background.

While perceiving goodness as the well-spring of a new culture, he insisted on a fine but clear distinction between the creative mind of culture and the original creative force of nature and the universe. Writing an inspiring poem, composing a symphony, or building a magnificent cathedral—none of these, he felt, touched the primordial ground of creation. Even the most refined and subtle cultural expressions still derived from thought and the self, the ego with its narrowly defined interest. "True creativeness does not need to express itself," he said. And, hinting at the holistic aspect of a new culture rooted in the individual life, "The greatest art is the art of living." *True, but one doesn't exclude the other. We as humans must create. After all nature constantly creates and destroys.*

IT WAS THE MONDAY AFTER THE FIRST TWO WEEKEND TALKS AT the Oak Grove, and we had almost twenty guests for lunch. Several trustees from the other foundations and practically all the KFA trustees were present. The atmosphere was rather more formal than usual, and the conversation centered around issues of art and culture. Krishnamurti was saying to one of the English trustees, "You've seen Chartres, haven't you? What a marvelous cathedral! Think of the enormous energy and cooperation it took to build something like that. It must have taken them decades, even centuries."

"And all inspired by religious fervor, for the greater glory of God."

"And completely anonymous, you understand? No one knows who the architect was. At that time, they didn't sign their work as they do today. Human beings can do the most extraordinary things when they set their minds to it. Going to the moon involved the working together of a hundred thousand people, I believe, but they did it."

A visitor from India started talking about the architectural wonders

of his country, about the temples, caves and mosques that had been created by people inspired by the religious spirit. He mentioned the cave
temples of Ellora and Ajantha, the Taj Mahal, Konarak and Puri. Krishnamurti had been listening to his account and now quietly interjected,
"And there is an island near Bombay where some monks carved temples
into the rock. It must have been over a thousand years ago. One of the
rock sculptures is of the god Shiva showing his three faces. It's an enormous sculpture."

Recognizing the description of a sight that I had visited some years
ago, I remarked, "Elephanta Island and the Mahesh-murti."

"This Tri-murti, as it's called," he continued, "is really an extraordinary image, full of depth and dignity. Imagine what the state of mind
must have been of those creating that monument!" There was a sense of
awe in his voice, as he contemplated the consciousness that had created
the sculpture of the three-faced deity. An interval of silence spread around
the table, as if the religious mind were manifesting among us. At last I ventured, "They must have been enormously inspired and devoted."

"No, sir," he replied. "They must have understood something, you
know, had an insight into the...religious mind."

He made an emphatic gesture, with intensely spread fingers. Everyone seemed to grasp what he was referring to: the religious mind, which
he held to be the key to the understanding of human existence and the
*sine qua non* for harmonious living and the beginning of a new culture.

AFTER THE CONCLUSION OF THE TALKS AT THE END OF APRIL,
he met with the staff at Pine Cottage for a number of discussions. As
often, he emphasized the importance of listening, "Listen with your
whole being, with all your mind and heart, and all your senses. Listen to
the sound of a tree, not of the wind or the leaves, but the sound of the
trunk, the silent sound of the roots." Later, during lunch, we were talking about music and some of the famous present-day performers of classical music, when Krishnamurti mentioned that somebody had sent him
a cassette recording of classical South Indian instrumental music. It was
quite exceptional, and he invited us to come and listen to it after lunch.

About ten of us trooped over to Pine Cottage and entered the small
sitting room adjoining his bedroom. It was furnished with simple ele-

gance. We seldom had occasion to enter his private quarters, so it felt like a privilege to be with him here. We were seated on some chairs arranged along the wall, and, although it was a relatively small space for ten people, it didn't feel crowded. I found myself growing silent within myself as I contemplated the intense listening that had happened within these confines for long periods of time.

By way of introduction, Krishnamurti said to us, "Now you can hear some excellent music — not the kind that you hear from the famous Indian musicians who make it to the West. They only get spoilt and corrupted by the publicity and money. So the music becomes second-hand, as they do it only for commercial reasons, for the money. But this is the real music, with tremendous integrity, not just for profit. It's sacred music." Krishnamurti's standards of artistic purity were uncompromising and austere, demanding not only technical excellence but also a dedicated selflessness. Without any motive, from sheer *joie de vivre*, one performed music for its own sake.

Presently, he turned on the player. Reverberating sounds of strings and percussion and the mellow strains of a bamboo flute evoked a different climate and landscape, and a different musical tradition. I followed my natural tendency and closed my eyes to harmonize with the drawn-out drone of the instruments. It seemed like an imageless revelation of pure sound, recreating a universe of sound within, telling a story of endless cycles of cosmic creation and destruction.

When the music was over and I opened my eyes, I thought for a moment I was looking at a new world. The people around me seemed to have new faces, as if an inner light were illuminating their features. A bond of silence and listening held us together for an instant, and one felt shy and strangely vulnerable. Then, without any comment or discussion, we thanked Krishnamurti for the listening treat and filed out of his sitting room to our respective places.

SEVERAL DAYS LATER, (IT WAS THE SECOND WEEK OF MAY), I was in the kitchen putting the finishing touches to this season's last lunch with Krishnamurti. I had turned on the desk top radio and was working to the sounds of Beethoven's *Choral* Symphony, which were pervading the sunny kitchen space. I lost track of time, because toward the end of the third movement, Krishnamurti entered the kitchen. I walked over to the counter to turn off the radio, but he quickly stopped me saying, "Oh no, sir, don't turn it off. It's Beethoven's *Ninth* Symphony."

"You really know it quite well, Krishnaji."

"Yes, of course. I lived all by myself in a log cabin up in the High Sierras and had only one record, which I played every day. It was Beethoven's *Ninth* and it was one of those old-fashioned turntables, which one had to wind up, and the loudspeaker enormous." He gestured to describe the old loudspeaker that opened like a horn of plenty.

"There was only one record there—Beethoven's *Ninth*—and I played it every day, for weeks on end, listening to every subtle nuance, every note and melody. After a week or two it seemed that I could distinguish the various instruments. Eventually I learned the entire composition by heart. I played it every morning at eleven o'clock."

"Why always at eleven o'clock, sir?"

"It was after breakfast, and I had cleaned the dishes. It was a moment of leisure, the morning sun shining into the room. It created a sense of order in the course of the day in the wilderness."

An image flashed across my mind: somewhere in the mountain world, in a small cabin amidst the towering sequoias, those thousand-year-old witnesses of silence, the young Krishnamurti placed a needle on the black record and, sitting on a wooden bench, listened with closed eyes to the musical strains of the deaf master.

As the choral voices on the radio started to intone the song of universal brotherhood, "*Freude, schöner Götterfunken...alle Menschen werden Brüder...*", I quietly gazed at Krishnamurti, as he stood next to me listening to the music. I felt a sudden, unexpected sense of great freedom. For a moment there was no hurry, no time or pressure, no next moment and no thought, only listening. Then, through the musical chords, I heard his voice asking, "What's for lunch, Michael?"

For an instant and without any reason, I felt like bursting into joyous laughter. Restraining myself, I smiled at him and replied, "Today, Krishnaji, we're having Mexican food: guacamole and jicama salad, enchiladas, corn-on-the-cob and black beans, and mango and papaya fruit salad accompanied by cookies, biscuits, that is."

"Ah, that's good. Can I help with anything?"

"Yes, sir," I answered enthusiastically.

It was a leisurely lunch with sixteen of us. Since Krishnamurti and

Mary Z. were leaving for England the following day, a great deal of the conversation centered around their departure and arrival time, the airline they were flying with, and other travel issues. Many of us wouldn't see him for nine months. But none of us, it seemed, were sad or sentimental, not only because he abhorred emotional behavior but simply because he was still with us at the moment and his presence was quietly overwhelming and complete.

All at once he said, "I must tell you a story I heard the other day. It's in ancient India. There is a yogi who is famous for his accomplishments and austerity. He owns only two loincloths—one to wash and one to wear. He visits the capital of the kingdom and his fame reaches the ear of the king, who politely invites the yogi to his palace. He greets him with due reverence, shows him around the palace, and takes him to the treasure vault, where he has enormous amounts of jewels and gold. He says to the yogi, 'Whatever you would like of my treasure is yours. Just tell me what you desire, and you can have it.' But the yogi proudly declines. 'Worldly possessions don't mean a thing to me. All I possess in the world are these two loincloths.' The king is impressed and says to him, 'Please stay with me for a day or two and teach me the secret of your great detachment and wisdom.' And the yogi accepts the invitation. A servant shows him to a bare room, where he can spend the night. In the middle of the night, there is an awful lot of noise, people shouting and running. Somebody throws open the door of his room and shouts, 'Run for your life! The palace is on fire.' The yogi dashes out of the room. There are flames and smoke in the hallways, and people running. As he is rushing out into the night, he sees the king in his robe next to him. And as they look back at the palace going down in flames, the king says to the yogi, 'Well, there go all my jewels and treasures. But I don't care: you have taught me that possessions don't matter, and that all one needs is a simple garment.' Hearing the words, the yogi suddenly turns and starts running toward the burning palace. The king doesn't know what the heck he's doing, meeting certain death. So he runs after him and catches up with him, 'What are you doing? Have you gone mad? You are meeting certain death in the flames. Why?' And the yogi turns toward him with fear and worry in his face and says, 'My loincloth, my other loincloth, I left it in the palace, I must save it, it's all I have.' And the king suddenly laughs, 'You are willing to give up your life for your puny loincloth? And you are teaching me about detachment and being free of possessions!'"

"So what's the moral of the story?" a lady asked. "Don't try to save your possessions when the house is burning?"

"No, it's about attachment," someone else remarked. "It doesn't matter whether one is attached to something enormous or something really small, it's still attachment."

"But isn't it about desire?" an older lady suggested. "Even to want to be free of desire is still desire."

"Don't be attached." Krishnamurti said, "Don't be attached to anyone or anything."

As we all rose from the table, everybody carrying their dirty dishes to the sink, I thought it was an appropriate good-bye story.

Unpretentiously, as he did all things, Krishnamurti helped with the clearing of the table, carrying pitchers, dishes and bowls into the kitchen. Seeing him helping with kitchen chores, guests and trustees alike promptly followed suit. Even those who normally wouldn't dream of lending a hand on this occasion adjusted their attitude and asked me what they could do to help. So I happily obliged by handing out rubber gloves, dishtowels, aprons and brooms, and giving brief instructions as to what needed to be done.

While everyone busied themselves with the clean-up job, Krishnamurti stood quietly between refrigerator and chopping table and observed the activity around him with patient amusement. I was putting the leftover food in plastic storage containers, and he asked me, "What are you going to do with that, sir?"

"We'll be eating it this evening, Krishnaji. It'll still be good. We usually make use of leftovers. I don't like to waste food or throw it away."

"Good."

He was getting somewhat impatient now and called out to Mary Z. who, with rubber gloves and apron, was busy at the sink. "Maria," he called with Italian zest, "we have to go. You still have to pack your things."

"I'm coming, sir," she responded and turned to look at him. "I'm just finishing these last few dishes."

He noticed I was placing the leftover cookies in a metal box. Coming up to me, he requested in a low voice, "Do you mind giving us a few of those biscuits for the trip?"

"Of course not, Krishnaji, I'll do it now," I answered and rolled a stack of about eight of them, first in some transparent film and then in aluminum foil. "This will keep them fresh. Do you think that's enough?"

"More than enough, sir, thank you," he replied. With that, he called out once more, "Maria."

"Yes, sir, I'm coming," she replied.

*Chapter 12*

# AN IMMORTAL
# FRIEND

### Starters

*Salad of mixed greens with vinaigrette or
yogurt & garlic dressing.
Greek salad, prepared with tomatoes, cucumbers,
bell peppers, olives, and feta cheese.
Broccoli and olive salad.*

### Main Dishes

*Home-made spinach lasagna, many-layered in
tomato and bechamel sauce,
with mozzarella and Parmesan cheeses.
Steamed asparagus, in a lemon & olive
oil dressing with a dash of herb salt.*

### Dessert

*Orange sunshine cake,
made with whole oranges and raisins,
served with whipped cream.
Fresh, seasonal fruit.*

JUST AS WE WELCOMED HIM ON HIS ARRIVAL IN OJAI, SO WE bade him farewell as he set out for Europe. A group of eight or ten of us had gathered that May afternoon beneath the pepper tree. We had loaded the luggage into the school van. The director was to drive Krishnamurti and Mary Z. to Los Angeles Airport, from where they would fly non-stop to London. All that was left now was a quick, unsentimental good-bye, and we would return to our regular work.

Krishnamurti, dapper in a sports coat and cravat, with soft leather gloves, stepped out of the house, accompanied by Mary Z. who was also elegantly attired for the journey. There was a round of hand-shaking, and Krishnamurti, who always felt and behaved like a guest, thanked each and everyone of us for having him here. We in turn thanked him for being with us. With that, they got into the van and drove off.

We looked at one another and sighed. It seemed strange to me, but all at once I felt alone. There was the sharp pang of separation, a sudden sense of absence, a void, like death. But it had a clean cut to it; it wasn't emotionally loaded, and it didn't leave a bitter taste in one's mouth.

SUMMER AND FALL ROLLED BY, AND I STAYED BUSY WITH MY normal school activities, which included cooking for the staff and students at the Oak Grove School, teaching some classes and going on field trips. Besides, I helped with the week-long or weekend Adult Center seminars at Arya Vihara, which were conducted every month by the German physics professor and his wife. By the time Christmas and New Year 1980 had come, my thoughts, which had never entirely left Krishnamurti, started to revolve around his return to Ojai in early February.

His arrival was like a fresh breeze bringing the scent of the new season. A week earlier I had started to set up the Arya Vihara kitchen for the upcoming luncheons there. During my absence, the sous-chef took over my cooking duties at the Oak Grove School. It was a welcome change, and I was thankful for the opportunity to be cooking for Krishnamurti and his guests for three entire months.

At the first lunch, after the usual questions concerning the details of his journey had been exhausted, he suddenly turned to the director, who was sitting across from him, and asked, "Do the children, the students trust you? Do they trust the teachers?"

"Well, up to a point they do. The older they are, the less they trust the adults."

"That's not good enough," Krishnamurti declared. "There must be trust: real trust, not just limited trust. They must feel completely safe, completely at home with you."

As the conversation continued, I realized that the keynote theme had been sounded. This time it was 'trust'. There was a certain pattern to the way the theme was first presented, although each year it changed and the form of the variations on the theme also changed. One year it had been 'responsibility', the next year 'psychological pressure', followed by 'interest and self-interest', and the year after that 'respect'. Krishnamurti usually raised the theme first at the lunch table, then developed it during discussions and dialogues with trustees, staff and parents. If there were any seminars or conferences with scientists and artists, he would often use this theme to approach the issues that were the focus of his investigation into consciousness, life, death and meditation. Invariably it was a living process of inquiry, an organic movement that unfolded like a flower. And, finally, the theme would be woven into the public talks at the Oak Grove.

"What is trust to you?" he was asking one of the trustees. "Do you trust anybody? Do you trust your wife? Do you trust partially, here but not there? What is trust to you, sir?"

The other man hesitated. "If I trust you," he said, "then I can rely on you, then I have confidence in you."

But answers like that seldom satisfied Krishnamurti. He usually imparted a very specific meaning to whichever key word he was using at the moment, giving it a depth and transparency that opened the door to a new perception of life.

"I don't mean reliance. Then I depend on you," he explained. "And I don't mean faith, either. That's what the Church has been saying for hundreds of years, 'Have faith, believe in Jesus.' That reminds me of a joke someone told me recently. Would you like to hear it? A Catholic is standing on a mountain and looks down into the beauty of the valley. Suddenly he slips and falls down the cliff and is barely able to hold on to the branch of a tree that is growing there. Below him is an abyss of a thousand feet. He doesn't know what to do, so he prays, 'Please, Lord, help me. Save me from death.' And a voice comes out of the sky and says, 'Have faith, let go!' And the man looks up and calls out, 'Is there anybody else up there?'"

While we were all laughing, Krishnamurti looked at us with bright eyes, eventually asking, "What is trust? Do you have trust? Not trust in something, some idea or ideal, just trust."

At the end of the meal, we got up with the question still unanswered. For me, it lingered on while I was sweeping the kitchen floor, and later throughout the day it recurred. As I kept pondering it, I thought I was catching a glimpse of what he was hinting at: trust as a state of mind, in which there was no fear, no worry, no suspicion and conflict; a mind without pressure, without a personal agenda. *Very true.*

*But what is the catalyst? H.*

A FEW DAYS LATER WE CANCELED LUNCH BECAUSE Krishnamurti wanted to take a day of rest, as he sometimes did to preserve his energies (he was eighty-five). I prepared a few simple dishes, which I carried on a tray to Pine Cottage. After placing the tray on the table, I asked him when I should return to pick up the dishes.

"Come in an hour, sir," he said. "Don't ring the bell, just come in. I'll leave the door unlocked."

When I returned an hour later, I was shocked by the scene I encountered in the dining room. Krishnamurti was not sitting upright at the table, nor chewing each mouthful thirty-two times, nor meditatively ingesting the harvest of the earth. He was bending over his plate in a very relaxed manner, holding his fork in one hand and a book in the other. He seemed to be deeply absorbed in reading the paperback. It was as if an image of mine was being shattered: he didn't do everything with full, 100% attention. Unable to contain my surprise I said, "You read while you're eating, Krishnaji?"

"Food is such a bore sometimes," he replied, then quickly added, "It's good, tasty food, sir. Only when you sit by yourself chewing it, it gets to be a bit of a bore."

His simple explanation pacified me and brought a joyful grin to my face. Collecting the dishes on the tray, I asked, "What are you reading, sir?"

"It's a thriller, by Rex Stout," he answered and showed me the title page.

As I was leaving Pine Cottage, he smiled and said, "Thank you, Michael. See you tomorrow."

THE NAME 'KRISHNAMURTI' MEANS 'LIKENESS OF KRISHNA', and refers to the divine hero of Hindu mythology, Krishna. While in Madras, I found it was a common name in South India: the telephone directory listed several pages of it in various spellings. In the Western world, to his and our amusement, his name was often mispronounced and misspelt. Some of the junk and fan mail he received was addressed to Krishna Murphy, Christian Murphy, Kristy Moorty, and Christoph Murphy, to name a few.

He had his own peculiar ways of referring to himself. During public talks he would often employ the term 'the speaker' and 'one', 'we' and 'you' in an attempt to avoid 'I'. Often he liked to poke fun at himself, with phrases like 'the man on the platform', 'the poor chap', 'the old boy', and similar expressions. But by far the most frequent way in which he referred to himself, both in public and private, was simply 'K'. Perhaps it was the anonymity of an alphabetic symbol that appealed to him.

AT ONE LUNCHEON IN EARLY MARCH WE WERE A RELATIVELY small, familiar group with a special guest, an older Indian lady, who had been a friend and associate of Krishnamurti for many years. She was sitting across from him, in a dark-red sari with a red *bindi* dot on her forehead. He was giving her his full attention, leaning forward over the table as they conversed. It seemed almost like a private conversation, although it occurred in the presence of twelve other persons. They were talking about people and events from long ago, as far back as the Theosophical days. Krishnamurti's recollection of these times seemed rather hazy. He kept asking the lady about the details of specific situations, and she kept reminding him what he had done and who had been present at that time. It sounded intriguing but also rather mystifying. At one point, he leaned back in his chair and wondered aloud, "Why wasn't that boy influenced and corrupted by all the adulation, the money and the power?" By 'boy' he was referring to himself as an adolescent during the early Theosophical days.

I had heard him ask a similar thing on a previous occasion. It didn't seem like a rhetorical question. There were enigmatic aspects of his life and person that appeared to be a mystery to him as much as to the rest of us.

"Was it the vacant mind?" he pondered "The boy was vacant, dreamy, almost moronic. Nothing stuck; everything just passed through that mind. It was like a sieve, not retaining anything." He questioningly looked, first at the lady, then at the rest of us, as if one of us might be able to provide an answer to the unusual events that had made up his life.

"When he traveled by train," he reminisced, half surprised and half amused, "they would reserve one compartment just for him. The two adjoining ones, behind and in front, were for his companions."

"But why?" I asked.

"To protect him," he laughed. "To see that nobody bothered him, and to keep him pure and uncontaminated. Nobody was allowed to touch him or his personal belongings. And there was always somebody with him."

"And the brother received the same treatment?" I asked, referring to his brother, Nityananda who died at Arya Vihara in 1925.

"Oh no," he replied, and, stabbing one slender long finger against his chest, added with an ironical laugh, "this was the Vehicle. All the others had to look after him. They used to prostrate themselves before him, practically worshipping him. But none of the adulation and fuss ever touched the boy. None of that meant a thing to him, you understand, sirs? Why was that? Why wasn't he corrupted by it all? Was it his vacant mind?" He fell silent, musing on the mystery of long ago.

THE FOLLOWING DAY WE LUNCHED ON GREEK SALAD, broccoli and olive salad, spinach lasagna prepared with a bechamel and a tomato sauce, asparagus, and orange sunshine cake for dessert. We were talking about the Oak Grove School and its relationship with the community, and Krishnamurti asked the director, "What does a simple worker at the check-out stand of the Meiner's Oaks market think of the Oak Grove School? Does he, or she, have any idea of what we are doing? Or do they think we are some odd Oriental cult?"

Some of us smiled at the question, which sounded naive but had a very relevant angle. The director answered, "Well, Krishnaji, I doubt if any of the lower middle-class workers have heard of the school or of you."

A teacher added, "They have probably seen the signpost as they've been driving by, so at least they know that there is a school."

"Unless they have children of their own, they wouldn't have any interest in a school," someone else suggested.

Krishnamurti wasn't satisfied with the answers. "No, sir. I know all that. If not the housewife in the market, take a fairly educated person who has some awareness of what's going on in the Ojai Valley and in the world." He started to laugh at his own train of thought. "All right, sir, take a very educated, fairly intelligent person, a doctor, a lawyer — no, not a lawyer — take the headmaster of Thacher School: what do they say about the Oak Grove School?"

The director responded, "Well, sir, you know that we just put up the large wooden sign at the entrance to the campus, and..."

"I know all that, sir. Please come to the point. What's the problem? Is it the name? The name 'Krishnamurti'?"

His incisiveness and unabashed honesty cut right through the sense of unease that arose, whenever the 'name' issue was brought up. A teacher spoke frankly, "Krishnaji, the name 'Krishnamurti' evokes apprehension, if not prejudice, in the average American. It raises notions of something alien, of strange gurus, sects and cults. The first association is with the Krishna Consciousness movement, which is world-wide. People who know very little about all this make an almost automatic association between these names — Krishna, Krishna Consciousness, Krishnamurti. It sounds the same to them, and in some way it *is* the same. Of course, it's a very superficial reaction, but many more have heard the name Krishna Consciousness than have ever heard of you."

"Then get rid of it," Krishnamurti declared very emphatically and without hesitation. "Drop the name, sir. The name doesn't matter at all. If it's a hindrance, get rid of it."

His action was immediate and without choice. Everyone else at the table, however, reacted with various degrees of shock to his suggestion. One trustee said, "But Krishnaji, how can we get rid of the name? We are the Krishnamurti Foundation."

Another person stammered, "We can't just remove the name — how can one...?"

A teacher said, "It doesn't make sense. What are we going to call ourselves, the Institute for Education?"

Sudden agitation gripped the group, as everybody voiced their views at once. I was watching Krishnamurti, whose words had triggered the emotional stir. He was leaning back in his chair, calmly folding his hands in his lap and observing with an aloof expression what was going on around him. He meant what he said. A name—whether it was his own or someone else's—was of little or no importance to him, particularly if it stood in the way of something greater and more vital.

The director said, "Krishnaji, you know that we just put up the new signboard." He was referring to a large wooden signboard, that had recently been erected at the entrance to the driveway leading up to the school campus. It read, 'Oak Grove School of the Krishnamurti Foundation of America', the second portion more prominent than the first.

"It took a lot of time..."

"Take it down."

"You mean...?"

"Remove the sign and replace it with one which only mentions the name of the school. That should take care of it. Finished. Basta."

As now, he had a rare capacity to cut through the meanderings of thought, through the long calculation of pros and cons, and arrive at a decision. But he was far from being infallible, as he was the first to admit. Especially in practical or personal matters his decisions, at times, turned out to be wrong. And we all-too-often tended to follow our desire to please him and did not challenge him sufficiently.

Wrapping up the issue, he remarked, "Maybe I should change my name to Christopher Murphy."

The tension which had built up around the table was relieved, and one of the trustees laughingly remarked, "That would solve a lot of problems, Krishnaji."

As a consequence of this conversation, the signboard in front of the school was taken down and replaced with a smaller one that simply stated, 'Oak Grove School'.

IN MARCH KRISHNAMURTI STARTED TO MEET REGULARLY with staff and parents on weekend afternoons at Pine Cottage. The luncheons on those days were well attended. Many of the teachers enjoyed the opportunity to ask him questions about his life, and he freely and without reservation answered their inquiries.

One of the teachers, who was sitting next to him at lunch on this particular day, was anxious to know about the celebrities he had met in California. Although he recalled meeting Stravinsky, Isherwood, Chaplin, Greta Garbo and John Barrymore, among others, he didn't have many anecdotes about them. It wasn't until she mentioned Aldous Huxley, the English novelist, that he became more eloquent and recounted the story of their long and fertile friendship.

"We first met before the war and would often visit one another, and keep up a correspondence. Once I went to see him and his Belgian-born wife, Maria, in the Mojave Desert, where they had recently moved. I had just started to write down some of my observations, and I showed Aldous what I had written. I used to be awfully shy at that time. But he was enthusiastic about it, saying it was very original, and urged me to keep on writing. He said he had never seen this style of writing in world literature before—a natural description followed by a philosophical discourse and a dialogue. He advised me to write regularly, perhaps a page or two a day, and so I've kept at it." He made a slightly apologetic gesture, as he sometimes did when talking about himself. "We used to take long walks in the hills, and he would give lengthy discourses on the flowers and plants by the wayside and the animals we encountered." A deep sense of affection shone through his words, as he talked about his friend who had died seventeen years earlier. "Aldous had tremendous knowledge about everything. He was a living encyclopedia. You could ask him about anything, and he would be able to give a learned lecture on it, whether it was religion, music or the arts, a rare insect or a plant." He paused and gazed at the young woman next to him. "But he realized that his immense knowledge was a burden and prevented him from experiencing things afresh. All that stored-up memory kept him from coming into contact with the new and original. And he was well aware of it. Sometimes he would say to me, 'I would gladly give up everything, all my learnedness and knowledge, to capture a glimpse of that, for one direct perception of truth.'" And Krishnamurti gestured emphatically, pointing at that which was beyond words. "We had a strange relationship—very affectionate and considerate. Often during our long walks together we wouldn't speak a word, or we would silently sit together."

"Didn't he also take psychedelic drugs at one time?" she asked.

"He wrote about it in *The Doors of Perception* and *Heaven and Hell*," I interjected.

"Yes, he experimented with them," Krishnamurti replied. Although I knew that he disapproved of drugs of any kind and dismissed the value of drug-induced experiences, I couldn't discern any judgmental tone in his voice. "He would tell me about his sensations: how the colors of the flowers became extraordinarily vivid and alive, and how the space between him and the flower disappeared."

He paused for a moment and smiled. Looking at our eager faces, he asked, "Does all of this interest you at all?"

When several of us enthusiastically answered, "Yes, yes," he gave one of his characteristic shrugs, indicating that it was entirely up to us. "He was blind in one eye," he continued, "and had impaired vision in the other. He used to practice a particular method of eye exercises, the Bates Method. He explained it to me in great detail, and I've been practicing it ever since."

"You do it every day?" I asked.

He nodded. "Every day for about half an hour."

"What do these exercises consist of?" a teacher who wore glasses asked with great interest.

Krishnamurti promptly demonstrated some of the simple exercises, like massaging the eyelids in a circular fashion, rolling the eyeballs in different directions, and focusing on objects at a distance, while covering one eye with one's palm. It was enjoyable to see the delight he took in minutely describing the various aspects of the Bates Method, and I marveled at the care with which he explained such seemingly trivial matters. On a previous occasion he had gone into great detail about how to spit-shine one's shoes, something which he did regularly. Another time he described to us how he had learned to walk properly in the mountains from an Italian captain of the *Alpini*.

Having exhausted his account of the eye exercises, he briefly returned to talking about his great friend from England. "Aldous used to smoke a lot. He finally got cancer of the tongue. That's what he died of."

*Part Three*

# YEARS OF COMPLETION

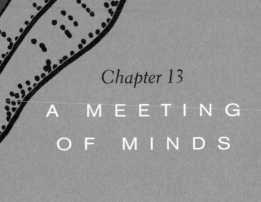

*Chapter 13*

# A MEETING
# OF MINDS

### Starters

*Tossed green salad with
vinaigrette or Roquefort dressing.
Pasta salad, made with angel hair pasta,
finely chopped olives, pine nuts, and pesto sauce.
Sliced fresh tomatoes, with thin slices of
mozzarella cheese and fresh basil.*

### Main Dishes

*Corn casserole: kernels of sweet corn in a
mixture of onions, bell peppers, and carrots.
Black beans à la cubana, cooked in a
tomato sauce with celery, bell peppers,
cilantro and mild chili powder.
Carrots and pineapple.*

### Dessert

*Tapioca pudding.
Fresh, seasonal fruit.*

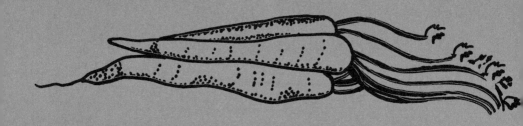

IN MARCH, 1980, PROFESSOR DAVID BOHM AND HIS WIFE SARAL came to stay with us for six weeks. They had been visiting Ojai regularly since 1976 around the time of the Talks, staying for a month or two in the upstairs guest apartment across from Pine Cottage. Over the years I was able to witness at close range the fascinating friendship between Krishnamurti and David, which had been flowering for twenty years.

I had first heard of David Bohm during the 1972 Brockwood Public Talks, when a student mentioned him as Krishnamurti's 'right-hand man', a description I found somewhat odd. He went on to tell me that Bohm, originally from the U.S., was a professor of theoretical physics at London University. At one time he had worked with Einstein and Oppenheimer and held teaching positions at universities in Brazil and Israel. As a trustee of the English Foundation, he and his wife regularly visited Brockwood Park and had dialogues with Krishnamurti, as well as with the staff and students.

The following year, 1973 in Saanen, I was going through a recently published book by Krishnamurti, *The Awakening of Intelligence*. The final chapter, entitled *On Intelligence*, contained an edited transcript of a riveting dialogue between Krishnamurti and Bohm. The two brilliant minds moved together and explored the width and depth of thought and intelligence. I had never before read or heard anything like it. A few days after this discovery, I had a brief chance encounter with David and his wife, as we met on our way to the tent where Krishnamurti was giving a talk that morning. But it wasn't until the spring of 1976, that we got to know each other better and became good friends.

IN THE COURSE OF THEIR FRIENDSHIP, KRISHNAMURTI AND David found that they shared not only a passion for uncovering the ways of thought but also a concern for language and its proper usage, with a fondness for tracing the etymologies of words. Both of them often demonstrated in their dialogues that returning to the root meaning of a word could provide a surprising insight—not only into its history but also into the actuality of what the word stood for. To their surprise, they discovered that they were using the same dictionary, which was neither the Oxford nor Webster's but the little-known *Universal Dictionary of the English Language* by Wyld & Partridge.

During the years of their cooperation, Krishnamurti and David engaged in many dialogues, some of which, like the 1975 series of twelve dialogues at Brockwood Park, were recorded. In 1976, seven discussions between Krishnamurti, David Bohm, and David Shainberg, a psychiatrist from New York City, were video-recorded for the first time and released under the title *The Transformation of Man*.

In the course of their conversations, they not only explored the nature of the mind but also sharpened their verbal accuracy by clearly defining key concepts. Krishnamurti had consistently used simple, everyday language to express his insights, at times employing poetic images. At heart, he held to the fact that 'the description is not the described, the word is not the thing'. That is, he used words to point to something beyond the word and therefore tended to be flexible in his use of language.

This was made clear when they fine-tuned the distinction between related concepts, like 'mind', 'brain', 'intellect', and 'thought'; 'awareness', 'attention', and 'insight'; and 'reality', 'actuality', and 'truth', often used interchangeably by Krishnamurti. Especially in the latter example, the clarification brought out some telling aspects of meaning. The word 'reality' derives from the Latin 'res' meaning 'thing', which in turn is related to 'reri' = 'to think'. Thus, our everyday reality consists of things that exist and that we can think about. Accordingly, even illusions, lies and deceptions are forms of reality—at least, in the brain in which they occur and in the real effects that result from the actions they can give rise to. Thus, a person suffering under the delusion that he or she is Napoleon will produce behavior characteristic of Napoleon. In contrast to 'reality' there is 'actuality'—'that which acts', or to use Krishnamurti's phrase, *what is*. 'Actuality' includes 'reality' but also transcends it, in that it denotes a dynamic wholeness, in which all things are related and interact and where their ordinary division is suspended and made whole. 'Truth', then, is beyond both 'reality' and 'actuality', like the ground or background which allows the actual to manifest. Ultimately truth is beyond comprehension and verbalization: sheer no-thing-ness.

All this defining of words, images and concepts was more than just semantic play—it corresponded to an actual process, in which two brilliant minds explored human consciousness to see if there was something beyond the perimeters of thought: the unknown, the limitless.

WHEN DAVID AND SARAL BOHM CAME TO STAY WITH US AT ARYA Vihara, it was a quantum leap in more than one respect, for both the staff and myself. The evening meal which I prepared for them at A.V. became a cultural event, of sorts. Any of the staff were welcome to join David and the A.V. residents for dinner and to participate in the dialogue, which usually started during the meal and continued afterwards in the sitting room. A great many of the teachers enjoyed the opportunity to converse with David in a relaxed atmosphere, gaining thereby a fresh perspective on the questions raised by Krishnamurti, as well as voicing their own views. These evenings with David were full of discovery and easy laughter.

One evening in March, 1980, after we had finished dinner and retired to the sitting room, a teacher new to the school was curious to know how two people as diverse in qualifications, temperament and background as Krishnamurti and David had met in the first place.

"How did it happen that you and Krishnamurti got to know each other?" she asked.

As he was sometimes wont to do, he left it to Saral to answer questions that concerned both of them. "It was in 1957," she began, "and Dave was working at Bristol University. One evening we were in the public library there, and I came upon a book entitled *The First and Last Freedom*. Going through it, I noticed a number of passages that talked about 'the observer and the observed', which reminded me of the work that Dave was engaged in in the field of quantum mechanics. So I showed him the book and as he went on reading it, he became more and more interested. Since we didn't know anything about the author, we eventually wrote to the publisher to obtain information about Krishnamurti. They sent us an address where we could find out more about him. When we contacted the office, which at that time was in London, they gave us the date and place of a talk he was to give there. We heard him speak for the first time in 1960."

"And how did you get to meet him in person?"

"After we heard his talks, Dave became very interested in talking with him in person. So we again wrote to the office in London and asked if a private meeting could be arranged, and they very swiftly responded, asking us if it was convenient for us to meet with Mr. Krishnamurti at such a place at such a time. He was staying at a hotel in London, and we went up to his room. He was very friendly, trying to make us feel comfortable. For a while it felt a bit formal, but he was very open and attentive when Dave started telling him about his work. He was listening with great intensity, asking Dave all sorts of questions, completely without reserve or any barriers between them. When Dave started talking about the observer and the observed, Krishnaji became more and more excited, saying 'Yes, yes, yes,' and finally he was hugging Dave." She started to laugh as she recounted the final part of the story.

The ten of us seated comfortably on the sofa and in the armchairs of the well-lit sitting room joined in her laughter as her narration evoked the encounter between the conservative, quiet professor and the energetic Krishnamurti, his senior by twenty years. David was also laughing heartily, vigorously slapping the back of his head with one hand, one of his peculiar gestures.

After that, their acquaintance grew into friendship and cooperation as the Bohms regularly attended the Talks at Saanen. In the natural splendor of the Swiss mountains, the two men went on long walks, talking over together the enormous problems and challenges that confronted humanity. When in 1968 a new, international foundation—the Krishnamurti Foundation Trust—was founded in England, Krishnamurti asked David to be one of its trustees. Subsequently, both David and Saral became deeply involved in the work of the new school at Brockwood Park.

AT THE END OF MARCH, 1980, KRISHNAMURTI STARTED TO HAVE regular afternoon meetings with both staff and parents of the Oak Grove. Just at that time, the Bohms arrived. Krishnamurti cordially welcomed them and made sure they had everything they needed in the guest apartment, less than twenty yards from his own quarters. He and Mary Z. came to join David and Saral and the rest of us for supper at A.V. that evening, a rare event, since they usually had supper by themselves at Pine Cottage. Krishnamurti invited David to come to the meeting with teachers the following day.

At the beginning of the dialogue in the living room of Pine Cottage, Krishnamurti asked David to sit in an armchair next to him and introduced him and Saral to the staff—even though many of us had already made their acquaintance. In public, he tended to be conservatively formal and also now referred to him as 'Dr. Bohm' and 'Professor Bohm'.

*Krishnamurti on the verandah of Arya Vihara*
California, 1930's

*Krishnamurti having lunch*
*on the patio at Arya Vihara*

California, 1977

*Krishnamurti in front of Pine Cottage*
1979 (Photo by Fritz Wilhelm)

*Krishnamurti planting a ficus tree at Oak Grove School*
Ojai, California, 1979 (Photo by Earl Scott)

*Fritz Wilhelm, Krishnamurti, and Michael Krohnen*

Arya Vihara, California, 1980 (Photo by Asit Chandmal)

*Saral Bohm, Dr. David Bohm, Krishnamurti, Michael Krohnen*

Arya Vihara, California, 1981 (Photo by Rita Zampesi)

*Krishnamurti, Pupul Jayakar and guests*
Arya Vihara, California, 1985  (Photo by Rita Zampesi)

*K walking with Michael Krohnen in the evening*
Rishi Valley, India, 1985 (Photo by Scott Forbes)

*Pepper tree as seen from Krishnamurti's room in Pine Cottage*
1983 (Photo by Michael Krohnen)

But half-way through the discussion he suddenly turned to him and asked, "May I call you David? After all, we have known and discussed with each other for over twenty years." It was an entirely sincere question, although both affection and light-hearted humor were present.

David replied, "Of course, Krishnaji. After all, I've been calling you Krishnaji all along."

Delighted laughter arose among us, shared by Krishnamurti and David, and a spirit of friendship communicated itself.

During lunch the following day Krishnamurti asked David, who was sitting across from him, "When shall we start our dialogue, sir?"

"Whenever it's convenient for you, Krishnaji. Maybe in the next few days?"

"Tomorrow afternoon?" Krishnamurti asked, looking questioningly at the teacher who was in charge of audio recording. "Would that be all right, sir?"

"Tomorrow in the afternoon?" the teacher said. "That would be Tuesday, April 1. Yes, I think that's all right, Krishnaji. What time? Four o'clock?"

The following afternoon, the two friends met in front of the fireplace of Pine Cottage, microphones attached to their lapels, to start a very serious and in-depth investigation of the condition of humanity. The trustees and several others of us were invited to attend the dialogue as observers. Krishnamurti was dressed in jeans and a cardigan, while David wore a sweater, a jacket and tie, as he usually did.

Krishnamurti started out by suggesting that humanity had taken a wrong turn a long time ago, which had led to endless conflict and sorrow. The 'I' and its patterns of division and becoming were at the root of conflict. Psychological time was the enemy of man. Proceeding tentatively, they concluded that the outward and the inward were not separate but one and the same movement. When that movement came to a stop, when the mind was silently with itself, there was meditation. Krishnamurti recounted one such event from his past. One night in India, he woke up at a quarter past twelve, and the source of all energy had been reached. Since this led to a complete sense of peace and love, he wanted others to get to this point, he told David.

Questioning whether there was such a thing as psychological evolution, they examined the difference between mind and brain, and the interrelationship of thought, knowledge, memory and experience.

Once psychological knowledge, which formed the 'me', came to an end, there would be no-thing-ness. This nothingness was everything, and everything was energy.

There were certainly several astonishing quantum leaps which occurred during their dialogue. For us, the listeners, it was a stunning circle of completeness. We could only marvel at the exploratory power of these two minds, how they pondered together during long intervals of silence, how they sometimes spoke at the same time but never lost contact with each other. It was a marvelous choreography from consciousness to emptiness. Wrapping up their conversation, they concurred that in the ending of time there was a new beginning, which was not of time.

The newly started thriller of a dialogue continued the next day, again with several of us present as observers. Krishnamurti and David picked up where they had left off, probing not only into the particular mind, with its patterns of becoming and conflict, but also into the universal mind and what was beyond. Having eliminated psychological time, becoming and desire, they moved step by step beyond nature and creation, beyond the universal mind, beyond energy, emptiness and silence, to an immensity where beginning and ending were the same. At one point they faced the paradox that what they were doing was putting the absolute into words. They agreed that it had to be done, even though the absolute could never be put into words. When finally they reached that which had nothing beyond it, which was without cause, they tentatively referred to it as 'the ground', where there was no beginning and no ending.

After taking this breathtaking journey to the very edge between the expressible and the inexpressible, they wondered how all this might be conveyed to an ordinary person. Despite the apparent difficulty, they felt it was necessary to do it since without some relationship with 'the ground', living didn't have any meaning. Krishnamurti suggested that the pursuit of this would lead to a marvelously ordered world. David, in turn, wondered what one would do in such a world, and Krishnamurti replied that, once the factors of conflict and disorder were gone, something else, which he called creativity, would come into operation. The professor thought it important to make this clear, because the Christian idea of heaven as perfection appeared rather boring, since there was nothing to do. "That reminds me of a good joke," Krishnamurti remarked. "A man dies and goes up to the Pearly Gates. St. Peter says to him, 'You've lived a fairly good life, not cheated or sinned too much. But before entering heaven I must tell you that we're all bored here. God never laughs, and the angels are quite moody, praying most of the time. So please hesitate before entering heaven. Perhaps you'd like to go down below and see what that's like. Then come and tell me what you prefer. But it's up to you. Just ring that bell over there. An elevator will come up and you just get into it and go down.' So the chap rings the bell and goes down in the elevator. The doors open and he is met by the most beautiful girls, who take care of him, et cetera, et cetera. 'By Jove', he thinks, 'this is the life.' And he says to the girls, 'May I just go and tell St. Peter?' He rings the bell, gets into the elevator and goes up. He says to St. Peter, 'Sir, it's very good of you to have offered me the choice, I prefer it down below.' St. Peter says, 'I thought you would.' The man rings the bell again and goes down. The doors open and two ugly fiends grab him and beat him up, pushing and kicking him. He moans, 'Wait a minute. Just a while ago you treated me like a king. And now this; why?' 'Ah, you were a tourist then.' "

We had already started giggling and laughing, while he was telling the joke in a somewhat breathless manner. At the punch line we burst into exuberant mirth. There was something entirely innocent about him, as he explored the absolute in dialogue with his friend and con-cluded it with a joke about heaven and hell. When the laughter died down he added, "Sorry. From the sublime to the ridiculous—which is good, too."

As we all got up, tears of laughter in our eyes and a sense of awe in our hearts, Krishnamurti suggested to David that they go on with their dialogue.

OVER THE FOLLOWING TWO WEEKS THEY ENGAGED IN A further six dialogues, during which several of the observers participated marginally. They explored the dominant role that man had given to thought and asked whether there could be an actual, physical mutation of the brain cells through direct insight. The meaning of death, and what was the action of a person who had touched 'the ground' in rela-tion to the rest of humanity were the concerns they addressed during the last two of their eight conversations in Ojai. The Ojai Talks, scheduled for the first two weeks in May, intervened. It wasn't until much later, in June and September, 1980, that Krishnamurti and David would conclude their investigations into the nature of the mind and the brain during another seven dialogues at Brockwood Park.

These fifteen dialogues of 1980, the final five of which were also videotaped, were seen as a coherent series and eventually published in book form under the title *The Ending of Time*.

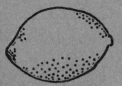

## Chapter 14

# FOOD FOR THOUGHT

### Starters

*Tossed green salad with vinaigrette or
creamy ranch house dressing.
Waldorf salad, prepared with apples,
grapes, celery and walnuts.
Cucumber salad with sour cream, lemon
juice & honey, and cilantro.*

### Main Dishes

*White bean soup, with onions,
celery and tomatoes.
Home-made spinach fettuccine, served
with a tomato and fresh basil sauce and
grated Parmesan cheese.
Whole baked zucchini.*

### Dessert

*Three types of ice cream and sherbet.
Fresh, seasonal fruit.*

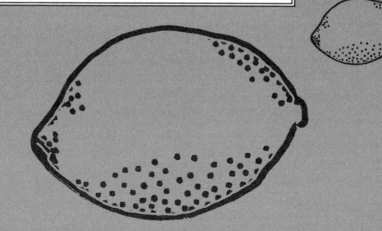

IN 1980 THE OJAI TALKS DID NOT OCCUR IN APRIL AS IN PREVIOUS years but at the beginning of May, since they were then less likely to be rained out. There were six talks on three consecutive weekends, with four intervening question-and-answer meetings. A professional crew videotaped them.

When, a few days after the conclusion of the Gathering, we bid Krishnamurti farewell beneath the pepper tree, he was full of a subtle energy, with an inner fire that touched all of us. Despite his delicate physique, he appeared to be at the height of his powers, at eighty-five years of age.

For the next nine months I was in Ojai, working at the school. But in my mind I was following his journey across the face of the globe—to Europe, India and Sri Lanka—eagerly awaiting news of his talks and discussions.

KRISHNAMURTI AND MARY Z. ARRIVED AT PINE COTTAGE in the late afternoon of Friday, February 20, 1981. They had come via England, where they had stopped over at Brockwood Park for five days on their return trip from Bombay. Krishnamurti looked frail and tired, not only on account of the long journey, but also because of the demanding program that he had gone through in India.

For lunch the following day I prepared a Waldorf salad, a cucumber salad with sour cream, a white bean soup, spinach fettuccini with a tomato sauce and baked zucchini, and for dessert, three types of ice cream and sherbet. It was the first day of the school's spring break, so only the regular guests showed up, bringing the number to twelve. More than anything else, Krishnamurti wanted to be filled in as to how the school was coming along and calmly listened to the director's report, every so often asking a question. I had to wait a while before the right moment arose to ask him, "Have you heard any good jokes recently, Krishnaji?"

I was sitting on the opposite side of the table two places away from him and used my loud voice to address him. He appeared startled for an instant before focusing his surprised gaze on me. His face lit up with a wide smile, and he didn't take more than a second to come up with the most recent one in his collection of jokes. Looking around the table, he prefaced it by asking, "Are there any Christians here? I don't mean to blaspheme or offend anyone." Since nobody declared themselves to be religiously affiliated, he continued, "The Lord and St. Peter are in heaven observing the action down on earth on a television monitor. They are amazed by what they see: people are forever rushing about, ceaselessly digging and constructing, building large cities, everywhere busy, busy, busy, from early morning throughout the night. The Lord turns to St. Peter and asks incredulously, 'What are they all doing, busy from morning till night, never resting, forever striving, battling, competing? What's the point of it?' St. Peter replies, 'Well, Lord, these people are your followers, they believe in you and obey you. And you told them to eat their bread in the sweat of their brows.' And the Lord says to St. Peter, 'But I was only kidding.'"

We started to laugh, but Krishnamurti gestured us to calm down, calling out, "No, don't laugh yet. There's more to come. St. Peter switches channels and they see a magnificent banquet hall in the Vatican with huge tables filled with expensive delicacies. There are caviar and truffles and the finest wines and so on. Hundreds of big men in purple robes are seated around these tables, feasting and laughing, drinking cognac and smoking cigars. They are the cardinals and bishops, having a feast. 'But what about these people,' the Lord asks St. Peter, 'they don't seem to be eating their bread in the sweat of their brows. If you ask me, they seem to be having a jolly good time.' St. Peter says, 'Well, Lord, these are the ones who *knew* you were only kidding.'"

When our exhilarated laughter had died down, he turned to me and asked with a twinkle in his eye, "What is the news, sir?"

I had been extremely busy the last few days, preparing the A.V. kitchen for his arrival, and hadn't spent much time following the most recent news developments. Taking a deep breath, I quickly tried to gather my wits about me. "Well, Krishnaji, you are probably familiar with most of these events. If you don't mind, I'll give a quick recap of the most important current affairs. As you know, last month Ronald Reagan was sworn in as the new president. By coincidence, after almost a year and a half of captivity, the American hostages at the American embassy in Teheran were freed around Inauguration Day. Meanwhile, the Soviet invasion of Afghanistan is continuing with much bloodshed, and the conflict between Iran and Iraq appears to be intensifying." In that vein I provided a headline survey of the world events of the last few months. Krishnamurti listened with full attention to my account, a smile playing around his eyes and lips. When I could not think of anything more to report, I turned to him directly, "And you, Krishnaji, have also been in the news. Mr. Lilliefelt and Mr. Hooker told us that Indira Gandhi visited you in Rishi Valley with many armed guards and under strict security. And, before that, you were invited to Sri Lanka and had a talk with the prime minister there. What was it like, sir?"

Krishnamurti gave a shrug and a characteristic gesture, indicating that all of that was of little importance. Alan Hooker and Theo Lilliefelt, both of whom were present at the table, had been with him in India in December 1980 and, on their return to Ojai, had provided an amusing and detailed account of the Indian prime minister's visit with Krishnamurti at the Rishi Valley School. Everyone now turned toward Krishnamurti, eager to hear an account of his visit to the jewel island, Sri Lanka, formerly known as Ceylon and Serendip.

Pulling a funny face as he looked at us, he asked, "You want me to tell you about it?"

"Yes, sir," several of us intoned.

"All right. The government of Sri Lanka had invited us to come as guests of the state. They put us up in the official guest house, owned by the government. Several dignitaries and ministers came to welcome us, and later we had an interview with one of them on television. There were several public talks, I think four of them. They reported it in the newspapers and on the radio and television. She was with me during this time and can tell you more about it," he added, pointing at Mary Z. He generally avoided recounting his personal experiences and sometimes even apologized when talking about himself.

Mary Z. readily went on, "Pupul Jayakar and Nandini Mehta were with us, and during the following days we were busy with press conferences and radio and television interviews. The day after our arrival, Krishnaji met the prime minister, Mr. Premadasa, a very nice man. The four public talks at Colombo were attended by thousands of people and broadcast live throughout the island. After this, Krishnaji held several dialogues with Buddhist monks and spoke at Colombo University. One afternoon the president of Sri Lanka invited us for tea. He was very interested in what Krishnaji talked about and asked for a private interview with him, which eventually lasted almost an hour and a half. At the end, he invited us to visit Kandy, in the interior of the country."

I had visited Kandy, the former royal capital of Sri Lanka, twelve years earlier. It was an attractive town by a small lake in the tropical highlands, famous in the Buddhist world for the Temple of the Tooth, which housed a relic of the historical Gautama Siddhartha Shakyamuni, the Buddha. During the time of the full moon in August, there was a week-long series of magnificent processions—thousands of Kandyan dancers in silver-filigree attire, accompanied by drummers and pipers, and hundreds of splendidly ornamented elephants—through the torch-lit streets of the town. The parade, known as 'Esala Perahera' and of religious significance, started and ended at the Temple of the Tooth. I had been deeply enchanted by the splendor of the procession and the sense of revelry among the hundreds of thousands of participants. Now I asked Krishnamurti, "Did you visit the Temple of the Tooth, sir, while you were in Kandy?"

"No, sir. The three ladies went while I took a rest," he replied, adding after a moment's quiet deliberation, "but twenty-some years ago I talked in Colombo, and they took us on a tour of the monuments and temples all around the island. When we visited Kandy at that time, they also showed us the Temple of the Tooth." A sparkle entered his eyes, and he explained with a wide smile, "They keep one of the holiest relics of the Buddhist world there, a tooth of the Buddha. So it was all very ceremonious and solemn when we entered the temple, and the head monk in saffron robes and with shaved head welcomed us and led us into the inner sanctum." He was laughing now at the memory of the event. "And they brought out a small box encrusted with magnificent jewels, in which they kept the tooth. They solemnly opened it, so that we could have a look at the tooth. It was a huge old thing, yellow and eroded." With thumb and index finger he demonstrated the size of the tooth, almost an inch wide. "And I was wondering if it really was a human tooth. It could easily have been a horse's tooth, that's how big it was."

We all burst out laughing at his description. He actually held the Buddha in the highest regard, probably more than any other religious figure in history. At the same time, he never relinquished his fundamental skepticism with regard to rituals and religious traditions, as he had just demonstrated.

DURING THE FOLLOWING WEEK THERE WAS CONTINUOUS rain, which at times intensified to heavy downpours and thunderstorms, covering the high mountain ridges of the valley with snow. Some of the teachers started taking turns to join us for lunch at A.V., but unfortunately Krishnamurti felt unwell for several days, and we had to lunch without him.

He took quite a detached view of the frailties that sometimes afflicted him, such as hay fever, sinus inflammation and hearing problems, joking light-heartedly, "First the teeth go, then the ears and then the eyes, and at last you also will go down into the earth."

Every once in a while, as now, I got to observe the veracity of this statement, not only in myself but also in Krishnamurti. He was feeling exhausted, probably as a result of his grueling program in India, followed by extensive traveling and the consequent change of climate. Besides, he had an upset stomach, maybe the onset of stomach flu. Around noontime I carried his lunch over to Pine Cottage and was surprised that he opened the door for me. Looking into his face, I was even more startled by a radical change in it. The lips were abnormally pulled in, shortening the distance between nose and chin and thereby altering the whole structure of the face. He was immediately aware of my astonishment, and, moving his hand exploringly to his mouth, he stated without embarrassment, "I've had some trouble with my teeth. Several had to be extracted, and the doctor put in some removable bridges. I forgot to put them in."

For some reason, I felt a deep sense of humility, as he explained to me the details of his health with complete openness. When I didn't respond to his statement, he continued, "You know, sir, my teeth have always been highly sensitive. It's probably in the genes."

Several days later, the first Monday in March and the beginning of school after the spring break, he came for lunch by himself, since Mary Z. had gone to LAX to pick up some friends, who were arriving from France that afternoon. He entered the kitchen, and we cordially greeted each other, when all at once I noticed that his mouth was puckered in. Hesitating for a moment, I said, "Excuse me, Krishnaji, could it be that you forgot to put in your dental bridges?"

He covered his mouth with one hand and said, astonished at his forgetfulness, "By Jove, sir, you're right. I forgot to put them in. I left them in the bathroom. I just have to go back."

He started to giggle to himself while he searched for something in his pockets. Finally he pulled out a set of keys. "Well, I've got the keys—I'll be right back."

Ten minutes later he returned with the dental bridges in place and his splendid face intact and asked, "What's for lunch, Michael?"

I told him what the menu was, pointing at the respective dishes, "There is, of course, the green salad, and a pasta salad, and an avocado salad, made with avocados, tomatoes, onions and bell peppers. Then we have baked potatoes, and a kind of quiche made with grated zucchini and cheese. This comes with a vegetable dish that is a bit like ratatouille, except it's made with zucchini, eggplant—or aubergine—and a tomato sauce."

He was paying close attention to what I was saying. It always surprised me that his keen interest extended to the minutiae of everyday life.

"And for dessert, Krishnaji," I said with a slightly exaggerated intonation, because of his fondness for a sweet treat, "we'll be having halvah. It's a Middle Eastern sweet made from sesame seeds and honey."

He raised his eyebrows with delighted surprise and, pointing at the dishes, remarked, "But the portions you prepared are rather small today, aren't they?"

"There are only five of us for lunch today, Krishnaji," I replied, "so we need a lot less than usual."

He nodded understandingly, "Who's coming for lunch, sir?"

"Well, the Lilliefelts are here, Mr. Hooker, you and I—that's all," I replied.

"Ah, good," he said, "we'll be *en famille*."

It was, indeed, a very relaxed and friendly meal. While reviewing the current world situation, we began talking about the communist system and the hegemony of the Soviet Union over the Eastern European countries. Erna Lilliefelt mentioned that in several of these countries, especially in Poland and Romania, there was considerable interest in Krishnamurti.

"It's like an underground movement, Krishnaji," she said. "They translate your books and secretly make a few copies, which then are passed around from hand to hand."

"And it's probably not without danger," I added. "Despite its relative independence from Moscow, the Ceausescu regime is dreadfully suppressive at home. Any form of dissent is brutally eradicated. I was reading the other day that everyone who owned a typewriter had to register it with the government."

"Why? To control any form of printed public information?" Alan asked.

"I suppose so," I answered. "It's also easy to make copies on a typewriter with carbon paper," I suggested. Turning to Krishnamurti, I asked, "Krishnaji, did you ever visit and speak in any of the East European countries?"

"I think it was in the early 1930s, when I spoke in Athens and traveled via Constantinople to Bucharest," he recounted. "The Queen — I've forgotten her name — invited us to the palace several times. But there were some fanatical, nationalist Catholic students, who had made threats against my life."

I gasped incredulously, "But why, sir?"

He uttered a soft laugh, "They saw us as a threat to their plans. We talked against organized religion, against nationalism, and so on. I did not really take the threat seriously but the government did. They posted armed guards at the door of our hotel rooms. Each time we came and went, there they were, following us around night and day. But nothing happened. As we were leaving the country, I all at once became violently ill on the train — throwing up, blood, and so on. I couldn't keep down any food for days."

I didn't quite understand the connection between the threats on his life and his getting ill, so I asked, "But what caused your sudden illness?"

"Somehow they must have secretly introduced some poison into my food. It was strange. I was the only one to get ill. I don't know how they did it," he said. "And it stayed with me for a long time."

"You mean the illness stayed with you?"

"Yes," he responded, "the illness, the poison, whatever it was. For years afterwards it recurred to varying degrees, and I only slowly recovered from it."

"Do you still suffer from it now?"

"Oh, no, now it's long gone," he said with a dismissive gesture.

We started talking about the Roman Catholic Church and its tremendous wealth and power, and how throughout history it had colluded with the secular powers, even if these happened to be totalitarian regimes, such as the Fascists.

Krishnamurti suddenly asked us, "Do you know Stresa?"

I thought he was talking about a person and asked, "No, I don't. Who is it?"

He smiled, "It's a town, a famous resort on Lago Maggiore in northern Italy. In the early thirties, while Mussolini was in power, I was invited to give several talks in Stresa. On the first day there were all the bishops, cardinals and generals sitting in the front row. I don't know why they came—perhaps they thought I was a guest of the state. I talked about freedom from authority, how destructive it was to follow anyone, and so on. The next day all the front rows were empty, and there was one old woman sitting in the back row."

We shared his laughter at the vivid scene of fifty years ago. Turning serious again, he continued, "No, sir. They can't listen to anyone questioning their authority. It was the same in Argentina. I was on a tour of South America speaking in various cities. In Buenos Aires, the newspapers were full of it, reporting every talk, with photographs and so on. They were broadcasting the talks, not only over the radio but also over loudspeakers at a number of street corners. But in the churches they were preaching against me, saying I was the Antichrist, and wanting to deport me from the country."

"And did they succeed?" a lady asked.

"No, not at all," he replied. "Some of the newspapers and intellectuals took my side, printing and distributing the talks in Spanish translations."

We were silent for a while, then Krishnamurti spoke up, "That reminds me of a good joke I heard the other day. The Pope dies and goes up to the Pearly Gates where he meets St. Peter. He says to him, 'You must be St. Peter.' St. Peter answers, 'And who are you?' The Pope is taken aback, 'You don't recognize me? I'm the Pope.' St. Peter picks up his list and goes over the names, 'Pope, Pope—I'm sorry, there is nobody here by that name. I'm sorry, but you can't enter heaven.' The Pope is shocked. 'There must be some mistake. It's impossible—I must be on that list. Please, look again: I'm the Pope!' St. Peter gets impatient and tells him to buzz off. By now the Pope is in tears and begs him, 'Please, St. Peter, I'm your successor and the representative of Jesus on earth. I'm the head of the Holy Roman Church. I have a right to enter heaven.' St. Peter is getting annoyed and says, 'I've never heard of anything so foolish. If you don't immediately buzz off, I'll call the angels with the flaming swords.' The Pope is in utter despair. 'No, please don't,

I beg of you. Can't you ask somebody who knows me? Maybe Jesus or one of the saints will vouch for me.' St. Peter gives in and says to the chap, 'All right, I'll go and ask inside. You stay here. And don't touch anything.' So he goes inside, and there are Jesus, his mother Mary, the apostles and several angels and saints. 'Excuse me, Lord,' says St. Peter, 'there is a chap by the name of Pope wanting to enter heaven. He claims to have been your representative on earth.' Jesus laughs, 'My representative on earth? That's rather absurd, isn't it? And I've never heard of anyone named Pope.' Turning to the others, he asks, 'Have any of you ever heard of a Pope?' No one seems to know the Pope, until suddenly the Virgin Mary speaks up, 'Wait a minute. Pope — isn't he the one who spread all the rumors about me and the Holy Ghost?'"

Bursting into laughter, the five of us shared the humor of this irreverent story. Outside on the porch, we heard the rain streaming down and a sudden clap of thunder.

"I've got to get back to the office," Erna Lilliefelt declared and, getting up from the table, collected her plate and silverware. I quickly got up and jumped over to take Krishnamurti's plate, as I usually did. "May I take your plate, sir?" I asked politely, and he looked up at me with a smile as I gathered his tableware. For some reason, I derived satisfaction from serving him in small ways like this.

"These are clean, sir," he said, pointing at the unused paper napkin and the glass. With that, he also got up and started helping with the clearing of the table.

After putting some of the leftover food in plastic containers, I carried them outside to the storage refrigerator in the small room in front of the kitchen. While placing the items inside the refrigerator, I noticed a large chunk of halvah sitting on one shelf. I could still taste the subtle sweet flavor of the halvah I had just had for dessert and suddenly craved more. I took out my pocket knife to cut myself a piece of the candy, when I suddenly heard a gentle voice ask from behind, "Could you please cut me a piece, too?"

I turned around to face Krishnamurti, who had followed me through the kitchen door and up the steps into the small front room. I felt a sudden sense of guilt coming on and for an instant was embarrassed — as if I had been caught red-handed. But Krishnamurti stood on the threshold of the room and smiled serenely, calming my momentary apprehension, which probably resulted from many occasions of secret childhood indulgences.

I remarked, somewhat apologetically, "This halvah is so delicious, isn't it?" Drawing a line with the knife across a section of it, I asked, "How much would you like, sir? This much?"

There was an amazing mirror-like quality about Krishnamurti as he quietly stood there, studying me with honest and undisguised openness. There was no division between us, but neither was there any sense of complicity. He looked at the halvah I was pointing at.

"Maybe a little more than that," he requested and then turned around to look closely at a three-dimensional topographical plastic map on the wall.

"I'd better take it to the kitchen and wrap it in some plastic film."

"All right, sir," he agreed and then asked, "What is this?"

"It's a map of this area, Krishnaji," I explained. "You see, this is the Ojai Valley. Here is the Topa Topa Range, and here we are, McAndrew Road. Of course, the scale of the mountains is exaggerated. There's Ventura, and in this direction there is Los Angeles."

"Hm, it's quite detailed," he remarked with a smile.

After returning to the kitchen, I wrapped the halvah in some film and handed it to him. Thanking me, he left through the back door toward Pine Cottage. Suddenly I realized that I had forgotten the piece of halvah. I swiftly cut myself a piece and started enjoying the smooth sweetness before continuing with the kitchen clean-up.

THE RAIN WENT ON FOR THE NEXT FEW DAYS, AND WE HAD rather small, intimate lunches at A.V. One day, there were only six of us at the table, and Krishnamurti recounted what he had seen earlier on the "Phil Donahue Show", a program he sometimes liked to watch.

"It's incredible, sir, the permissiveness of this society," he said to Theo Lilliefelt, who was sitting across from him. "The other day, there was a—what do they call them?—a dancer, a male stripper on the show. He demonstrated his dancing, practically naked, and the women in the audience were screaming and clapping, all excited. It was so utterly vulgar." He shuddered at the recollection of it. "But it's not only that, they reveal all sorts of intimate sexual details, washing their dirty linen in public. Everything goes, and they are so casual about their relationships, about their marriage. One woman said that she doesn't love her man any more because there is another man who is much nicer, more handsome, and all the rest of it, and she will leave one and move in with the other. Imagine it, sir—to say this in public!"

"Well, Krishnaji," one lady said with a gentle smile, "women now have equal rights and enjoy the same freedom that men have been enjoying."

"Equal to whom? Free to do what?" Krishnamurti asked with some passion. "They say this is a free country. And everybody feels free to do what they want—to follow his or her pleasure, not giving a damn about anyone else. Without any respect, without any sense of responsibility for their own actions or for others, without any kind of restraint." He looked at us searchingly, almost as if accusing us of a similar attitude.

"It's part of the overall culture, of the ethos of America," I suggested. He turned toward me and I felt a wave of strong energy rushing at me.

"No, sir," he said firmly, "that's not good enough. America is setting the standard for the rest of the world. Everywhere, even in Russia and India, they are following her example. The younger people there imitate the dress, the dance and music—you know, rock 'n' roll, the sex and films. Where will it lead to? Everyone for himself and to hell with the other!"

"It's worldwide decadence," Theo said.

"Maybe the institutions of marriage and family are obsolete," a lady suggested.

A sudden smile softened Krishnamurti's face and, turning to all of us, he asked with enough sincerity in his voice to make it sound like a serious question, "So what happens when one egotist marries another egotist?"

I didn't know how to take the question, whether to consider it from a serious or comical point of view. I was thinking of oneness, the elimination of the egotistic attitude, and so on. After several tentative answers had been rejected, he offered the simple answer, "Two egotists."

## Chapter 15

# KEY TO THE
# MYSTERY OF LIFE?

### Starters

*Tossed green salad with
vinaigrette or tahini dressing.
Pasta salad made with
finely cubed celery, carrots, peppers,
zucchini, pine nuts, broccoli flowers,
olives and sun-dried tomatoes.
Avocado salad with cubed tomatoes,
bell peppers, minced garlic,
cilantro, and lemon juice.*

### Main Dishes

*Baked potatoes stuffed with
onions and mushrooms.
Quiche prepared with grated zucchini,
cheese, eggs, parsley, onions, and celery.
Aubergine Provençale: cubed eggplant
in a tomato sauce.*

### Dessert

*Halvah, made from sesame seeds and honey.
Fresh, seasonal fruit.*

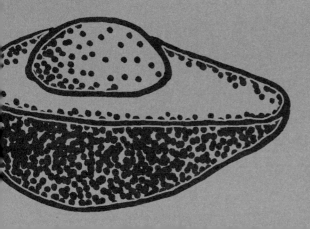

DURING THE NEXT FEW WEEKS, THE OPPORTUNITY TO HAVE quiet, intimate lunches with Krishnamurti became rarer, and the pace of activity quickened. He had several meetings with the staff and parents of the school, before an educational conference, partially funded by a U.S. government program, started on March 20. A professor from San Bernardino State University organized the three-day event, attended by almost thirty professors, teachers and students. Krishnamurti discussed with them the meaning of education, the nature of knowledge and thought, the role of a teacher, and the relationship between *what is*, insight and right action. All four sessions were videotaped by a professional camera team and subsequently published in book form.[4]

During the following days there was a flurry of activity, as guests, friends and associates came and went and often stayed for lunch. Among them were David and Saral Bohm, who again stayed in the guest apartment for about a month. They had a hectic program of their own, and David's speaking engagements forced them to leave before the beginning of the Ojai Talks in early May. It was the first time in five years that they had missed them.

At the end of March, Krishnamurti had several weekend dialogues with staff and parents at Pine Cottage. These meetings now took place at eleven o'clock in the morning, which required that I prepare lunch the previous evening and early in the morning, unless I wanted to forgo participating in the dialogues. I cherished these meetings with Krishnamurti. Their illuminating beauty lay in the fundamental simplicity with which he started the inquiry into the significance of education and living. The question he pursued over two meetings was, 'How does one inquire?' It opened the door to an investigation as to how our minds actually examine a problem and eventually led to 'respect' as the holistic attitude necessary to face the complexity of our lives. "Respect is listening," he stated.

IT WAS DURING THE LATE '70S AND EARLY '80S THAT Krishnamurti became fascinated by the computer, by the increasing importance it was having in human affairs, and its role in the development of the human mind. What particularly intrigued him was the computer's extraordinary capacity to out-think and out-perform its creator in most mechanical mental tasks. During his talks and discussions, and also at the lunch table, he often mentioned its positive impact on our lives, without neglecting to see its negative aspect.

Toward the end of March, an Indian friend of his, Asit Chandmal, who provided him with a lot of information about the function and role of computers, visited us for several days. On April 1, 1981, the Bohms returned to Ojai from a seminar they had attended in Los Angeles. During lunch that day the conversation, primarily between the three of them, revolved around electronic devices and artificial intelligence.

Krishnamurti was saying to David, "Sir, there is a great similarity between the brain and the computer. Both are based on memory, are storehouses of knowledge, and function according to programs. The computer can do anything the human brain can do. And it can do it a thousand times faster and more accurately."

Asit added, "The Japanese are planning to create the fifth generation of computers, which will replicate the processes of the human brain. The government is investing vast amounts of money in this project. There already are some prototypes, which can learn from the data input they receive and modify their own programs. And the geneticists are working together with the computer scientists, researching the use of the brain's hydrogen and carbon molecules, instead of silicon, in the making of computers."

David was skeptical and stated in a measured way, "I doubt that any such linkage of the organic and the machine will lead to anything."

Krishnamurti pursued his line of questioning, "Sir, if the computer takes over most mechanical tasks, what is left for the human brain? Maybe the computer won't be able to compose music like Mozart and Beethoven, or write poetry as Shakespeare and Keats did. It will probably never be able to look at the stars and appreciate the beauty of nature and the universe. But most other work will be done by computers and robots, so what will happen to the human brain? Will it atrophy?"

I was puzzled, as were several other listeners around the lunch table. "What do you mean by that, sir?" I asked.

"There are really only two ways for the brain to move: one is toward the inside, into itself, into self-inquiry and so on. Which is what we are talking about. The other is toward the outside: more entertainment, diversion, amusement, stimulation—you know what's happening. So what is left for the brain to do? Almost all of its functions have been taken over by the computer. Right? There is a tremendous increase in the leisure available to the human being. And unless the brain finds a totally different approach, it will atrophy like a muscle that is not being exercised any more. It will simply wither away, shrivel up. It's happening now, sir!"

Not everybody at the table seemed willing to accept this kind of prediction and quite a few objections were raised. Krishnamurti usually enjoyed being challenged and continued with calm certainty against a tide of skepticism: "The computer is not limited by borders, nationalities and governments, as we are. It's beyond all those, and it can outthink us. It will probably invent its own god, which we will worship. I must tell you a good joke about this. A man enters a room full of computers and the scientist there tells him to ask any question he may have. So the man asks, 'Is there a god?' The scientist enters the question, and the computers start to flash and buzz. After a while the answer comes, 'Now there is.'"

As we were laughing, Krishnamurti looked at us with something like pity and skeptical amusement: "Yes, sir, face it." Turning toward David and Asit, he said, "It's getting late. Shall we continue this conversation this afternoon?"

They agreed, and a few hours later, at four o'clock that afternoon the three of them met in the living room of Pine Cottage. Trustees, guests and staff who had the time and leisure to attend were there. The dialogue focused on the new technology of computers and what it entailed for the future of humanity. They inquired into thought and knowledge, intelligence and insight, in relation to the man-made machine. Krishnamurti was intrigued by various future aspects and applications of computers, while David appeared more skeptical of some of the rather far-fetched claims put forth by their Indian dialogue partner. Eventually, though, they concurred that the human brain had infinite capacity—something the computer lacked.

Toward the end of their conversation, Krishnamurti repeated his warning that the computer would create its own god and that we might become its slaves, unless there was a radical transformation of the brain cells through insight. And he recounted another story about man, god and computer: "A person is praying to God. And there is a computer in the next room, one of the highly advanced super-computers. And the computer says, 'Who are you praying to? God is here.'"

ON THE FIRST WEEKEND OF APRIL, ANOTHER CONFERENCE, organized by David Bohm, took place at Pine Cottage and A. V. On three consecutive mornings, Krishnamurti met with several professors of sociology, religion and philosophy, a rabbi from New York City, and the poet Kenneth Rexroth, who lived in Santa Barbara. I was familiar with and admired his poetry, and his elegant translations of Oriental verse. I was, therefore, thrilled to meet him in person. It was a bit of a shock to see that he had difficulty walking with a cane, at times needing the support of his wife. Besides, he was on a very restricted special diet. Despite his declining health, however, he established a fine rapport with Krishnamurti during these discussions. (He died the following year.)

Throughout April, there was an abundance of meetings involving Krishnamurti, David, the trustees, staff and parents, and also between David and the school staff. This led up to the public talks in early May, which again attracted thousands of people from all over the world— although, of course, Californians were in the majority.

The day after the sixth and final talk of the series, Krishnamurti had an important appointment in Los Angeles. He was to be interviewed by Keith Berwick at the NBC studios for a television talk show called "Odyssey".

I was just on my way over to the office to hand in some bills, when I noticed four people huddled in front of the open garage next to the huge pepper tree. They were Krishnamurti and Mary Z., dressed up for the trip to the metropolis, and two trustees, the Lilliefelts. They appeared rather agitated and at a loss, as they excitedly discussed among themselves. I went on into the office and settled my accounts. Five minutes later, on my way back to A.V., I noticed three of them still standing there, helplessly perplexed, while Krishnamurti was impatiently pacing back and forth. My curiosity aroused, I stepped up to them and said, "You look like you're having a problem."

Mary Z. explained, "The car won't start, and we have to be in Los Angeles by four-thirty."

Although utterly ignorant of how cars work, I suggested a few standard starting problems. "Could it be the battery?" I asked.

"That's the first thing we checked," she replied. "But the lights are working, so it can't be that."

"Does the engine turn over when you turn the ignition key?"

"That's the puzzling thing. When one turns the key, nothing happens at all. None of the dash board indicators come on."

"Is there any sound?"

"No sound at all, not even a click."

"Let me try one more time, Mary," Theo, the white-haired, former U.N. diplomat suggested.

She handed him the key, and he went into the garage to sit in the driver's seat of the grey diesel Mercedes.

Krishnamurti, in the meantime, had kept on pacing about, looking rather pensively absorbed, as if confronted by a mystery, the clue to which he might discover any moment. "No, it's something else," he announced, shaking his head in puzzled wonderment. "I'm sure it's something else."

Theo stepped out of the garage and, handing the keys back to Mary Z., stated with a frustrated shrug, "Nothing, nothing at all."

"Shouldn't we perhaps call the Triple-A man?" his wife Erna suggested. "It may take a while for him to come but that way you could still get there on time."

"If it can be started at all," Mary Z. wondered, then agreed, "Well, yes, I suppose we'd better give them a call."

"I'll do it from the office," Erna said, energetically walking toward the office. "I'll use my card number."

"Well," said Mary Z., with a half resigned, half cheerful tone, tossing her head upward in a characteristic movement, "I might as well give it another try." And she walked over to the driver's seat to try her luck.

In the meantime, Krishnamurti was deepening the mystery by walking in circles, evidently looking for the missing link, every so often making a mystifying pronouncement. "It must be something else, something we aren't thinking of."

Mary Z. emerged from the garage, indicating with a helpless gesture her evident lack of success.

"It must be something else; somehow, we are not seeing the obvious," Krishnamurti insisted, as if there were an extraordinarily simple solution that none of them, including himself, were able to put their finger on.

"Can't you simply use the other car?" I asked, pointing at the closed garage door on the left.

"It's not there," Mary Z. plaintively explained, "it's at the service station being serviced."

Just at that moment Erna reemerged from the office, exclaiming, as she approached, "It won't be long. They'll be here within ten minutes." And, holding out her hand toward Mary Z., she asked with a short laugh, "Why don't you let me give it a try in the meantime?"

Mary Z. passed her the key, and she went to try her luck.

Pondering the root cause of it all, I hesitantly voiced my conclusion, "It must be the electrical system."

Nobody paid any attention to my suggestion, and Krishnamurti momentarily stopped his intense perambulation to address Theo, "It must be something else, sir; something very simple and obvious, which we don't see. But what could it be?"

Comical images flashed before my mind's eye, as I frantically tried to solve the problem by systematically going through all thinkable and unthinkable possibilities. Looking at the two dignified older gentlemen conferring with earnest miens, I had the image of Sherlock Holmes and Dr. Watson confronting an enigma and studying the clues. Then the notion crossed my mind that this was a sort of lottery: tremendous fortune for the lucky one who figured out the answer to the puzzle.

Erna reappeared, joking with an unembarrassed laugh, "It won't start for me, either."

"What is the possibility we didn't think of, sir?" I heard Krishnamurti ask Theo.

The thought of hitting the jackpot crossed my mind: What if it would start for me? I hesitantly approached Mary Z. and asked, "Do you mind if I give it a try?"

She gave a short, slightly exasperated laugh, handing me the bunch of keys, "Why not? We may as well all try. What difference does it make?"

I looked at the key which had the well-known Mercedes symbol on it. As I walked into the garage, I was aware of the empty space to the left, where Krishnamurti's coupé was normally parked. I let myself sink into the leather upholstery of the car, taking note of the immaculate state of the interior after many years of use. I introduced the key into the ignition and turned it. Nothing—no click, no signals, no engine roar.

I got out and returned the key to Mary Z.

Krishnamurti was still harping on the same theme, wondering out loud, "What could it be? What did we overlook? Something very, very simple."

Just then a loud noise came from the invisible portion of the driveway. "That must be the automobile club," Erna ventured.

We turned around to watch the tow-truck come into sight.

Mary Z. was, at that moment, looking alternately at the key and something else in her purse. Just as the truck pulled up next to us, she said in a quiet, firm voice, "I think I made a horrible mistake. I'm sorry, I think we've been using the wrong key."

Krishnamurti gave a sudden, clear laugh, in which there was neither reproach nor judgment, "Ah, that's it! That's what we couldn't think of."

Mary Z. walked quickly over to the car with the newly discovered second key from her purse, while Krishnamurti laughed joyfully, patting Theo on the shoulder, who joined in with him in a comradely fashion. Erna, meanwhile, walked over to the driver of the service truck. "I think we just found the problem," she explained, just as the engine of the Mercedes started firing. The man, exhibiting no sign of exasperation, as if he was used to this type of thing, said laconically, "Well, I still need your membership card."

While this was being taken care of, Mary Z. backed out the Mercedes, just barely able to maneuver past the truck, and Krishnamurti swiftly got in on the passenger side. As they drove off, I walked down the narrow trail through the orange grove to the A.V. buildings. Suddenly by myself, the whole scene passed before my inward eye and I couldn't help but laugh out loud with my whole being. What I had just witnessed offered itself as an illustration of the way we approach many of the fundamental issues and conundrums of life. We keep trying the wrong key, while the right one is there all the time, extremely close at hand, much closer at hand than one can possibly imagine.

Two days later, on May 20, we once more said goodbye to Krishnamurti and Mary Z. beneath the pepper tree, as they departed for Brockwood Park and the distant shores of different continents.

AT THE END OF THE SCHOOL TERM IN JUNE, WE RECEIVED startling news through the worldwide network that connected the various Krishnamurti Schools and Foundations: David Bohm had suffered a massive heart attack in London. We were shocked to hear that he had had to undergo triple by-pass surgery and, for several days after the operation, hovered on the threshold between life and death. Krishnamurti went to see him before and after surgery, trying to calm his old friend's acute apprehension of dying. Not surprisingly, coming face to face with death was a shattering experience for him, leaving a lasting imprint. It seemed to deepen his sense of humility.

David only gradually recuperated from this ordeal and henceforth had to take great care, both with his diet and his daily activities.

APART FROM GIVING TALKS AT THE USUAL LOCATIONS, Krishnamurti spoke twice before packed audiences in Amsterdam in September, 1981. While he was pursuing his annual wanderings around the globe, we at the Oak Grove School were busily involved with a growing number of students, that was approaching one hundred. In addition to my regular cooking and teaching responsibilities, I also found myself substitute teaching a Spanish language class for several months, since the Spanish teacher had unexpectedly left.

While wrestling with the formidable challenge of interacting with a whole new generation in the classroom, I also concerned myself with the question of transformation, which Krishnamurti had raised so often and so urgently. I asked myself, 'Do I really want a complete, radical transformation? What are the implications of that question? Is it a valid question? And, if it is, what is the point of answering that question on the verbal level? A mere verbal answer is meaningless. The only true answer is the actual doing.'

I realized that the crucial element in transformation was time. It could only happen in the active present, in the actual moment. As soon as I measured, compared, projected it into the future, transformation was an illusion. Only when there was no gap in time between observation and action, when it was instantaneous, could change occur. It was in the field of the everyday and ordinary, as much as at the roots of consciousness, that it operated. But I also knew how easy it was to deceive oneself and invent the fanciful notion of having been transformed. Watching was everything.

AT THE END OF THE SCHOOL SPRING BREAK, ON FEBRUARY 14, 1982, Krishnamurti returned to Ojai. He appeared in fabulous form, raring to go. The following day—Washington's Birthday—there was a luncheon for him and the trustees. He wanted to know how the school had been doing in his absence, especially since the plans to set up a high school (in a building yet to be constructed) were well on their way. Eager to talk with the teachers, he asked to meet with us at Pine Cottage the following afternoon.

The theme which he raised during the discussion was 'respect and disrespect'. "Do the students respect you, the teachers and adults?" he asked us. "And do they have a feeling of respect toward nature, toward the earth?" It was a theme that was to dominate our meetings and dialogues for months to come.

THAT WEEKEND, KRISHNAMURTI CHECKED INTO A HOSPITAL IN Los Angeles to undergo a hernia operation. Mary Z. accompanied and stayed with him during the four days of his recuperation at the U.C.L.A. Medical Center. When he returned to Pine Cottage on Ash Wednesday, February 24, the small, faithful 'welcoming committee' was waiting for his arrival. It was painful for us to see him in such discomfort. Ever so slowly he emerged from the Mercedes, leaning on the door to steady himself. Almost involuntarily I stepped closer and reached out toward him to lend some support. But he waved me away and said very firmly, "No, sir, I have to do this myself." With that he inched his way, step by step, up the flagstone path toward Pine Cottage. Another teacher and I walked slowly behind him, in case he should stumble or slip.

He took more than two weeks to recuperate fully, and it wasn't until Saturday, March 13, that we resumed having our regular lunches at A.V. That afternoon he had a discussion with Dr. Jacob Needleman from San Francisco State University and his Indian friend, Asit Chandmal, who kept him informed about the latest developments in the computer world. The following Monday, as the rains kept pouring down, we had a small but extraordinary lunch, that included Asit, the trustees, and the A.V. residents. The conversation centered around computers, and artificial and human intelligence. At one point, Krishnamurti referred directly to 'his' intelligence, making clear he wasn't claiming it as his own by specifying, "It's neither mine, nor yours; it's intelligence." He didn't think of intelligence in the conventional sense—as memory, the accumulation of knowledge, or the clever calculative capacity—but rather as the simple, impersonal force of observation that operated in the active present and was able to function in the most complex field. He asked, "Is K's brain just a freak occurrence, or can other humans also have such a brain?"

One of the lady trustees wondered, "How would you describe that brain, Krishnaji?"

"It's vacant, simple, unpreoccupied, but also alert and very watchful. It doesn't record any personal hurt or psychological injury," he explained, as all of us listened, full of attention.

Eventually the conversation moved to goodness and evil. Krishnamurti maintained, "There is a reservoir of goodness, and it has no relationship whatsoever with evil."

I had some difficulty grasping what he meant and suggested, "Evil, then, is an illusion?"

"No, sir. Evil exists, evidently," he insisted. "But it cannot touch the other; it has no relationship with goodness." As I was on the point of continuing with my questions, he stopped me, saying, "Kindly listen to this, sir. Simply listen."

But, despite carefully listening, I found it difficult to understand what for him was so simple.

The rains continued to fall and it was getting noticeably colder. During the conversation the next day, Krishnamurti started wondering about modern teenagers, about teenage sex and pregnancies. Suddenly he asked the director, who was sitting across from him, "Are there any prodigies among your students?"

"Do you mean child prodigies, Krishnaji?" the director asked.

"Yes. Like Mozart or Beethoven," he replied. "Who else was a child prodigy? Maybe Aldous Huxley. Was K a prodigy? Did the boy have some extraordinary talent?" After a moment's deliberation, he enumerated several points which seemed to suggest otherwise. "He was dreamy, vague, almost moronic, couldn't retain a thing. All he was interested in was sports and mechanical things, taking a watch apart and putting it back together again, and later disassembling and reassembling a car engine."

A lady suggested, "Maybe it was this vagueness, Krishnaji, this emptiness of mind that was an early indication of what later manifested as the genius of K—a talent, not in a special field, but of a different order."

Krishnamurti was hesitant to accept such a suggestion without careful examination. It was only after lengthy deliberation that he allowed, "Well, perhaps K could, in a certain sense, be considered a prodigy."

During lunch the next day, with the rain still streaming down, we talked about some of Krishnamurti's personal traits. Not having any emotional attachment to himself, he did not mind that we asked questions about him, as long as it was an impersonal investigation into the phenomenon called K.

"K is very simple," he said, "there is a sense of innocence and trust about him. He is open and without suspicion, even towards strangers. I must tell you a story about when I was staying at Mrs. Zimbalist's house at Malibu some years ago. In the afternoon, I would take a walk on the beach by the Pacific Ocean. One day, a man whom I had never met before approached and asked me whether he might accompany me. I said, 'All right, come along.' And together we strolled along the beach, not saying very much, just looking at the waves and the beautiful scenery. Then he asked whether we could sit down together for a moment. I said, 'All right.' So we sat down on a dead tree trunk, a piece of driftwood. We sat quietly for a while, looking out over the vast blue expanse. Then he asked me if he could hold my hand. So I gave him my hand, and we sat there holding hands for several moments."

The small group of people at the table were quite spellbound by his unusual story. It had the effect of a thriller on me, with its sense of danger and sexual undertones. At the same time, I was astonished at his naiveté in placing himself in a possibly hazardous situation. But he did not seem to take note of our sense of apprehension and continued, "After we had been sitting there quietly, holding hands, and looking at the lovely scenery, he asked me if he could give me a kiss."

I involuntarily held my breath.

"So I said, 'All right,' and he gave me a peck on the cheek."

The sense of suspense intensified as we, his listeners, asked wordlessly, 'What next?'

"That's all," he concluded, taking everybody in at one glance.

Somehow I felt suspended in the thin air of my own imagination. Thrown back upon myself, I quietly marveled at his innocent and guileless openness. Like a child, free of fear and distrust, he seemed to be ready to be everyone's friend.

When he arrived for lunch the next day, I noticed that he was still walking rather slowly and carefully. I held the screen door open for him, and after our initial greeting he immediately proceeded to tell me, "No more desserts, no more sweets—finished."

I was shocked. "But why, Krishnaji, what happened?"

"Yesterday we went to the hospital here for another check-up—you know, because of the operation. They tested my blood and found that the blood sugar level continues to be too high. So I have to cut out all sweets, sugar, honey, and so on."

"Oh, that's too bad," I said regretfully. "What about carrot juice? Can you still take that?" For some time he had enjoyed having freshly squeezed carrot juice with his meal.

"That's out, too."

"And yams, sweet corn, and raw or cooked carrots?"

I was eager to find out all aspects of his new diet, slightly alarmed at the prospect of extensive food restrictions.

"Vegetables are all right, even raw carrots," he explained. "I must only avoid high concentrations of sugar, such as are contained in carrot juice."

"What about fruit juices?" I continued, making mental notes.

"Out," he replied with easy finality.

"Can you still eat fruit, like apples, pears and so on?"

"Sparingly—maybe one or two per day, that's all."

For a moment a wave of sympathy rose in me, as I recalled how much he enjoyed a sweet treat, or a spoonful of ice cream for dessert. But any kind of self-pity or nostalgic regret was far from him, and he suddenly looked at me incisively and said, "Of course, sir, you must continue to make desserts for the others. They shouldn't be cut short because I can't have any sweets any more. It would be ridiculous to subject them to my dietary restrictions."

The sovereign ease with which he could give up things on a practical level was matched, if not surpassed, by his ability to end mental and psychological involvements from one moment to the next—as if no time were involved in taking a decision but only the immediacy of perception. It was a capacity that astonished me, a creature attached to pleasures, sensations and entertainments, who had to struggle to give up so-called bad habits. This inner freedom, however, did not exclude personal loyalty, nor a subtle, immovable firmness in adhering to his course of action.

EARLY ON THE MORNING OF MARCH 24, KRISHNAMURTI AND Mary Z. left for New York City, where he was to give two talks at Carnegie Hall the following weekend. The next day, in pouring rain, David and Saral Bohm arrived at Arya Vihara. Although he had fully recovered from his operation, David had lost much weight and looked pale and marked by his brief brush with death.

## Chapter 16

# THE ENERGY
# OF EMPTINESS

## Starters

*Mixed salad with lettuce greens,*
*sprouts and red cabbage,*
*with vinaigrette or tahini dressing.*
*Tomato salad with fresh mozzarella and basil.*
*Tabouli made from cous-cous,*
*parsley, fresh mint, currants,*
*sun-dried tomatoes, and pine nuts.*
*Hummus dip of garbanzo beans*
*served with pita bread.*

## Main Dishes

*Saffron rice.*
*Eggplant Parmigiana, made from*
*broiled eggplant slices powdered*
*with cinnamon, in a rich tomato sauce*
*and slices of mozzarella and Parmesan cheese.*
*Whole zucchini, briefly baked to perfection.*

## Dessert

*Three different types of ice cream.*
*Fresh, seasonal fruit.*

KRISHNAMURTI AND MARY Z. RETURNED FROM NEW YORK CITY on April 1. During lunch on the following day he enthusiastically told us about the large crowds that had filled the hall to overflowing. He was amazed that tickets for his talks were being scalped in the street at rather steep prices.

I was serving myself a helping of dessert—giant sequoia strawberries with ginger cream—when I looked out of the window of the corner servery and noticed a great horned owl sitting on an upper branch of the tree next to my cottage. Several of the large owls had been nesting in the trees at A.V., spending the daytime hours high up amidst the dangling foliage of the white-barked lemon eucalyptus trees around the parking lot. At dusk and into the night one could often hear their low-toned, mellow hooting.

With sudden excitement I thought that Krishnamurti might like to look at the winged creature. He was extremely fond of animals and often told of his encounters with bob cats, bears and tigers in the wild. It was extremely rare that I had a chance of showing him something wild and beautiful, so I rushed back into the dining room and, without much ado, breathlessly announced to him, "Sir, come and look, there is a great horned owl up in the tree."

Without any hesitation he got up and walked into the small room with me. No one else at the table seemed excited at the prospect of seeing a live owl. I eagerly stood next to him and pointed up into the tree. "There, Krishnaji, on the second, no, the third branch to the left. Can you see it?"

He was peering up where I was pointing but had difficulty discerning the unobtrusive shape in its camouflage plumage. Turning his head this way and that, he finally said, "I can't see it, Michael. Where is it?"

For a moment I was afraid that my discovery might fly away before I could share it with him, so I said, "Excuse me, Krishnaji, but it may be easier to see if we step outside for a moment."

He didn't object. We walked through the kitchen, out the door and around the corner, until we stood ten yards from the smooth, white trunk. Looking up at the strands of crescent leaves gently swaying in the breeze, I saw that the owl was still in the same place. In fact, it had taken note of us and was going through the strangely endearing, characteristic owl motions of pulling its round, flat face into its shoulders and moving its head rhythmically from side to side, as if wanting to check us out. Its horn like protrusions and large, round eyes were clearly visible. With sudden excitement I pointed at it, whispering, "Can you see it, sir, can you see it? It's moving its head back and forth."

Krishnamurti stood there, slender and fragile, like a little boy, with his head thrown back, and squinted into the bright afternoon light, shading his eyes with his left hand. All at once he exclaimed softly, "Ah yes, now I see it."

I felt relief and a sense of unexpected exuberance. There was a space of silent and intense watching as we stood there in the sunlight. The bird was watching us in return.

"It's really quite big, isn't it?" he remarked after a while.

"It must have an enormous wingspan."

Several moments of silent observation passed before he grabbed my arm with a characteristic gesture and led me toward the door, saying, "All right, sir."

Reentering the dining room I found the other guests still sitting chatting. I had the odd sensation that, for a moment, I had stepped into another world of bright colors and discovery and was now back in the narrower space of familiarity.

THE RAINS CONTINUED UNABATED THROUGHOUT THE following week. Krishnamurti met with the school staff four consecutive times, talking about the trust we all needed to have to be able to build the school he envisioned.

On the weekend of April 16–18, a professional television crew came to film four dialogues between Krishnamurti, David Bohm, Dr John Hidley, a local psychiatrist, and Dr Rupert Sheldrake, a British biologist, who had recently developed a challenging new theory. He named it 'morphic resonance', proposing that members of a common species, like monkeys, or humans, shared learning and any significant new discovery through 'morpho-genetic fields', biological channels of transmission, even though the individual members lived far apart and had no physical contact with one another. The four discussions at Pine Cottage, produced on videos as *The Nature of the Mind*, were sponsored by a private foundation that funded mental health projects.

BY THIS TIME, LATE APRIL, THE RAIN HAD FINALLY STOPPED AND we were again enjoying bright, clear days. During one lunch I served home-made fettucini with tomato-sauce and Parmesan cheese, a garbanzo bean dish, and steamed artichokes with a simple mayonnaise and mustard sauce. Krishnamurti was generally fond of Italian and Provençal cuisine, and I had, therefore, assumed that he liked artichokes. Since we lived close to Watsonville, the so-called artichoke capital of the world, we were blessed with a plentiful supply of the 'royal thistle'. Large, gorgeous specimens were available at bargain prices at the local markets. I had developed a fondness for the fleshy leaves and served them regularly, going through the laborious and sometimes painful process of trimming each single thorn protruding from the leaf top.

I was in the middle of enjoying the heart when I noticed Krishnamurti skeptically studying an artichoke leaf in his hands. He said to the person across from him, "It's really a terrible bore to tear all these leaves apart. And there is so little on them." The lady made a noise as if to concur with his critical assessment of the artichoke situation. I, however, felt momentarily stunned into sudden disillusionment. Recovering from my speechlessness, I tried to speak up in defense of the flower heads, "But Krishnaji, they are not only delicious but also an excellent source of vitamin B-12."

He showed himself unimpressed by my claim and said, in a slightly ironical tone, "It takes forever to eat them."

"I thought you liked them, sir," I said plaintively.

Some moments later, he turned toward me and asked, "What's the news, sir?"

It felt like a welcome diversion from my artichoke disappointment, and I started to recapitulate the most recent developments in the Falklands War between Britain and Argentina. I concluded it by quoting the great Argentinian writer, Jorge Luis Borgès, whose brilliant assessment of the deadly conflict I had just read in a news magazine: "It's like two bald men fighting over a comb."

Krishnamurti broke into delighted laughter. "That's very good—two bald men fighting over a comb! I must remember that."

As the conversation went on, it centered around human conflict, especially war and how it affected the collective and individual consciousness. David Bohm characterized war as organized conflict, resulting in a form of public mania, which had its roots in the belief that one's own country was superior and always right. As an illustration he cited the opening words of the former German national anthem, 'Deutsch-land über Alles' (Germany above all), and the saying, 'My country right or wrong', which exemplified the powerful effect of nationalist slogans on individual thinking. Krishnamurti compared it to a form of obsession, which totally corrupted the ethos and behavior of a society. He proceeded to recount an event from his life.

"It was during the war years when I was here in California. I was walking down the main street in Santa Barbara, when a woman approached me with a box in her hand. She said her fiancé had just sent her a gift from the front, somewhere in the Pacific, and she wanted to show it me. She opened the box, and I recoiled. There was a shriveled-up human head in it. She asked me if I wanted to buy it as souvenir. Imagine it, sir!"

Everybody at the table was horrified, imagining the bizarre scene. Referring back to the recent dialogues on mental health, several people started talking about abnormal states of mind, such as the control of the mental faculties by demons and other strange psychic forces.

One lady asked Krishnamurti, "Do you think that a consciousness can be possessed by demonic forces? I don't mean madness or hallucinations, but other entities."

After a moment's deliberation he replied, "May I tell you a story? It was quite a few years ago in London. I was staying at a friend's house in the suburbs, and one afternoon I was looking out of the window when a Rolls-Royce drove up the driveway. A chauffeur got out and opened the door for a lady, made-up and elegantly dressed. She rang the doorbell. I was alone in the house and answered the door. The lady introduced herself and asked if she could talk with me in private; it was a matter of some urgency. So I asked her into the house. She came straight to the point and told me that she was a very successful, high-class call girl. She had made a fortune sleeping with hundreds of men of the highest social standing—aristocrats, politicians and businessmen. Six months earlier one of her lovers, whom she adored above all others, had left her for good. She told me all of this very matter-of-factly, very calmly. One evening she was alone in her house, sitting in front of the fireplace. Staring into the flames, she playfully started to conjure up the spirit of her former lover in her mind. She was shocked when suddenly a phantom materialized out of the fire, assuming the form of her former lover. She went on to tell me that she had then sex with this phantom. She had found it exciting and pleasurable, and so the same thing happened on the following nights, but only when she was by herself. It went on for months. But the phantom became more and more powerful and started to gain control over her. It told her what to do, and its wishes became more demanding, telling her exactly when they would meet again, and so on and on. She was possessed by the phantom, and it ruled her life. She wanted to put a stop to the whole thing but saw no way out. She didn't want to consult any psychologist or priest or any other professional. So she discreetly asked some of her friends in high places if they knew anyone trustworthy who could advise her in a most sensitive, private matter. Our name came up, and after attending one or two of the talks, she felt confident that I might help her in her curious predicament. She hadn't told a soul about her fantastic experiences; I was the first to know about them. She was close to tears as she told her story, evidently in deep distress. I agreed to help her on condition that she do exactly as I told her. She promised. I asked her to leave one of the rings she was wearing and return after three days. During that time she was not to have any sex, nor to remain alone in her house at night, so the phantom couldn't contact her. When she left, she offered a large sum of money for our help, but I did not accept it. I placed her diamond ring on the mantelpiece above the fireplace. That's where it remained for the next three days. I didn't touch it or do anything with it. Three days later, the lady arrived in her Rolls-Royce. I returned the ring to her and told her to wear it at all times, resume her normal life and see what would happen. A week later, she called me. She was overjoyed. The phantom had been expelled. Even when she was alone at night in front of the fire, the phantom did not make its appearance. It seemed to be banned once and for all. She thanked me profusely, again offering money, which, of course, I could not accept."

We were spellbound in our seats, listening to his bizarre tale. It had such a touch of the magical and supernatural about it that it seemed to spring from the fantasy world of A *Thousand-And-One Nights*, rather than from his lips. There was an interval of stunned silence, during which one could practically hear our internal strings of credulity being stretched to their limits. Then, as if on command, everyone excitedly started talking at the same time, reviewing the details of the eerie story with one another.

Krishnamurti was quietly and with calm amusement observing the impact of his story on us. Then, raising one hand, he called out, quickly recapturing everyone's attention, "Just a minute. That isn't the end of the story. There is still something to come, a final twist." He smiled. "A few months later, we were dining out in a restaurant in the city, and this same lady was there at another table with some friends. She recognized and greeted me from a distance. When I was by myself for a moment, she hurried over and said she had something important to tell me. She apologized profusely for taking my time and thanked me once again for my help in her distress, then proceeded to tell me that, as time went by, she had started to feel bored and lonely; just a month ago she again conjured up the phantom, just for fun, and now the whole thing was happening all over...."

His face assumed an ironic expression as, with raised eyebrows, he studiously examined each face for its reaction to the *dénouement* of the story. There was a wide spectrum of responses, ranging from outright indignation, doubt and incredulity, to amusement. My own reaction bordered on wild laughter, that I felt welling up within myself but restrained. I wondered if there might not be an astonishing parallel between the call girl's state of mind and that of most of us here. We might claim to want our consciousness radically changed, our lives selfless and without conflict, but what would happen if, by magic and without any effort on our part, we were transformed into fuller and more complete human beings, with alert but empty minds? Would we not clamor for the safe, accustomed haven of our old self, that well-worn garment of memories, which had become us, which was us? Would we not scurry back under the sheltering roof of the familiar home, rather than stand alone in the vastness of the open skies? Pondering this, I had to admit that I didn't really know the answer. So I asked Krishnamurti, "And what happened after that?"

He gave an expressive shrug. "Well, nothing...it just went on, I suppose."

He did not provide any further explanation, and we were left to our own devices to make head or tail of this unusual anecdote. Soon after that we cleared the table and went back to what we normally did.

A FEW DAYS LATER SARAL BOHM INFORMED ME THAT THERE would be an additional guest for lunch: he had been a student friend of David's at UC Berkeley. Both became exponents of quantum mechanics and had at one time taught in Brazil. His name was Richard Feynman and he taught at the California Institute of Technology at Pasadena. Among other things, he was a Nobel Laureate in physics, having received the prestigious prize in 1965 for working out a new way to treat quantum electrodynamics and also for his exemplary and highly entertaining lectures on Quantum Theory, which were later published as a textbook on the subject.[5] Saral mentioned discreetly that he had been diagnosed as having a terminal form of cancer.

He was in his 60's, a distinguished-looking, handsome man, a few years younger than David. He was of slim, medium build, with an expressive face, fine features, a high forehead, and full, swept-back, light brown hair. He was dressed with chic in casual Californian style, exuding an air of easy, nonchalant self-confidence. He clearly was a scientific celebrity of the highest order.

I had prepared a tomato salad with fresh mozzarella and basil, a hummus dip of garbanzo beans, tabouli, served with pita bread, saffron rice, eggplant Parmigiana and baked zucchini, followed by ice cream. There were about sixteen people for lunch that day.

In his usual modest way, David introduced his friend to Krishnamurti. They politely shook hands and exchanged greetings. But it was clear that Dr. Feynman was primarily present because he was visiting his old college friend, David, and less out of interest in Krishnamurti and his work. Krishnamurti was quietly watching the guests serving themselves. When Dr. Feynman approached, he directed him to the chair at the head of the table, saying, "Please sit here, sir, so you can be next to Dr. Bohm."

While David placed himself on Dr. Feynman's left, Krishnamurti took his usual seat, the first place on the right, across from him. I sat three chairs away. I had been expecting that at one point or another a lively conversation would evolve between Krishnamurti and Dr. Feynman, or between the three of them. But nothing of the sort seemed to materialize. Some of the teachers, however, were eager to put questions to the illustrious guest and to gauge his thinking on various topics.

Krishnamurti appeared rather quiet and withdrawn. I had seldom seen him so reticent during a meal. Even so, he was most intently watching what was going on. Dr. Feynman seemed to be used to being the center of attention. Without any sense of undue assertion, he enjoyed the role of eloquent raconteur. I had just been wondering whether he had any interest in Krishnamurti and his teaching when one of the teachers asked circumspectly, "Do you think, sir, that philosophy has any role in education?"

Dr. Feynman answered swiftly, "I have never been interested in philosophy. I don't know anything about it, nor can I say anything about the subject."

The questioner wasn't easily deterred and continued by focusing on questions of psychology and education. Several others joined in, and Dr. Feynman evidently felt more at ease with these topics. He began to talk about his family, how he interacted with his children, and so on. Gradually, he caught everyone's attention as he reminisced about his own upbringing, about his nature walks with his father, who pointed out to him the small and great wonders of the earth, explaining various phenomena by inventing imaginary words. We were all listening spellbound to his fascinating and amusing narration. One could tell that one was in the presence of a gifted teacher and entertaining story teller, a brilliant scientist, and possibly a wonderful person.

Krishnamurti had been silently following the animated story, and one could sense the respect in his quiet watching. There was a reciprocity between him and Dr. Feynman, as they kept a cautious and respectful distance from each other—a polite stand-off. Clearly, Dr. Feynman was here to visit his friend David Bohm, nothing more, and Krishnamurti fully respected and left it at that.

After lunch, Krishnamurti remarked to one of the teachers who accompanied him on his way to Pine Cottage, "Did you notice it, sir, about Dr. Feynman?"

The young man was puzzled and asked, "I'm sorry, Krishnaji, I don't understand what you mean."

"He was a very unhappy man," Krishnamurti said cautiously. "I watched him carefully."

The teacher was mystified by this assessment but didn't pursue the issue, since he had to go to the office, while Krishnamurti went on to Pine Cottage. It might well have been an accurate observation, especially if one takes into account Dr. Feynman's terminal illness.

Saral Bohm later told me that David and Dr. Feynman had spent most of the rest of the afternoon huddled around the coffee table in their apartment, conversing in a kind of 'scientese', as she put it, communicating through a code of mathematical equations, formulas, and other rather enigmatic terms, comprehensible only to a few highly specialized initiates of quantum mechanic lore.

A few years later, Dr. Feynman became nationally famous on two counts: as the brilliant chairman of the commission of inquiry into the disaster that befell the U.S. space shuttle *Challenger* in 1986, which shortly after take-off exploded, killing all seven astronauts on board; and as the author of a best-selling autobiography, which revealed his great humor and skill at story-telling. More recently, I happened to watch a television documentary in the Nova series, aired on the Public Broadcasting System, which featured a lively interview of Dr. Feynman. To my surprise, he was recounting verbatim the same stories about his childhood and family that he had told us at the A.V. lunch table.

Dr. Richard Feynman died in 1988.

WE WERE GLAD THAT THE RAINS HAD STOPPED IN TIME FOR the soggy ground to dry up before the start of the public talks on May 1. Apart from regular dialogue meetings with Krishnamurti at Pine Cottage, everybody had their hands full with preparations for the two-week event.

During a luncheon in midweek that was attended primarily by 'the regulars' and a few trustees from overseas, we began talking about ancient Greece and its prodigious success in handing down its basic ideas and institutions to our present-day world: its political, cultural and scientific influence was everywhere. I knew that apart from Chartres Cathedral, the Shiva sculpture on Elephanta Island, and the *Winged Victory of Samothrace* in the Louvre, Krishnamurti most admired the ancient citadel of Athens, the Acropolis, with its fabulous columned temple, the Parthenon. He had visited the birthplace of democracy several times in the 1930's, and again in 1954 and 1956, expressing himself exuberantly about these architectural masterpieces. He had even declared himself to be in love with the marble statue of the Goddess of Justice, Themis.

A few days earlier I had read a newspaper article about the destructive toll which car exhausts and other industrial pollution was exacting on the two-thousand-year-old marble relics in the congested Attic metropolis. Thinking this might be an interesting piece of information, I began by saying to Krishnamurti, who was sitting next to me, "The acid rain and sulfur oxidants are quickly eroding these marble monuments which have survived for almost three thousand years. In less than a few decades all of these irreplaceable masterpieces will be..."

He turned toward me as I was talking, and a pained expression crept into his face. Suddenly he interrupted me with a tone of tremendous hurt, "No, sir, please, don't talk about it. You don't know...it's too...it's too..."

He didn't complete the sentence but let it trail off into unspecified agony. All at once I felt horribly awkward, almost as if I had transgressed by having broached this painful subject. For an instant, I actually thought some of the people across the table were eyeing me with silent, judgmental reproach. What had I done? I felt like apologizing although, on second thoughts, it seemed rather ludicrous to do so. I shot a furtive, sideways glance at Krishnamurti. He was quietly chewing away, with half-closed eyelids, without any visible sign of pain. I breathed a silent sigh of relief— I had let my innate guilt conditioning get the better of me.

BEFORE WE KNEW IT, THE TALKS HAD STARTED. DURING THE second and fourth question-and-answer meetings he brought up an old theme, delivering it with a force that hit all the way home. "Why hasn't man changed?" he asked with tremendous passion, restating the same question more directly a week later, "Why haven't you changed?"

There was no answer—unless one wanted to rationalize. One could only hold the question within oneself and ponder it, live with it.

During the weekend talks he addressed issues such as 'order, fear and thought', 'knowledge, death and love', and, finally, 'the religious life and meditation'.

On Friday, May 21, another seasonal cycle of living with Krishnamurti ended, as he and Mary Z. departed for England.

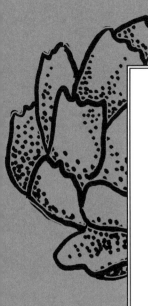

### Starters

*Tossed green salad with vinaigrette
or creamy mustard dressing.
An assortment of raw vegetables: sliced
bell peppers, zucchini, celery,
mushrooms, grated red cabbage,
carrots, and beets.
Steamed artichokes, served with
a mayonnaise-mustard sauce.*

### Main Dishes

*Steamed quinoa, garnished with
parsley, raisins and pine nuts.
Azuki beans, prepared with
onions and soy sauce.
Baked kabocha squash.*

### Dessert

*Fresh raspberries,
served in a sauce of cream and cognac
with whipped cream on the side.
Fresh, seasonal fruit.*

DURING THE FOLLOWING MONTHS, THE OAK GROVE STAFF continued to wrestle with putting into action its 'Intent'—the statement composed by Krishnamurti in 1975, which declared that the purpose of the school was 'to bring about a radical transformation in the consciousness of mankind'.

On a personal level, I kept wrestling primarily with questions of relationship and sex and became absorbed in the nitty-gritty of day-to-day living. All the while, though, I continued to write poetry and to examine my life in the extraordinary mirror of Krishnamurti's teaching. My blemishes had not disappeared, I had not changed at the roots of my consciousness, and I felt that all I could do was watch my limitations and shortcomings without judgment, effort or choice. In that there was a great freedom, which I also felt in my daily contact with the wild nature of the valley and mountains.

KRISHNAMURTI, IN THE MEANTIME, FOLLOWED HIS REGULAR itinerary from Europe to India. The two special events during this time were two talks he gave at the Barbican Center in London in June, and four talks in Calcutta in November, 1982.

THE PREVIOUS WEEK WE HAD HAD A SERIES OF DESTRUCTIVE rainstorms. Now the air was clear and unpolluted, and the land was washed clean and shining; it was February 9, 1983, the day of Krishnamurti's return to Ojai. Mary Z., who had been here since last November, drove to LAX to pick him up on his arrival from London Heathrow.

Ten of us were waiting beneath the pepper tree. I felt a great sense of joy welling up in me as the gray Mercedes sedan came into sight and pulled up in front of the garage. Krishnamurti, dressed in his elegant traveling clothes, got out of the car. He looked fragile and thin and a little bit tired, as he greeted each one of us in turn. Turning to look at the undulating skyline of the hills, taking in the beauty of the land with one sweeping glance, he exclaimed after an interval of silence, "What a country this is! So rich and beautiful, so vast!"

The following day, a Thursday, we had a small luncheon with only eight people. As we were amiably conversing about Krishnamurti's time in India and his journey to California, I took the opportunity to ask him, "Have you heard any good jokes recently, sir?"

He was relaxed and in the right mood to respond, "All right, sir. There are three good jokes I've heard recently. In the first one, God has just completed the creation of the world, with its oceans and continents and all the creatures, including the humans. As he surveys his work, an angel points out that there is one small spot in the center of Europe that's been left blank and empty. The Lord says, 'I must have over-looked that spot. What shall we do with it?' And the angel answers, 'If I may suggest it, Lord, why don't you create a land of milk and honey, called Switzerland—with snow-peaked mountains, streams, forests and green meadows, where cows graze that produce the best milk in the world?' The Lord replies, 'That sounds good. And what about the humans there?' And the angel suggests, 'Why not make them clean, orderly, and hard-working, with the greatest respect for money?' And the Lord says, 'So be it.' And so it was done. After some time the Lord wants to see what he has created and goes down to Earth. He walks among the mountains, enjoying the beauty of the scenery. After a while he comes to a small village, very clean and orderly. As the day is getting hotter, he feels a bit thirsty. So he walks up to one of the cafés with out-door tables and chairs. The owner immediately recognizes him and comes running, greeting him with great respect, 'O Lord, please sit down. It's an extraordinary honor that You visit our small town and my humble café. Is there anything, anything, that we can do for You?' The Lord is pleased and says, 'By Jove, I noticed your splendid cows grazing out there. Give me a tall glass of cold, fresh milk.' 'Immediately, O Lord.' And the man trots off and returns with a tall glass of fresh, cold milk with foam on the top, and places it in front of the Lord. He drinks it down with much enjoyment. He's just getting up from the table when the owner comes running and, with a respectful bow, places a small plate with a strip of paper in front of him. The Lord looks at it and asks the man, 'What is that?' The owner bows again and explains, 'With all due respect, O Lord, that is the bill.'"

We laughed out loud at the joke and the way he told it, how he enacted with small gestures and facial expressions the roles of the Lord and the bistro owner.

One lady asked, "Do you make up all your jokes?"

He replied, "Oh no, not at all. Somebody tells them to me and sometimes I remember them—if they are good jokes. I only invented one joke, and that was a long time ago. The following story I was told in India. You may have heard of Birla, the industrialist. He's from Calcutta, tremendously rich, and for many years his company has had a virtual monopoly on passenger cars built in India, with the Ambassador. They are not very well-made vehicles, not very comfortable, and they often break down. So Birla dies and goes to heaven. St. Peter meets him at the Pearly Gates and asks, 'Who are you, please?' 'I'm Birla,' he replies, slightly annoyed at not being recognized. St. Peter goes through his list of names. 'B—B—Birla. I'm sorry, your name is not on the list. I don't think you can enter heaven.' Birla protests angrily, 'I'm Birla, the industrialist. I must be on that list. Look again. B—i—r—l—a.' St. Peter is taken aback by the man's arrogance and says, 'I don't know anybody by that name.' 'By Jove,' Birla exclaims, 'everybody knows me—everybody. And you're trying to tell me...' Peter says politely but firmly, 'Please, sir, don't get excited. That won't help you up here. Your name is not on the list. I've never heard of you, and I'm afraid that you won't be allowed into heaven.' For a moment Birla is crushed and falls into a morose silence. St. Peter feels pity for him and says, 'But perhaps you can provide us with a good reason why we should let you in.' Birla immediately perks up and says, 'I have helped the cause of many religions by spending millions upon millions for the building of temples, mosques, and churches.' St. Peter replies, 'That's quite natural, all rich people do that: they want to become famous and save paying taxes. But that hardly qualifies you to enter the heavenly paradise.' By this time Birla is feeling quite frustrated and shouts, 'Now look here, my dear chap, there is nobody in the whole of India, maybe in the whole world, who has done so much for his workers and their families, built hundreds of hospitals, homes for orphans and the aged, schools and universities.' St. Peter says, 'I'm not sure whether that counts either. After all, these people have given their energy, their labor, their lives, so that you could become rich. No, no—none of that matters in heaven. What we ask, which is the real question: what have you ever done for God?' Birla frantically searches his memory and finally brightens up, saying with satisfaction, 'Well, sir, for decades we have been manufacturing the famous Ambassador car. And, whenever somebody opens the door to get into their car, they exclaim, 'O my god!'"

We were still laughing when Krishnamurti began narrating the third of his new jokes. "An American multimillionaire who lives in England wants to become a proper, perfect English gentleman. So he goes to Huntsman on Savile Row and has a dozen of the best suits made for him, complete with Jaquet ties and topcoats. Then he asks the tailor to refer him to the best shoemaker. 'Why, sir, just next door, there is Loeb's.' He goes there, has his feet measured, and orders a dozen of the most beautiful, handmade shoes. When he asks for the best place to buy a cane and umbrella, they send him next door. Proceeding from one shop to the next, he is gradually outfitted with the best of everything, looking every inch the perfect English gentleman. The next time he goes to see his tailor for some alterations, he has his Rolls-Royce pull up in front of the shop. The tailor, with whom he has become good friends—they're in the same club and so on—immediately notices that he is in a horrible state, very depressed and gloomy. So the tailor asks the American, 'What's the matter, sir? You look as if something dreadful has just happened.' 'Yes, I really feel terrible. I can't get over it,' sighs the rich man. 'But why, sir?' exclaims the tailor. 'You've got the very best of everything: excellent car, best clothes and shoes, umbrella, gloves, et cetera. You look every inch the perfect English gentleman. How could you possibly feel depressed?' By now, the American is almost in tears. 'Because we've lost India.'"

Everybody round the lunch table was in tears, they were laughing so hard. It wasn't only the joke and the way he had told it that were so hilarious, but also the fact that he had enumerated the very stores on Savile Row that he himself frequented for his clothes and shoes.

The following Sunday was the beginning of the Chinese New Year, the Year of the Pig, and sixteen people came for lunch. We had Greek salad, a carrot and ginger salad, couscous with toasted almonds, ratatouille, fried tofu with green onions and parsley, a selection of cheeses with fruit and garlic bread, and datenut bread and ice cream for dessert.

After some initial small talk, Krishnamurti started a serious conversation by asking the director, "Why do children at a certain point in growing up turn into 'monsters'? You know what I mean: cruel, inconsiderate, selfish, and so on."

One person asked, "Do you think that happens with all children?"

"More or less," Krishnamurti replied, "maybe more so with boys than with girls."

"It's also culturally modified," the director said. "In India, the children are so well-behaved, obedient and respectful, especially when they are younger."

Krishnamurti concurred, "Yes, it's really quite remarkable. I say to them, 'Let's sit still for five minutes,' and immediately they all assume a cross-legged posture, close their eyes and are absolutely still for five minutes. Could you get American children to do that?"

A lady trustee protested, "But Krishnaji, it's a totally different culture. The children in India are conditioned from early on to act and sit in a certain way, to obey. It's really quite different here."

A teacher suggested, "Here they are too excited and nervous. Maybe it's the diet and the entertainment, all the junk food and the constant peer pressure."

Krishnamurti didn't disagree with any of what was being said but pursued it further by asking, "Can one show them responsibility, sir? You know what I mean by that word 'responsibility'? Can one give them responsibility?"

The teacher asked, "Do you propose, Krishnaji, to give the student a specific responsibility—for an animal, for a small space in the classroom? Is that what you mean?"

"No, sir. Not just responsibility for a tree, an animal, a plant, and so on. Any specific example is too narrow. Can one convey to him or her a sense of responsibility for everything—for the earth, for nature, for all of mankind? Do you understand?"

"But how could one do that? That's an awfully large responsibility for a child—all of humanity."

"You see, sir, you are making a problem of it. You are asking 'how'—which is the method. Don't make another problem of it. It's not: I don't have responsibility, how do I get it? But rather: listen in silence, observe, watch—can you show that to the student?"

"I think of responsibility as something that I'm accountable for."

"That's what is usually meant by that word. It also implies duty, a burden, and so on. We mean something quite different by responsibility—namely, the ability to respond. To respond adequately to a challenge, to what is happening. And to be able to do that one has to listen, observe, be choicelessly aware of the whole situation."

Responsibility became one of the main themes over the next two months, when Krishnamurti met with the staff nineteen times at Pine

Cottage. Apart from asking us repeatedly why we didn't change, he explored the questions of confusion and disorder, cause and effect, and finally asked, "What is a sharp, a good mind?" This question led to an inquiry into the brain, consciousness, mind and intelligence.

This year Krishnamurti seemed to be full of an inexhaustible energy. More than ever, he was burning to convey his insight, meeting frequently with staff and parents, with trustees and committees, in addition to his unusually busy public speaking schedule. It was also around this time that Krishnamurti started a remarkable diary, which, unlike previous notebooks, he did not write down but dictated into a cassette recorder while still in bed early in the morning. These lyrical reflections on nature and the human mind were later transcribed and published as *Krishnamurti to Himself*.

AT THE END OF MARCH, DR. AND MRS. JONAS SALK FROM THE Salk Institute in San Diego visited us. During dinner at A.V. the inventor of the polio vaccine began an animated conversation with Krishnamurti about the troubled state of the world and what could be done about it. What is compassion, what is enlightenment, and how can they affect the world? were some of the questions they raised. Although they agreed on a number of issues, their views did not entirely converge. The following day, Sunday, March 27, they had a videotaped dialogue in the more formal setting of Pine Cottage.

There was no lunch at A.V. for the next two days, since Mary Z. and the Lilliefelts had gone with Krishnamurti to their lawyer in Oxnard. He was giving his deposition in a lawsuit filed by the Foundation against Rajagopal. This was one in a series of lawsuits and counter-lawsuits, which had been going on since 1969. The Foundation was seeking to recover written and other recorded material by Krishnamurti, as well as assets given to him for his work, from the K & R Foundation, controlled by Rajagopal.

After spending most of the day at the lawyer's office, the four of them had supper at A.V.—a rare occasion. During the meal they were still preoccupied by the lengthy legal proceedings, conversing about various aspects of the deposition. Krishnamurti was visibly strained, having been subjected to very hostile questioning by the other party's attorneys. In order to avoid further harassment and a possible appearance in court, it was decided to withdraw the lawsuit, an action formalized on April 1.

IN THE LATE AFTERNOON OF MARCH 30, DAVID AND SARAL Bohm arrived at Pine Cottage. Krishnamurti made a point of joining several of us beneath the pepper tree to welcome the professor and his wife. He greeted his old friend with affectionate care, inquiring after their welfare and making sure that they felt at home in the upstairs guest apartment. David looked pale and exhausted from the long journey, while Saral appeared as bubbly as ever.

The following day, when Krishnamurti met the school staff for a discussion in the bright living room of Pine Cottage, he politely asked Dr. Bohm to sit next to him, offering him the seat of honor. David was very quiet and spoke only a few times, when addressed directly.

This year there was a peculiar pattern to the comings and goings of Krishnamurti and David Bohm: as soon as one arrived, the other promptly departed. Five days after the Bohms' arrival, Krishnamurti and Mary Z. took off for New York City, where he was to give two talks at the Felt Forum, Madison Square Garden, on April 9 and 10. During the luncheon prior to his departure, he urged David to have dialogue meetings with the school staff, a request he gladly complied with.

At lunch two days after his return from New York City, Krishnamurti briefly described the talks, which had been attended by over four thousand people, and the several interviews he had given to newspapers and magazines. But his mind was concerned with the school, and he soon delved into discussing what type of school he envisioned, emphasizing that he wanted a 'strong' school, which would last for hundreds of years.

During Monday lunch, Krishnamurti asked David and Saral, who were to travel to the San Francisco Bay Area on Wednesday, about the seminar they were going to participate in. It was going to take place at a Christian College, with a number of Christians partaking. Krishnamurti asked in a general manner, "How will Dr. Bohm talk to the Christians about the psyche?"

While outside abundant rains poured down from dark-grey skies, everyone pursued the question with much light-hearted laughter, although in the end we were rather short on concrete advice. In the afternoon, Krishnamurti met with the staff at Pine Cottage and forcefully raised the question of what constituted a 'strong' school. It was based on learning and thinking together and implied the cultivation of curiosity and doubt.

At lunch the following day, David raised his own question, which he put to Krishnamurti: "What is the relationship between watching, awareness, choiceless awareness, concentration, attention and insight?" An unexpected, fully fledged dialogue ensued, primarily between Krishnamurti and David. It was a conversation full of subtlety, fine differentiations, and sudden clarity. Everyone at the table was spellbound, while the rains kept streaming down without abeyance. A few brave spirits tried to join in the dialogue by offering their respective views. But the subtle force of the flow of meaning seemed to be too unremitting for anyone but the two main players to keep pace with. Most of us listened quietly and intently.

More than an hour had passed since everyone at the table had finished eating their dessert. Every so often, somebody took a sip of water or juice; otherwise, only the deepening exploration into insight seemed to matter. It was as if discharges of energy flashed back and forth between the poles of these two brilliant minds, illuminating the entire field around them. Suddenly there was a pause. A deep sense of silence permeated the room, and the only sound that could be heard was the noise of the rain pounding the wooden decks and roofs. Then, with a verbal handshake, they agreed, "Only insight acts."

As we rose with quiet wonder from the table, one of the trustees plaintively remarked, "We really should have taped this conversation."

ON THE DAY OF THE BOHMS' DEPARTURE FOR THE BAY AREA, Krishnamurti met with the staff and asked what role entertainment played in the life of the child and in our lives. "Can you show the child about conditioning? Not only his conditioning, but also learn about your conditioning at the same time?"

After exploring the separation of life into work and leisure, he asked one of his deceptively simple questions, which had the impact of a deep probe into one's consciousness. "Do you really love what you are doing?"

Unless one really loved what one was doing, how could one possibly help the child, educate the child?

A WEEK LATER THE BOHMS RETURNED FROM THE SEMINAR in the Bay Area, only to see Krishnamurti and Mary Z. depart for San Francisco the next day. He was to give two talks at the Masonic Auditorium over the weekend. Since I too was going to drive up north on the following day to attend these talks, I apologized to the Bohms for not being able to look after them during their time in Ojai.

IT WAS A GREAT THRILL FOR ME TO VISIT SAN FRANCISCO, a city where I had lived for several years in the late 60's, and to again hear Krishnamurti speak at the Masonic Hall. During the second talk, on Sunday, May 1, I was deeply moved as he evoked the image of two friends walking side by side along a wooded path in dappled sunlight, talking over together the great questions of life—birth and death, joy and sorrow, peace and conflict, freedom and love. He proceeded to point out that the words 'friendship' and 'freedom' were closely related: their common root meant 'love'.

AFTER HIS RETURN TO OJAI, KRISHNAMURTI AND DAVID SPENT five more days together, before David and Saral left on May 8 for Toronto, where they had an engagement. This meant they missed the Ojai Talks, which started the following weekend.

An hour after their departure we had a meeting with Krishnamurti at Pine Cottage, during which he asked us, "What is action?" Step by step we went into the whole complex question of action and found that action based on thought, memory and knowledge—clearly the great majority of our everyday actions—was limited. And limitation implied division and, therefore, conflict. Division was conflict, a simple law.

Because of Krishnamurti's advanced age—he was 88—the 1983 public talks at Ojai were shortened from three to two weekends, so that there were now four instead of six talks and two instead of four question-and-answer meetings. But one could certainly not discern any diminishing of energy in him, as he mounted the platform amidst the grove of live oaks to address the three thousand people gathered in front of him. On the first Sunday, he described how he was walking with the audience, as with a friend, along a sun-dappled trail, exploring earnestly and without barriers the serious questions that persisted throughout one's life. During the first question-and-answer meeting, on Tuesday, May 17, he defined the word 'guru', which so often was misapplied to charlatans and self-styled saviors. Making resolutely clear that he was not a guru and had no followers or disciples, he explained that 'guru' derived from a Sanskrit word meaning 'heavy, weighty, grave'.

"So a guru is someone who points out and dispels illusions, and thereby eradicates ignorance," he said, "not someone who imposes his ignorance on others."

Some moments later he expanded on the meaning of the word 'mantra', which originated from the Sanskrit for 'to measure, think' and came to signify 'to ponder over not becoming, and to abandon all self-centered activities'. He emphasized that this was the true meaning of a mantra—not the cheap, exploitative practice of selling for a lot of money a syllable, which, they claimed, produced a quiet state of mind.

"You might as well repeat the word 'Coca-Cola' over and over again," he quipped amidst laughter from the audience. "It'll have the same effect of mesmerizing you."

For many years, Krishnamurti had been lashing out at the commercial exploitation of the human quest for truth. Any religious practice and teaching for financial gain was anathema to him. Truth was not a commodity for sale, nor could it ever be monopolized, organized or owned by anyone. Because of this, he was adamant in insisting that no fee was charged for attending his talks and dialogues, nor for any of his public or private interviews. The only charge ever made by the Foundation for a talk was when the cost of renting a public facility, such as the Masonic Temple, the Santa Monica Civic Auditorium, or Carnegie Hall needed to be defrayed through the sale of tickets.

Krishnamurti's unambiguous insistence on free attendance at his talks actually posed something of a problem for the trustees and financial officers of the Foundation. Both the Foundation and the School were very dependent on the donations of people interested in supporting Krishnamurti's work. And, although the Talks at the Oak Grove took place on home territory, they still incurred considerable expenditure. Two people with slotted boxes were posted at each entrance to the Oak Grove, requesting a donation of three dollars for the talk. Whoever refused to pay could still enter, but had to endure the disapproving look of the collectors. Despite this and the requests for donations delivered by a trustee prior to a talk, the income seldom, if ever, covered the costs.

An unusual thing happened at the end of the first question-and-answer meeting. Just as he was leaving the Oak Grove, Krishnamurti was served a legal writ against him and the other trustees of the Foundation. Rajagopal had initiated another lawsuit, even though the Foundation's lawsuit had been withdrawn.

THROUGHOUT THE TALKS THERE WERE MANY GUESTS, including several trustees from overseas, who regularly came to lunch with Krishnamurti at A.V. Hence, it was a very busy time for me in the kitchen, and we had lively get-togethers around the lunch table.

During one of the mid-week luncheons the conversation focused on the various organized religions and the enormous amount of conflict and suffering they had caused throughout human history. One of the trustees was saying, "Look at the recent conflicts involving Muslims — Iran and Iraq — and the ongoing struggle Israel has with the Palestinians and her other Islamic neighbors; look at the fights between Muslims and Hindus in India, and so on. Islam really is a religion of the sword."

Krishnamurti responded, "Face it, sir: Christianity has caused more wars and bloodshed than any other religion on earth. I wonder if it's because it claims divine revelation, directly from the horse's mouth."

"But so do Islam and Judaism," I said amidst laughter. "In some respects they all recognize the biblical scriptures as a common source of revelation. They all believe in one God."

"But their most important sacred texts are different," a teacher pointed out. "The Torah, the New Testament and the Koran — each of these books is said to contain the one and only, ultimate truth."

"They are the religions of 'the Book'," Krishnamurti said. "When a religion is based on one book, like the Bible or the Koran, you have people who are bigoted, intolerant, narrow-minded. You can see it, sir. The book says so, and that's that. If the Christians and Muslims were to allow doubt, the whole thing would collapse."

"But the Hindus also have their sacred scriptures," one lady objected, "and so do the other Asian religions."

"The Hindus and Buddhists have a great number of so-called sacred books, but none of them is considered the exclusive authority. They have a long tradition of inquiry and doubt. They have fostered skepticism: you can question everything. And the Hindus have 100,000 gods—you are free to choose your favorite one among them."

After the ensuing laughter had quieted down, he mused, "I wonder if the Pope and the bishops and all the other preachers really believe in what they are saying. They seem to be fairly educated people, and yet they carry on about virgin birth, ascension to heaven, sitting on the right hand of God, and all that other nonsense. They must have some doubts in their minds. They say all this and see the gullibility of the people and go home and laugh themselves silly, don't you think?"

He looked at us questioningly. Most of the people around the table had some Christian or Jewish elements in their background and seemed somewhat skeptical of what he was proposing. I found it difficult to accept such utter cynicism and hypocrisy on the part of these religious professionals.

"Why, Krishnaji?" I objected. "Why would they pretend to believe in these things and mislead everyone?"

"That's fairly simple," he responded, "there is much gain in it, much profit, power, prestige. Look at the Catholic Church, how fabulously rich it is. Enormous land holdings, buildings, fantastic art collections, jewels, gold and treasures—one can't imagine the wealth. Or the millions of dollars the evangelists and preachers are collecting in this country. And everybody bows to you, and kisses your hand. Think of the prestige and honor the bishops and cardinals get. So there are many reasons and rewards for getting involved in this racket. But I still wonder if they really believe in all these dogmas, doctrines and fairy tales."

Several people expressed a certain incredulity that the Pope and other high-ranking religious dignitaries would deliberately engage in a scheme of deception and exploitation.

"At some level of their being they must believe in what they say and represent," one teacher insisted.

Krishnamurti didn't reply directly to the various objections but went on with his own line of reasoning, "The other day I saw a chap on television, you know, one of the fundamentalist preachers—what do you call them?"

"Televangelist," a lady answered.

"Yes, a televangelist. He was talking to his congregation: hundreds, maybe thousands of them, young and old, in a large modern church. They were singing and praying, wearing robes and all that business, and the chap says, 'There will be a white hole in the constellation of...'" He looked around searchingly, "What's the name of that famous constellation?"

"Pleiades?" someone suggested.

"No, not the Pleiades."

"Orion?" I proposed.

"Yes, that's it. There will be a white hole in the constellation of Orion, and Jesus will appear in it with all his angels and apostles, and he will take his followers, 12,000 or some number, with him through the white hole into heaven. And the camera showed the faces of the audience, all worshipful, with tears in their eyes, believing all the rot the man was saying."

While narrating the televangelist story, he had adopted a theatrical attitude, thrusting out his arms and mimicking the preacher's cloying histrionics. We watched his performance with increasing fascination, with some tittering here and there, which finally exploded in exuberant laughter. It was not only his expert parody which was so hilarious, but also the notion that Krishnamurti the 'World Teacher' could be sitting in front of a television set, watching the televangelist go through his *spiel*. On a number of previous occasions he had described several Christian reverends, who performed on their own television channels, soliciting funds by selling religion, miracles and healing.

"One can't imagine the gullibility of the people there," he went on, rather more seriously, as a tone of incredulity crept into his voice, "all of them completely gullible, soaking it up, buying every word of it. And everything he said was based on the Bible; it was supposed to be the absolute, literal truth. The absurdity of it all!"

A trustee asked, "What is the name of the preacher you were watching, Krishnaji?"

He had forgotten the name—after all, there were dozens of preachers on the airwaves. But his recollection of other telling details—the kind of smile, the robe, the style of preaching and singing—was both witty and phenomenal. A guessing game ensued, in which most of us participated, revealing our fairly wide-spread knowledge of the more prominent religious entertainers. After everyone had finally agreed which preacher he was referring to, he contended, "That man cannot possibly believe what he is telling those people."

At this point, practically everyone was ready to concede that large-scale deception and exploitation was taking place on television in the name of religion. Large numbers of the public became all-too-willing victims, because of loneliness, despair and confusion. Even so, there was a peep of dissent from the inevitable but-voice. A teacher suggested, "Okay, they deceive and make money, and so on, but I'm sure they believe in Jesus, and the Scriptures, and...."

"No, madam," Krishnamurti countered emphatically, "that's just not good enough. Any old bird can claim a belief in Jesus and carry on with his sordid business—that's just too easy."

I sometimes felt that he was too categorical in his blanket rejection of things Christian. "But what about the mystics?" I asked, changing the subject. "Meister Eckhardt, St. John of the Cross, Hildegard von Bingen, Theresa of Avila—didn't they have some insight into, some contact with, the sacred during their lives?"

"As far as I understand, sir," he answered, "the Christian mystics were still rooted in Jesus, in the Church, and the whole Christian belief system. They never went beyond it."

I fell silent, not knowing what to answer.

"None of the religions of the book can really question what they are based on," another teacher stated. "They cannot go beyond the source of their revelation. They believe the book contains the unalterable, fixed truth."

Krishnamurti concurred, "No book contains the truth. Truth is a living thing. How can it be fixed? They have stopped inquiring, that's why they are dead. And you know what the word 'religion' means? I've looked it up in the dictionary. They don't really know the origin of the word, but there are two possible root meanings. One is 'gathering, collecting, binding'. And it also means 'pondering over, observing, caring'. We are saying, religion is the gathering of all energy to find truth."

We fell silent. All at once I could see religion—not as an institution, not as an organized hierarchy, not as a belief system with temples and churches, books and dogmas — but as a living endeavor, as a flame burning in the mind.

Soon after we rose from the table and carried the dishes into the kitchen, Krishnamurti lending a helping hand.

ON THE DAY OF THE LAST TALK, SUNDAY, MAY 22, I HAD THE rare opportunity of watching a feature-length film with Krishnamurti in the same theater. It was at five o'clock at the Ojai Playhouse, the local movie theater in the heart of town. There were several hundred guests, who had come to see the premiere of the film, *The Challenge of Change* produced by Evelyne Blau, a trustee of the Foundation. The subject of the film was none other than Krishnamurti himself.

Just a few minutes before the scheduled start of the film Krishnamurti and Mary Z. arrived and quickly took their seats in the back rows of the theater. I thought it remarkable how shy he was, practically making himself invisible, only hours after an illuminating talk on religion and meditation.

The film portrayed him and his work from the early theosophical days until the present, telling the story of a fairy tale life, that seemed to spring directly from *A Thousand-And-One Nights*.

A FEW DAYS LATER, ON MAY 27, WE HAD AN EARLY LUNCH at 12:30, so that Krishnamurti and Mary Z. could leave at two o'clock to catch their flight to England.

It had been an extraordinary season. More than ever, Krishnamurti's coming and going had been like a powerful storm, which stirred up everything and everyone. Afterwards, nothing was quite the same; until, of course, our habitual patterns set in again, like dust settling on bookshelves.

# Chapter 18
## A CULMINATION OF DIALOGUE

### Starters

*Shepherd's salad, a salad of many
different greens with vinaigrette
and blue cheese dressing.
Marinated artichoke hearts,
olive and tomato salad.
Grated carrot and ginger salad.*

### Main Dishes

*Leek and potato soup.
Pasta primavera: short ribbon pasta with
green peas, carrots, zucchini, red and green
bell peppers, garnished with pine nuts and
fresh basil, served with grated Parmesan cheese.
Steamed green beans with slivered almonds
and finely chopped parsley.*

### Dessert

*Fruit salad with yogurt,
sweetened with maple syrup.*

WHILE WE WERE STRUGGLING TO REGAIN OUR BEARINGS after his departure, Krishnamurti was confronted with a series of difficulties at Brockwood Park. In April, a fire had badly damaged his bedroom and sitting room, so that he had to use different quarters for some time. In June, Dorothy Simmons, the principal of the school, had a stroke. Four administrators were appointed to take over her duties, which led to a rift between staff members. A long, drawn-out struggle ensued, despite Krishnamurti's attempts to bring about harmony. A more creative event in June was the meeting of Krishnamurti and David Bohm at Brockwood Park. Two dialogues between the two old friends were video-recorded and entitled *The Future of Humanity*.

Some time in August, 1983, we received the electrifying news that Krishnamurti would be coming to Ojai in early September, shortly after the conclusion of the Brockwood Park Gathering; he would stay with us for a whole month. The reason for this unaccustomed visit was that, because of the lawsuit Rajagopal had initiated, a date had been fixed for Krishnamurti and Mary Z. to make their depositions in Ventura. The appointed day was September 20 and this, of course, required their presence in California.

THE DIRECTOR ASKED ME TO GO WITH HIM TO THE AIRPORT to pick up Krishnamurti, Mary Z. and Dr. Parchure, an Indian physician accompanying him. It was a bright, sunny day as we drove the school van along the Pacific Coast Highway to LAX. The flight was on time, and we didn't have to wait long.

The director suddenly pointed out a small group of passengers coming up the walkway toward the exit. Then I made out Mary Z., who was pushing a wheelchair with someone in it. I didn't immediately recognize Krishnamurti, since he was bundled up in blankets. Dr. Parchure, his personal medical attendant, was pushing a baggage cart piled high with suitcases. The director and I walked over to welcome them.

Krishnamurti looked vulnerable and tiny, like a child, with a blanket wrapped round his legs and torso. He was looking agitated and flushed, with a rare color in his cheeks. After we had loaded the luggage into the back of the van, the five of us set out on the drive north.

It was the first time I had gotten to ride with Krishnamurti in the same vehicle. Somehow, I thought of it as something special, a privilege, although I wasn't sure why. As we were driving through Santa Monica, Malibu, Oxnard and Ventura, Krishnamurti was taciturn, looking out the window at the shimmering blueness and the parched yellow hills. Mary Z. was sitting up front with the director, asking questions about the school. Dr. P. was on the seat behind them, reading a magazine. Krishnamurti was sitting on the left in a row by himself, while I brought up the rear. Every so often, I thought I felt powerful vibrations of silence emanating from him, permeating the vehicle. But my own thoughts, the noise of the car, and the heavy traffic on the highway distracted me from the quiet immensity.

THE FIRST LUNCH, THE FOLLOWING DAY, SEPTEMBER 8, consisted of marinated artichoke heart, olive and tomato salad, a carrot and ginger salad, leek and potato soup, pasta primavera served with grated Parmesan cheese, and steamed green beans adorned with slivered almonds and lots of finely chopped parsley. For dessert I made a fruit salad, with yogurt sweetened with maple syrup. It was a small luncheon with only eight of us.

Mary Z. told us about Krishnamurti's experience on the flight from London Heathrow to LAX. He was in the first-class section of the Boeing 747, when one of the flight operators, noticing his interest in the technical details of the plane, invited him into the cockpit. He was fascinated by the many dials, screens, monitors and meters necessary to operate this giant flying machine.

One of the teachers jokingly remarked, "You really should be wearing the captain's hat, sir."

We proceeded to calculate how many miles he might have traveled throughout his life. Assuming that normally he circled the globe at least once a year—taking into account his early voyages by steamer—we arrived at an approximate figure of more than a million miles. We were awed. All at once, he recalled a joke he had heard recently. "It's the maiden flight of the first fully computerized, fully automated, pilotless and crewless supersonic jet across the Atlantic," he recounted, with a charming twinkle in his eye. "The airplane is fully booked after an enormous media campaign. The passengers are seated and the take-off proceeds smoothly. Once in the air, the automatic intercom clicks on to welcome the passengers, 'Welcome, ladies and gentlemen, on our maiden flight from London to New York on the first fully computerized, pilotless and crewless aircraft. The computerized flight system is certified to the highest safety standards. Relax in your seats and enjoy your flight, while the robot flight attendants serve you refreshments. Rest assured that absolutely nothing can go wrong, nothing can go wrong, nothing can go wrong....'"

While we were still enjoying a good laugh, I remembered my newsman's hat and began, as soon as everyone had quieted down, "Well, Krishnaji, you may have heard of the recent air disaster—it happened just two days ago—when the Soviets shot down Korean Airlines flight 007 over Sakhalin island...."

This started everyone talking, since the event had dominated the news for the past forty-eight hours.

THROUGHOUT MY LIFE I HAVE BEEN A MOVIE FAN, PREFERRING shows on the big screen to TV monitors, and going to theaters as often as I could. Of course, I try to avoid the brainless fare and find the rare masterpiece. Every so often, the conversation at the lunch table revolved around the most recent film releases. I would sometimes give a review, after I had seen a movie in Ventura or Santa Barbara—or, less frequently, in Ojai. Krishnamurti was usually quite interested in my critique but, at some point or other, would cut short my learned discourse by simply asking, "Was it good?"

He didn't seem to go for art films, social or romantic dramas, or films with a message. He preferred action yarns—adventure, westerns, thrillers, and the like. During one lunch in early September we were talking about the so-called 'spaghetti westerns', that had brought fame to Clint Eastwood. Krishnamurti, who liked the tough actor, admitted to enjoying his films. A lady guest expressed undisguised shock. "How can you like all that shooting and killing, Krishnaji?" she asked.

He looked at her with quiet attention. An impish twinkle crept into his eye, as he replied, "But they're not really killing each other. It's all make-believe: They're using blanks, and the blood is ketchup or red color. After they're shot and fall down, they get up again. It's only for show."

The lady wasn't entirely convinced and stammered, "But why, why...?"

Krishnamurti politely disregarded her fluster. Leaning back in his chair, he said, "And I like the scenery, the background of mountains and valleys. And it's lovely to see the horses running at full speed and jumping over rocks and gullies."

I was always surprised by his capacity to invoke a poetic mood with the barest minimum of words, drawing a quick sketch of a situation with just a few verbal strokes.

Someone mentioned the film *E.T. — The Extraterrestrial*, which had been a huge success in the U.S. and overseas. Several of us reviewed and praised the tale of the visit to earth of the endearing creature from outer space. All at once, Krishnamurti became intrigued by what he heard and started asking questions about the film. I pointed out that a theater in Ventura had matinee showings of the film. Erna Lilliefelt promptly suggested to him that they go to one of the early shows. His eyes lit up, and he gladly accepted the suggestion.

The day after his cinematic experience, some of us asked him, "Krishnaji, how did you like the film?"

He became a bit dreamy-eyed at the recollection of the story of the extraterrestrial and simply said, "I liked it." After a moment's deliberation, he added, "It was really adorable. Such an enchanting creature, E.T."

Erna quipped with a smile, "Well, Krishnaji, you are E.T. You are the Extraterrestrial."

He didn't say anything but only smiled. We broke into delighted laughter at the analogy, and soon he joined in.

AT LUNCH ON SATURDAY, SEPTEMBER 15, THERE WERE ONLY eight of us. The conversation was about the time when Krishnamurti was first introduced to upper crust English Victorian society, under the tutelage of Annie Besant. He fondly remembered her, referring to her as 'Dr. Besant'.

Alan asked him, "Did you ever meet George Bernard Shaw? He was supposed to be a good friend of Annie Besant's."

Krishnamurti laughed, "He liked to refer to himself as GBS. The first time I met him was shortly after my brother and I had arrived in

England. I was awfully shy in those days and hardly ever spoke a word. One day we were invited to dinner at a mansion, I think it was in Wimbledon. We sat at a long table, festively made up, with candles and crystal, servants and all the rest of it. Dr. Besant was sitting at one end of the table, my brother and I to either side of her, and at the other end of the long table was GBS, with his long white hair and beard. The other guests were high society people and the conversation was very polite and subdued, when suddenly, in the middle of the meal, GBS called out in his loud sonorous voice, 'Annie, I've heard you are raising a new Messiah from India.' "

Krishnamurti paused and, with an impish grin, pointed a long tremulous index finger at his chest. We started to laugh, and Erna asked, "What was the reaction of the other guests?"

"There was a silence for a moment, then they all laughed."

"And what about you, sir?" I asked. "How did you feel?"

"Well, I was just sitting there and couldn't run away. I felt horribly embarrassed, and blushed, and wished the ground would open up and swallow me whole."

At that, our laughter intensified and, for a moment, we shared wonderful, liberating mirth.

BECAUSE OF THE UPCOMING DEPOSITION IN THE LAWSUIT, the lunch table conversation sometimes centered around lawyers, judges and the prevalence of litigation in modern societies.

"That reminds me of something that happened in India some time ago," Krishnamurti began. "I was giving a talk in Bombay, and afterwards a man came to see me. He was an older man with white hair, of dignified bearing, and he told me his story: he had been a judge at the high court for many years and had a family with several children. One morning he said to himself, 'For many years now I have been passing judgment on all sorts of people—criminals and robbers, as well as corrupt businessmen and politicians. But I don't really know what truth is, or even if justice exists. So how can I possibly practice justice, if I myself don't know justice?' And so he decided to follow the Indian tradition, retired from his post, left his family—after taking care of their welfare, of course—and wandered off into a remote forest to meditate and find out truth. He meditated for twenty-five years all by himself in the forest, you understand? For twenty-five years he carried on, and then the other evening he came to hear the talk in Bombay. When he came to see me afterwards, he had tears in his eyes. 'I heard what you said,' he told me, 'and suddenly I realized that I have been deceiving myself: for twenty-five years I thought I was meditating, but I have only been hypnotizing myself.' That's what he said. And for someone who had practiced meditation every day for twenty-five years to admit that he had deceived himself; that is something enormous—the nature of a human being like that."

Krishnamurti fell silent after this dramatic story, as did all of us around the table. What would I do, I said to myself, if I suddenly discovered that my life had been one long self-deception? I really didn't know.

SEPTEMBER 19 WAS THE FIRST DAY OF THE NEW SCHOOL TERM. On the following three days there weren't any lunches at A.V., since Krishnamurti, Mary Z. and the Lilliefelts were busy giving depositions in Ventura. The lengthy legal proceedings, however, were far from being concluded: they dragged on for several more years and were not settled until June, 1986.

On October 10, Columbus Day, Krishnamurti, accompanied by Mary Z. and Dr. P., departed for England, where he resumed his regular traveling schedule, continuing to India in November.

IT HAD BEEN A STORMY SEASON AT THE SCHOOL. A NUMBER OF parents, joined by several of the teachers, were up in arms, rebelling against the school administration and some of its recent directives. It seemed a curious coincidence that, after Brockwood Park and the Rajghat School in Varanasi, Ojai now should be experiencing turmoil and conflict of its own. Discontent was not entirely unknown at Oak Grove, since many people who joined Krishnamurti schools came more often than not with high expectations, demanding nothing less than perfection—if not from themselves, then at least from those around them. And since, with one or two notable exceptions, we were all ordinary mortals, the clash with reality for those who expected an instant paradise of rare, enlightened human beings was starkly sobering. Krish-namurti sometimes quoted a well-known saying that hinted at this, "We've met the enemy—it is us."

THE PREVIOUS YEAR TWO DIRECTORS HAD BEEN PUT IN charge of the Oak Grove School, one for administrative, the other for educational matters. On February 21, 1984, the two directors drove to the airport to pick up Krishnamurti, Mary Z., and David and Saral Bohm. It was the only time that, by a rare coincidence, Krishnamurti and David arrived at LAX at the same time. And it was unusual for us, the welcoming committee, to greet the two great friends simultane-ously beneath the pepper tree.

Krishnamurti was rather tired and didn't come for lunch the next day. But the day after that he joined us at the lunch table and at one point told us a joke he had heard recently.

"You may have heard this joke—about the naming of the divine child in Bethlehem," he began. "The child was in the manger, sur-rounded by oxen and sheep, while his mother, Mary, and Joseph were discussing what name to give him. Solomon was suggested, Moses, and David, but they couldn't quite agree. At that moment, the Magi, the three wise men from the East, entered the stable. Paying homage to the new-born child, they placed offerings of myrrh and frankincense before him. The third chap, who was very tall, knelt down to present his gift of gold. As he got up, he bumped his head on the low rafters of the stable and exclaimed in pain, 'Jesus Christ!' Mary turned to Joseph and said, 'That's a nice name. That's what we'll call him.'"

While we were still laughing, he looked around the table and said apologetically, "I hope I'm not offending anybody."

One of the trustees asked him about his time in India. He gave only a brief indication of his busy program and the difficulties that he had encountered there, before we adjourned for the day.

During lunch the following day, Friday, February 24, David Bohm initiated a conversation by putting a question to Krishnamurti, who was sitting next to him. He apparently had a great many questions on his mind and was keen on formulating and examining them with him. A lucid flow of meaning started to move between the two minds, like waves from one shore to the other. Several people, including myself, felt confident enough to contribute to the conversation. This added to the dynamics of the dialogue, bringing all of us together in one movement. The spontaneity of the discussion enhanced the feeling of togetherness. Starting with a simple question and a simple reply, it swiftly took on the weight and depth of great seriousness.

Erna Lilliefelt had apparently noticed a recording device under the counter by the window. She leaned over to me and whispered, "Why don't we record this?"

I whispered back, "Yes, a good idea—but we haven't got a blank tape."

She persisted, as was her natural tendency, "Can't we get one? Perhaps run over to the office?"

Meanwhile, Krishnamurti and David had formulated the question, "Is there a global outlook? And what does it imply?"

This was a question of deep concern for me, not least because I had been teaching a course at the High School, called 'Current World Affairs', which was directly related to this issue. For an instant I experienced resistance at the prospect of missing out on a portion of the illuminating dialogue. Then suddenly I remembered and whispered to Erna, "I've got some tapes in my room. I'll quickly go and get them."

It took me less than a minute to return with two blank tapes.

The exploration of the global human situation continued over our dirty plates. Everyone's attention was focused on the two friends, whose energies were passionately locked, though they exchanged their views with graceful ease.

For a moment I felt awkward, as I started to set up the cassette recorder, right next to Krishnamurti and David. They halted their deliberations and turned toward me with half puzzled, half amused expressions on their faces. There was a space of silence. To conceal my embarrassment, I briskly asked them, "I hope you don't mind if I record this conversation."

Neither of them saw any reason to object to my request and signaled their consent with a brief nod, before returning to the subject at hand. I slipped a blank cassette into the machine and punched the record button. The small wheels started to turn.

"How can one convey a global outlook to one's students?" Krishnamurti asked, thoughtfully pausing before he continued. "What do we actually mean by 'global outlook'? Can one live according to the perceptions one gains through such a global outlook?"

"Clearly, a global outlook must be related to wholeness, the wholeness of life," David suggested.

"Yes sir, not to be fragmented; not to see and think one thing, say another, and then do something altogether different."

We added our two cents' worth to the discussion. At one point, Krishnamurti asked David, "Sir, do you think there could be something like a global religion?"

For a moment there was excitement but also laughter, as we envisioned an organized form of global religion. But it soon became apparent that Krishnamurti rejected any such proposition out of hand, especially when it was suggested that his teaching constitute the basis for such a worldwide set-up. The notion was anathema to him and quite contrary to what he had in mind.

"We want to set man free," he declared with great seriousness, "not invent new fetters for him."

David pointed out that the various world religions had started out with an intent to be for the whole of humanity and to bring together all human beings. But each organized belief system eventually claimed to possess the truth, exclusive of all others, and had subsequently caused division, conflict and untold suffering throughout the course of history. He matter-of-factly stated that the question, 'Should there be a global religion?' was highly theoretical and, therefore, not beneficial to pursue. Krishnamurti concurred with his assessment, and we left it at that. We rose from the table in unison and carried our dirty dishes into the kitchen. There seemed to be a strange bond that united us for that moment. All sixteen of us had examined something together, had been of one mind for the past two hours, thanks in large part to the two catalysts.

The director and I briefly discussed what to do with the tape-recorder and the recording. Although we weren't sure whether there would be a follow-up to this highly unusual dialogue, we agreed that I hold on to the recorder for the following days, just in case a similar opportunity arose again. There had been numerous recordings of Krishnamurti, Dr. Bohm and others in dialogue, but the settings were always carefully stage-managed. Here, for the first time, we had recorded a conversation that occurred completely naturally—a lunch table conversation that yet had the full depth and scope of inquiry.

THE NEXT DAY WAS A SATURDAY, AND I EXPECTED approximately twenty guests for lunch. Before starting with the meal preparation in the morning, I set up the recorder, so that I could immediately go into action, if and when another dialogue occurred.

Krishnamurti looked across at David, who was still chewing his last morsels of food, and asked with a brief smile, "Well, sir, shall we continue where we left off yesterday?"

Taking a quick sip of water to clear his mouth, David smiled his endearing, open smile. Pushing one hand through his full but graying hair, he replied, "Well, yes. Where did we leave off?"

In fact, they found that they had left off at a point beyond which it made no sense to continue. Yesterday's inquiry into global religion had been left on the doorstep of the individual consciousness. The only conundrum was that Krishnamurti repeatedly and convincingly demonstrated that there was no 'individual' as such. He said, "We are not individuals. The word 'individual' means 'not divided'. But we are divided, fragmented human beings, both within and between ourselves; therefore, we are not individuals."

I could follow his argument and grasped it intellectually, but I was far from seeing it as a rock-solid fact. Clearly, to have this insight in the context of 'you are the world, and the world is you' necessitated an exceedingly subtle perception.

I looked at Krishnamurti who seemed to be weighing a question in his mind. He fully and carefully regarded David and finally asked, "What is honesty, sir?"

As so often, the form and content of what he said were extremely simple, but a deeper significance—which lay beyond the words—was conveyed non-verbally. David did not take the question lightly, nor was he tempted to offer a quick, simplistic answer. He started by carefully considering the etymological root of the word 'honesty'. There was a playful quality to this type of investigation, that both Krishnamurti and David liked to engage in, and it was just this marriage between the playful and the serious that allowed actual meaning to blossom forth. David had a great capacity for memorizing words, their roots, and their original meanings. "'Honesty'," he explained, "is related to and has the same basic meaning as 'honor'. And 'honor' signifies 'official dignity, repute, esteem, reward and good name.'"

Krishnamurti pulled a skeptical face, objecting less to the etymological definitions than to accepting these meanings for the present investigation. "No, sir, that's what the politicians are concerned with — you know, good name, reputation and all the rest of it, while actually they continue to be deceitful, ambitious and false."

"Well," David said, "the meaning of honesty, as we now understand it, is 'uprightness, trustworthiness, integrity.'"

That appeared to reconcile Krishnamurti to the true significance of the word 'honesty', since he seemed intent on establishing a connection between it and truth, moral behavior, and no deceit.

Halfway through the conversation, Krishnamurti suddenly halted and looked at David with an expression of surprise, "You have a meeting at the school this afternoon, don't you?"

David nodded quietly and Krishnamurti went on, "Well, it's almost three o'clock. We'd better stop, don't you think?"

Krishnamurti had encouraged his friend to conduct a number of discussion meetings with both School staff and Foundation trustees during his stay at Ojai, which this year lasted only two weeks. Without any sense of rivalry he promoted his friend, transcending the trivial, possessive delineations which institutionalized bureaucracy all too easily sets up. The following day, he asked him, "How did it go?" And David gave a summary of the meeting.

WE CHECKED THE RECORDINGS FROM THE PREVIOUS TWO lunch dialogues but found the sound quality to be inferior. We, therefore, exchanged the old recorder for a newer model. It was a recording device with something of history, in that Krishnamurti had used it for his solitary dictations, published under the title *Krishnamurti to Himself*. Somehow, I felt elated to get to use this state-of-the-art machine.

Now the discussions became more formalized. One of the trustees would introduce the session by saying into the table microphone, "February 26, 1984: after-lunch table discussion at Arya Vihara, Ojai, California, between Mr. J. Krishnamurti, Dr. David Bohm and others." Fortunately, the sense of free-flowing inquiry and uninhibited participation by those present was not affected by these formalities.

It was Sunday, and there were nineteen guests around the table. For the moment, everybody seemed possessed of a sense of leisure, unpreoccupied by any extraneous obligations. It was the end of lunch and Krishnamurti whispered to David—as if by now it was the natural thing to do, "Shall we start?"

And they delved right into the dialogue, while some of the guests were still spooning their dessert, ice cream. Neither of them had a pre-formulated question. It was, indeed, as if they were taking a stroll along a wooded path in the dappled light, talking over the prevailing patterns of life and consciousness.

Krishnamurti used the analogy of 'the ebb and flow of life'. Both agreed that the movements of life were unified and of the same nature—the outgoing and incoming movements of consciousness were one and the same, just as the ocean tides are movements of the same water, differing only in the direction of flow. The outer created the inner; the inner influenced and shaped the outer. Which of the two came first and was predominant was the perennial dilemma of the chicken and the egg. In fact, at a most telling moment in the discussion, Krishnamurti suggested that there was no 'inner', at least not in the sense in which we usually thought of it. If any true 'inner' existed, it was the unknown and unknowable. After some deliberation, they both con-curred on this vital point.

I was both intrigued and mystified by the proposition. Although I was far from grasping its essence, I glimpsed enough of its truth to be tantalized.

Krishnamurti proceeded to enter the realm of everyday living by inquiring into right action. It was action which did not contain within itself the seed of division and incompleteness and, therefore, was free of the need for further adjustment. As he put it, "Can I live without a sin-gle problem? Can I be free to watch and observe?"

Putting the question negatively did away with the multitudinous pos-itive formulations of what constituted happiness, enlightenment, etc.. As he pointed out, "Our brains, from early childhood, have been trained to solve problems. But we have created most of the problems which con-front us. Problems are a form of stimulation; we are addicted to them. Without any problems, we feel dead."

He suggested that we needed a brain entirely unpreoccupied and free of problems in order to solve the problems that naturally arose—at the very moment they occurred. Although it sounded like a circular rid-dle, the proverbial 'Catch-22', it was eminently logical and practical. For most of us listening he seemed to be offering a description of what lay beyond the sunlit horizon. We could see it clearly, but how to get there? What prevented us from grasping what he was hinting at and, in one fell swoop, making it an instantaneous actuality? Was there a gap, a barrier, which distorted our perception? Or did it require a total action, an internal, undivided immediacy, which we were somehow incapable of?

We seemed to be on a roll. By now, the after-lunch dialogue had become a standard feature. The guests virtually expected me to bring out the cassette recorder so we could get started.

It was the fourth dialogue, Monday, March 27, 1984, and Krishnamurti began by asking David, "Sir, is there anything beyond the brain — except nature?"

In the ensuing conversation it was suggested that we live almost exclusively in a world of our own making — the interpreted, analyzed, manipulated world of our daily life, shaped and created by thought. From the chairs we sat on, the table we ate off, the cars we drove on linear roads, to our professional lives and social interactions, and the whole inner make-up of ideas and memories — all of that was created by the brain. And although the human being, through the instrument of thought, manipulated, exploited and tried to control nature, the totality of nature clearly lay outside the scope of the brain. Nature was the larger context, the matrix and ground from which we sprang and of which we were but minuscule parts. Nature had evolved the brain.

Eventually, Krishnamurti asked, "Is there something apart from nature and the brain which has created its own reality? Is there something that is qualitatively entirely different?"

The trend of the inquiry reminded me distantly of the *Ending of Time* dialogues four years earlier, because David suggested in response, "Perhaps nothingness is that quality, is that state."

As they tried to define that which was ultimately indefinable, they equated it with love, truth and beauty, and saw it as the source of attention. Now Krishnamurti moved into the more practical sphere by asking, "Is it possible to completely empty the brain of its psychological content?"

He seemed to imply that nothingness could not manifest, become 'operative', as it were, until this psychological emptying had occurred, which, of course, implied a complete abandonment of self-interest, even the annihilation of the structure of the self: the 'I' and the 'me'.

Most of us sat silent, as the afternoon sunlight streamed in through the curtained windows and reflected off the dark surface of the table, unable to say anything. 'How? How?', one wanted to ask. But we knew better than to ask for a method.

Suddenly, Saral remembered that David had another afternoon dialogue session with the staff at the school pavilion. We got up quickly from the table, the vital question still alive in our minds.

SEVERAL TRUSTEES REVIEWED THE DIALOGUES RECORDED on the new recorder and found them to be of inferior quality. The background noise of tableware, shifting chairs, thuds and coughs had distorted the sound. They suggested that we use the high quality reel-to-reel Nagra recorder usually used for recording public talks, formal dialogues and interviews. I felt apprehensive about this change, since I would have to use a separate microphone to pick up the sound signals and headphones to adjust the auditory levels of the recording. Besides, the threading in and switching of the reel tapes was a rather sensitive affair, not recommended for someone who easily turned into a nervous fumbler, like myself.

At the opening of the fifth after-lunch dialogue, Krishnamurti joked, "Before we all go to sleep, what are we going to discuss?"

Nobody seemed to have a relevant question on their mind, so, after an interval of silent deliberation, he asked simply, "What is corruption?"

After a brief semantic examination, which revealed that 'corruption' meant 'fragmented, broken up', we looked at possible historical causes for the pervasive corruption of human society.

Krishnamurti hesitated to allow the concept of 'society' into the dialogue, since it suggested an entity that was separate, externalized, and both autonomous and anonymous. Invariably, it negated the responsibility of each single human being.

"Society is put together by human beings, it is what we are," he insisted. "Society is not different from us. We are society."

He, thus, firmly anchored the essence and relevance of our discussion. For him, there was nothing theoretical about it. To drive home the point to each one of us present, he altered the phrasing of the question into a simple, direct, "Why am I corrupt?"

He asked the question for us—he clearly felt that he was not corrupt.

Nor had I ever witnessed any indication that he might share that common and destructive quality with the rest of us. This inescapably confronted us with the question, as in a mirror. He repeated it intermittently, and the relentless force of self-inquiry inherent in this simple formulation pushed everyone against the wall. Any answer we came up with was swept aside as rationalization and roundabout excuse.

David suggested that people had lost faith in the integrity of society. Someone else cited overpopulation and the concomitant pressure for survival, the search for security, and competition. But Krishnamurti again and again returned to the original question, dissatisfied with any explanation. Vicariously he asked, "Why have I become like this? Why am I corrupt? What has made me corrupt?"

I could observe within myself that one really shied away from seriously putting this question to oneself. Probably not many of those at the table, including myself, really perceived the fact of their corruption. David saw what Krishnamurti was driving at and rephrased the question in an objective form, true to the scientific method, "How does corruption affect the brain?"

Krishnamurti however insisted on putting it right on everyone's doorstep, "Put yourself that question: 'why am I corrupt?'"

Probing for the inner cause of this pervasive corruption, he tentatively offered any number of answers, which none of us had entertained.

"Is it knowledge?" he asked. "Is it the tremendous importance given to the intellect?"

He never seemed quite ready to accept an answer, even his own. He remained in a state of not-knowing; he kept on probing, pushing, questioning, never allowing any formulation, however plausible, to become a conclusion. A conclusion was a dead end for him. Finally, after repeating the question, "Why am I corrupt?" between twenty and thirty times over a two-hour period, he made that enormous quantum leap that only he seemed capable of. It was the unthought-of, inconceivable *dénouement* of a spellbinding psychological thriller, in which we were all participants, victims, perpetrators. And the 180-degree turn from the horizontal to the vertical plane, imbued with clarity and simplicity, was something none of us had envisioned.

Even so, he refrained from insisting that his proposition was right. The beauty of the argument dwelt in questioning the question, or rather the motive behind it. He suggested that wanting a conclusion—which essentially implied knowing the cause, which then in turn would become knowledge—was itself corruption. Wanting to find the cause of a problem was the same thing. That which had been causing corruption, that is, thought and knowledge, were also asking the question.

Was this a case of leading the argument *ad absurdumn*?, I asked myself. Or was it the beauty of an investigation into *what is*, a movement from nothingness into nothingness? To positively clarify the point he was making—and I think he fully meant what he said at that moment—Krishnamurti simply stated, "I don't want to know."

Who could keep pace with that?

THE FOLLOWING DAY, FEBRUARY 29, NO DIALOGUE OCCURRED during lunch. Perhaps everyone needed a breather, or there was a need to get down to the nitty-gritty, since only money matters were discussed. The day after that, however, Krishnamurti was ready for another dialogue session with David Bohm and our assortment of minor minds. Starting out with one of his deceptively simple questions, which yet had the potential of leading to the gateway of actuality, he asked, "What is time?"

There were various explanations, definitions and tangential views put forth, but he was intent on making the examination factual, personally relevant, and immediate. "What does time mean to you?" he wanted to know.

As we voiced our perceptions, the various aspects of time gradually manifested. There was the past, the present, the future, becoming, continuity, death, change, beginning and ending, memory, thought and knowledge, and the now. But he wanted to explore the everyday fact of time, the simple or complex actuality of it. He wanted us to look deeply into our own minds, not theoretically but actually, while we were speaking and listening. Finally he stated, like a magician who makes things disappear, "There can only be change if there is ending. If I look for change, there is no change. So I won't look for it. Ending without a future means no time."

I think we understood what he meant as far as word and meaning went; but at the fundamental level, where word and action did not differ, none of us seemed quite to be there. A brief moment of stillness preceded the noise of chairs being moved and tableware clinking as we got up from the table.

THE NEXT DAY, KRISHNAMURTI AND MARY Z. WENT TO Los Angeles, and there was no lunch. But on Saturday, March 3, I recorded another after-lunch dialogue between Krishnamurti, David and various trustees and teachers. It differed substantially from the previous six conversations, both in topic and quality. In fact, because of the sensitive and specific subject matter, David spoke only minimally.

The school had been experiencing a number of difficulties. The lunch guests were primarily staff and trustees, and everyone seemed to be preoccupied by the recent complaints and reproaches. The previous day, Krishnamurti had received a serious letter of complaint from a parent group, and he was quite upset. As we were talking over the issue, he appeared to become more furious, fiercely challenging all of us, who sounded rather apologetic and complacent. When someone usually quite close to him spoke of trust, he impatiently turned on her with the words, "What do you mean by trust? Why should I trust you?" It resembled a verbal battle during which nobody was allowed to get away with a careless remark.

The problem of the school did not go away. The questions were how to structure it, especially with the recent addition of a high school; who was in charge and responsible; how to relate to the parents; what role did Krishnamurti's teachings play in the affairs of the school, and did they conflict with the academic curriculum? Krishnamurti discussed these matters with trustees, parents and staff time and again during the coming months. There was no easy solution; it was an ongoing labor of love, if it was to make any difference at all.

DAVID AND SARAL BOHM LEFT THE FOLLOWING MORNING, on March 4, to meet various commitments of their own. Thus, they did not attend the Ojai Talks of 1984. It turned out, in fact, that these six unusual lunch table conversations at Arya Vihara were the very last recorded dialogues between Krishnamurti and David—a meeting of brilliant minds, a rare walk of two great friends along the shaded trails of life.

*Chapter 19*

# C R E A T I V I T Y

### Starters

*Tossed green salad with
vinaigrette or garlic dressing.
Greek salad, made with chunks of tomatoes, onions,
bell peppers, topped with olives and feta cheese.
Greek-Indian cucumber salad, with yogurt,
cumin powder and cilantro.*

### Main Dishes

*Asparagus soup.
Vegetarian moussaka, made with
layers of eggplant,
bulgur wheat and walnuts,
with a bechamel sauce
flavored with cinnamon.
Zucchini in tomato sauce.*

### Dessert

*Persimmon cream, made with
ripe Kaki persimmons and cream.
Fresh, seasonal fruit.*

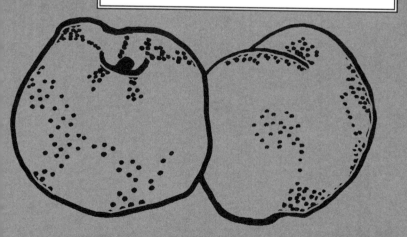

IT WAS A HIGHLY UNUSUAL EVENT. KRISHNAMURTI HAD BEEN invited to give a talk at the government-operated National Laboratory Research Center at Los Alamos, New Mexico, birthplace of the atomic bomb and the atomic age. Forty years earlier, Richard Feynman had worked there on the Manhattan project which David Bohm had almost joined.

On March 20, 1984, Krishnamurti spoke to several hundred resident scientists about 'Creativity in Science'. Although he didn't entirely negate the possibility of creativity occurring in the realm of science, he politely suggested that it was unlikely that what he considered to be creativity would flower in the present location. On the following day, he answered questions and answers regarding the same topic by the assembled physicists.

During lunch on the day after his return to Ojai, he and Mary Z. recounted some of their impressions of their three-day trip to Indian country to the few of us around the table. Finally he mused, "I wonder if any of what we said really affected them. The scientists are so rooted in knowledge, always gathering more and more of it. How can they put all of that aside?"

A lady trustee suggested, "But, Krishnaji, there must have been at least one or two among them who really listened to you. And perhaps some of what you were saying sneaked beyond the barrier of knowledge, and some seeds were left behind."

"That reminds me of a lovely story I heard recently," he said. "And, please, I'm not comparing the scientists to the people in the story, who happen to be robbers."

We all started to laugh at the droll way in which he introduced the telling of his anecdote.

"It was a family of robbers, and they had been robbers for many generations. The father would take his two sons out to rob people and teach them how to steal. After a profitable robbery, he would go to church with them and thank God for his kindness and light candles in the church, because this was their vocation. So one day they are returning from a successful heist, their pockets filled with money and stolen jewels, and are crossing the large square in front of their house. A crowd of people has gathered and they are listening to a man giving a sermon. As soon as the father hears what the man is talking about, he tells his sons, 'Quickly, cover your ears!' One of the two brothers obeys, but the other is curious to hear what the man is saying. And the preacher is telling his listeners, 'It's wrong to rob and steal from another person. Don't ever hurt a fellow human being, but be kind to one another.' He hears these words but continues with his life as a robber. And he lives in pain and inner conflict for the rest of his life."

"But couldn't he have changed his life and given up his robbing and stealing?" I asked.

Krishnamurti turned toward me, and I felt a powerful wave of energy. "Hey," he said with surprise and then widened his eyes to a comical expression, "you are not getting the story, Michael. It's his life, it's his livelihood."

The teacher next to me explained, "He hears the truth but doesn't act upon it. Therefore, it turns to poison and disturbs his life ever after."

"Well, yes," I said with an embarrassed laugh, "I understand that. But if he had changed his life, it wouldn't be a story—or would it?"

ONE WEEK LATER, ON MARCH 29, KRISHNAMURTI MET THE school staff at Pine Cottage at four o'clock in the afternoon. For some reason, several questions about food and the vegetarian diet were raised. Food was an issue that had been regularly examined from the very beginning of the school in 1975, and it came up again and again during staff and parent meetings. Naturally, food was an important concern, and it needed to be addressed in the proper context of culture, conditioning, health and right living. Although not all the trustees, nor all of the staff, and certainly not all the students' families were vegetarians, there had been an agreement from the beginning to maintain a vegetarian campus. Krishnamurti himself had been a vegetarian throughout his life, never tasting meat, fish, or fowl, but he was not at all interested in vegetarianism as a sectarian issue, a cause, or a movement. At one point he had clarified the question, "Nutritionally and scientifically it is not necessary to eat meat. One can live very healthily, normally, and have plenty of energy by having the right kind of food. Which means no meat."

But he was deeply concerned as to how divergent rules about the eating and non-eating of meat might affect the child. "Here we say, don't eat meat. They go back home, and the whole family eats it. Won't the child feel confused? Here this, there that. Are we creating an inner conflict in the student?"

As we carried on a lively debate about it, everybody adding their two-cents' worth, Krishnamurti kept simplifying our convoluted approach, clearing away the personal, emotional underbrush.

"I'm clearing the decks as we go along," he said with a slightly impish smile. "Look, sirs—keep it simple. No vegetarian-*ism*. I am not interested in vegetarian-*ism*. I am not a follower of vegetarianism. We are not vegetarians."

Some of us were slightly startled. What?

He noticed it at once and clarified, "No *ism*. There is no place for any *ism*, any dogma or ideology. I simply won't kill. It's wrong to kill. That's all."

We sat there in illumined silence. Suddenly everything seemed simple, clear and self-evident. His insight had cut through the deep-rooted entanglement of pros and cons, argument and counter-argument—in fact, to the very heart of the matter. A shy silence filled the bright room, and with quiet emphasis he added, "To kill another human being is the greatest evil."

We were held suspended by an exquisite stillness; then he all at once injected some light-hearted humor into the gathering, "But don't come to me and ask whether it's wrong to kill vegetables."

A lady teacher promptly felt impelled to sustain the argument and asked, "Well, in a way, it is like killing, isn't it? If I cut the cabbage and cauliflower from the ground...."

"But, madam, you've got to live! You can't just live on air and water." A punctuating pause. "No sir, you see, you continue with this...." His voice trailed off, leaving the sentence unfinished. "If you are an Eskimo and you live in the icy wastelands, what do you do? There are no vegetables and all that. So you hunt to stay alive, right?"

Nobody objected.

"But we are in California. There are all kinds of vegetables and fruit around, all year long. So it's easy to live on a vegetarian diet and be healthy and full of energy."

The issue came up again during lunch on Monday, April 2. Eight of us were discussing vegetarianism, drugs, smoking, alcohol, and so on, and whether the school could deal with these problems through rules. Seeing the necessity to have some rules at a school, we puzzled over the question of how to avoid the conflict they brought about in the students.

The following Sunday morning, Krishnamurti met with the staff and inquired into the ending of the self, pointing out that knowledge was the self. To entertain the notion that the sense of self, that seemingly immutable feeling of identity was nothing but a bundle of memories was both liberating and exhilarating for me.

There were only six of us for lunch on Monday—it was the day of the Academy Awards ceremony in Los Angeles. We were having an easy, delightful conversation, a conversation among friends, talking about experiences that touched upon the realm of the supernatural, the miraculous and extrasensory.

"I must tell you a story which happened to me in India some time ago," Krishnamurti began and looked at us with a serious expression. "This is not imaginary but factual. A group of us were sitting on a stone terrace overlooking a lawn and a small rose garden. It was a lovely evening, and we were conversing in a leisurely fashion when, all at once, the servant came and announced that there was someone who wanted to see us. It was a poor itinerant *sannyasi*, and he wanted to give us a demonstration. So we agreed. He requested that a newspaper be brought. Then he asked the servant, who was holding the newspaper, to fold it down the middle, then once more, and then again. All this time he was sitting cross-legged on the lawn, on the side opposite the rose bushes, about ten or fifteen yards from us. Next, he told the servant to place the folded newspaper at the bottom of the stairs to the terrace. He asked us to watch the newspaper very carefully. He just kept sitting there, with closed eyes, but he never touched the newspaper or handled it. As we were closely watching the newspaper, it started to shrink. It gradually became smaller and smaller, until all at once it had entirely disappeared. It had vanished into thin air. The whole newspaper was gone in just a few moments."

Krishnamurti held out his slim, elegant hands and illustrated the process by bringing together his palms. Suddenly, as they almost touched, he dramatically jerked them apart. "Gone!" He studied our mystified faces. Everyone appeared incredulous and impressed.

I might have questioned the eyewitness report more skeptically, if it hadn't been told by Krishnamurti. Instead I only asked, "It completely disappeared into thin air?"

"I was watching him and the newspaper like a hawk, and also the others were carefully observing the whole event. I couldn't figure out how he did it." As if to certify the reliability of his fellow observers, he added, "None of us had touched any alcohol."

We quietly contemplated the story, waiting for him to offer an explanation of the magical event, but none seemed to be forthcoming. After an interval of silence, I wondered out loud, "But why did he do it? I mean, why did he come to demonstrate his magic to you?"

"I'm not sure," Krishnamurti replied. "Maybe he was drawn by the presence of the group, maybe by the presence of K. Afterwards we offered him money, but he refused it. Accepting money for this would have made it cheap, you know." He made a small dismissive gesture as if to indicate that the tradition of many of the Indian *sannyasis* was outside the realm of commercialism.

"But was it real?" Erna asked.

He gave a short delighted laugh, "Oh, yes, it was real."

He clearly enjoyed seeing us puzzled by the mystery and letting its enigmatic aspect puncture our consciousness, which was either too gullible or which hardly ever dared step beyond the parameters of cause and effect.

"But what did it mean?" someone asked.

"Maybe it didn't mean anything at all. Many of the *yogis* and *sannyasis* in India gain an extraordinary power through constant practice. If you work at it every day with all your might, you can accomplish astonishing things—walking on hot coals, materializing or dematerializing things, fasting for weeks on end, levitating, holding your breath for a long time, and so on and on. At the end of it, you ask, what does it all mean? What of it? What difference does it make if you can sit on pins or hold your breath for half an hour? Do you see, sir?"

"But why do they go through all the struggle to gain these powers?" I asked.

"Ah, that's fairly simple, isn't it? So they have some importance, have power, impress people. For some of them, as for that chap, it's a special gift and they don't take money for it. But many of them go through extraordinary deprivations—denying themselves and their bodies any comfort or enjoyment—just to achieve this. And they do it. It can be done. The most incredible things can be done if you set your mind to it. But this other thing—what we are talking about—that's something entirely different. That has nothing to do with any of these tricks and magical powers."

I thought I understood what he meant. Yogic feats required a gathering of energy, focused one-pointedly on the perfection of a specific skill, almost like an athlete, while he demanded a total and radical change of the human consciousness, so that one could live intelligently and without conflict.

"I have to tell you another story about this," he added, and his face took on a puckish expression. "We were staying at a house in Bombay," he continued. "Two *sannyasis* passed by the house, an older guru and his young disciple, or *chela*. They were on some religious pilgrimage, walking the length of India—a thousand miles—walking, you understand, not by car or train. The old man sensed the presence of a great being in the house and sent the *chela* to inquire if he could enter the house and see us. So we agreed to see him, and we all sat in one room, and Pupul Jayakar was there, and the old boy made sure that he wasn't sitting on the same mat as she was."

"Why didn't he want to sit on the same mat?" I inquired.

A humorous twinkle came into his eyes. "Well," he explained, "any contact with a woman was against his vow of chastity and would have polluted him, so sitting on the same mat with her...," he started to laugh, gesturing descriptively, "You see, through the mat, he would be touching her, or perhaps the other way around—she would be touching him." His laughter enveloped all of us. Calming down, he went on, "So he asked that some water be brought, and they poured it over his hands, catching it in a basin underneath. He had it passed around, saying, 'Taste it.' So we tasted it."

I felt a certain revulsion at the idea of tasting water poured over another person's hands, but Krishnamurti continued unperturbed, "It was regular clean water. He asked that the water be thrown away, and that fresh water be poured over his hands a second time. Again he asked us to taste it, and it had the definite fragrance and taste of rosewater. I was watching the chap very, very closely. I doubt if he could have introduced anything into the water. The others agreed that it smelled and tasted like rosewater, and they had been watching him as well. It wasn't a trick, you understand? How do you explain something like that?"

We racked our brains, but we couldn't come up with an explanation of the causal connections underlying these mysterious phenomena. Krishnamurti wasn't on the point of offering his, either.

Our amiable conversation continued amidst much light-hearted laughter as I talked briefly about current world affairs, such as the withdrawal of U.S. forces from Lebanon, how the abolition of Roman Catholicism as a state religion had affected Italy, and some of Margaret Thatcher's recent pronouncements on European Union. This apparently reminded Krishnamurti of something amusing, because he quietly started laughing to himself. He revealed the source of his enjoyment as Paul Theroux's *The Kingdom by the Sea*, a book he had been reading over the last few days. Some of the character description of the English he found so comical and accurately observed that he broke out in loud laughter while telling us about it.

Throughout his life, Krishnamurti sustained a curious love-hate relationship with things British. Britain was at the height of her imperial power when the simple Brahmin boy from the South Indian backwaters was introduced to the pinnacle of western culture. Aristocrats took him under their wing, imbuing him with the standards of proper living. Although he had the impeccable manners of a prince, he was occasionally confronted with racial discrimination because of his dark skin. He maintained a skeptical attitude toward the stuffy and often silly conventions, in which British society abounded. Quite knowledgeable about the eccentricities of the ruling classes, he liked to poke fun at their absurdities. Especially the monarchy, the cornerstone of the empire, was anathema to him. He saw it as a grotesque and obsolete institution. Curiously, we had a few royalists among us, who fondly followed the royal antics in the news media. Whenever any tabloid gossip about Prince and Queen was brought up at the table, Krishnamurti would cover his ears with both hands and exclaim with anguish, "No, no, don't talk about that rubbish. What rot it all is!"

TWO DAYS LATER, KRISHNAMURTI, ACCOMPANIED BY MARY Z. and Asit Chandmal, departed for New York City, where, on the weekend of April 14 & 15, he gave two public talks at the Felt Forum in Madison Square Garden. Two days later he was invited to speak at the 'Pacem in Terris' Society at the United Nations.

THE DAY AFTER HIS RETURN, SATURDAY, APRIL 21, THERE WERE only five people for lunch. I was preparing a meal of Greek salad, cucumber and yogurt salad, asparagus soup, vegetarian moussaka and zucchini in tomato sauce, with persimmon cream for dessert, when Krishnamurti briskly entered the kitchen. He didn't look tired from his ten days in the Big Apple, but rather energized. After we had exchanged greetings, I asked him, "How did it go, Krishnaji?"

He wasn't quite in the mood to provide me with a detailed account of the past few days, other than to say there had been a large audience and that it had actually gone quite well.

I noticed that he was nursing one hand, a finger of which was bandaged. "What happened to your hand, Krishnaji?"

He looked at it and replied with a dismissive gesture, "We went to a restaurant, and someone closed the car door on it as I was getting into the car."

I winced at the thought of the penetrating pain.

He quickly added, "Of course, he didn't mean to do it. He just was not paying attention. But now it's almost healed." This triggered another memory which got him fired up. "And we had some wonderful food. They were small, round things, green, and melted in one's mouth, simply delicious. Can you make those, sir?"

I had never before heard him rave about food. He had often declared—quite truthfully, no doubt—that food bored him. I was both surprised and slightly taken aback by his request to duplicate a culinary feat with only the most rudimentary description. I quizzed him for greater details, but his culinary perception was rather vague: he could give only a general description of the items—green, roundish, cylindrical, maybe made from spinach, and definitely Italian, very delicate. I promised to give it a try if I could find a recipe that came close to his description. When I later asked Mary Z. about the mystery dish, she confirmed that it was *gnocchi verde*, spinach dumplings.

Curious about the restaurant, I asked him, "What kind of a restaurant was it, Krishnaji?"

"It was fairly small but excellently appointed: the finest tableware, crystal and all that, in the Italian part of town. It was called 'Il Nido' which means 'The Nest'. When we went there, I spoke Italian with the *maitre d'* and the waiter, and they showed us to the best table in a corner by the window. Everything was first class. We went there almost every day," he recounted, with a beautiful expression on his face, mirroring the delightful experience.

"What kind of dishes did you have, sir?"

His memory faltered a little. "There was pasta—homemade, of course, wonderfully light and delicious. And they had the most marvelous tomato sauce, made from fresh tomatoes with just a touch of basil—very simple and delicately fragrant."

I made a mental note to prepare a sauce like that. But there is always a tremendous handicap when one tries to recreate a specific dish, especially if it has been made by a master chef, as the one at 'Il Nido' doubtlessly was. Even the most precise recipe won't necessarily enable one to equal the original. Several factors may be responsible for this: the legendary tiny ingredient, which the chef retains as his personal secret, or, more likely, a certain intangible quality, hard to define but having to do with touch, expertise and timing. This is not to say that cookbooks are useless. On the contrary, recipes are often a wonderful link between word and reality. But it is a tough proposition to recreate a dish previously tasted at home or in a restaurant, because invariably many complex factors combine to make a taste experience.

"They also had excellent wines," Krishnamurti remarked.

"But Krishnaji, I thought you didn't drink."

He smiled at me reassuringly. "No, sir, I don't drink wine—but the others did. I tasted a drop or two—just to see what it tasted like."

Although he disapproved of alcohol as an escape, he had many friends of French and Italian origin who quite naturally took wine during their meals. He didn't seem to mind, and often his host or hostess would offer it to his guests as a matter of course.

I went on a hunt for a *gnocchi verde* recipe and soon found one. Carefully following the prescribed steps, I prepared and served them for lunch. Afterwards, I asked Krishnamurti whether they resembled the ones he had had at the restaurant. He responded with polite honesty, "Not quite, sir."

A few days later, I gave it another go. This time Krishnamurti hesitated, savored the texture and the flavor, and declared, "Well, it's a bit closer, but still not quite the same."

I left it at that, giving up the desire to imitate or compete—at least, in regard to spinach dumplings.

THE END OF APRIL WAS A TIME OF SUBTLE CHANGE. THERE WAS
continuing unrest and dissatisfaction at the School, without a resolution
in sight. Krishnamurti was full of energy and straining to do new things,
wanting to meet new challenges. A gentleman from Washington, D.C.,
who had been a speech writer for successive U.S. government adminis-
trations, came to visit us at the end of April. He was an eloquent and jocular man, very interested in Krishnamurti and his work, and suggested
that he give public talks in the very citadel of global power. Krishnamurti liked the idea and, after careful deliberation, agreed to take on the
challenge. Definite plans and preparations were set in motion for him
to speak at the Kennedy Center in Washington, D.C., one year hence,
in April 1985.

OUR NEW FRIEND FROM WASHINGTON, D.C., ENJOYED
telling jokes and had a good repertoire. Krishnamurti liked his outgoing
nature, and they traded jokes and anecdotes at the lunch table. After
hearing a slightly *risqué* joke about the Pope, entitled 'Tutti Frutti',
Krishnamurti told one that I had not heard before.

   "Two friends, one of them a bishop, die in a car crash. They go up
to heaven and meet St. Peter. Neither of them has sinned too much, so
he lets them in. And he says to them, 'If you have any special request,
tell me now, and I'll see to it that it gets done.' The bishop, a religious
person, asks to see God. St. Peter is startled by his request and tries to
dissuade him, 'Seeing God is a very sensitive affair—it's very shocking.
Few people can stand it. If I may advise you, please don't insist on this.'
But the man is adamant and insists on his wish. Finally St. Peter gives
in and tells him, 'Very well, if you insist. Just don't blame me afterwards.
Go that way and follow the signs: 'God'. And don't forget to come back
here.' Off he goes to see God, while his friend waits with St. Peter for
his return. It takes ten or fifteen minutes before he returns. He is a mere
shadow of himself, as pale as a ghost, and staggering about in deep
shock. His friend is concerned to see him in this state and says, 'By Jove,
what's happened to you? What was He like?' But the man can only
moan, 'She's black.'"

   This earned a good round of laughter. After we had turned more
serious again, we started talking about organized religions, sects and
cults, and especially Christianity. I was actually quite startled when, out
of the blue, Krishnamurti addressed our guest and said boldly, "Jesus

Christ may never have existed. There is no objective, independent document from that period which mentions his name. All we really know is what the apostles and evangelists wrote fifty or a hundred years later, and they might have just invented the whole thing."

Practically everyone at the table seemed to be as startled as I was, especially since Krishnamurti was quite in earnest when he made his statement. All too often his views were unquestioningly accepted, but now he was suddenly confronted by a small storm of vociferous protest, "But Krishnaji, that's really too far-fetched. How...?"

He quite enjoyed stirring up controversy. Eventually it became clear that he had read a book by an Italian historian, Emilio Mella, who claimed to have done the most painstaking research into the records kept by the Roman authorities, who administered Judaea and Palestine at the beginning of the Christian era. "The Romans at that time kept meticulous records of all the executions within their jurisdiction," he explained, quite convinced by what he had read. "And none of them contains the name of Jesus."

"But, Krishnaji, that doesn't mean that the person Jesus never existed," a lady objected.

"And documents do get lost," a teacher concurred. "This was two thousand years ago."

An unusually animated back-and-forth of logical and historical arguments ensued, before Krishnamurti finally conceded that in all likelihood there had been someone called Jesus (or Joshua). But, he insisted, this religious teacher differed substantially from the images of popular tradition and had nothing to do with the figure official Christendom had created.

It was after lunch a few days later, and Krishnamurti was just carrying some pots into the kitchen, when the doorbell rang. I went to answer it and found a middle-aged man standing on the threshold with a bouquet of flowers in his hands. He solemnly asked me whether he could see Mr. Krishnamurti. I vaguely remembered having seen him before. He was a self-styled spiritual teacher, with his own system of beliefs in which he tried to combine Christian elements with aspects of Krishnamurti's teachings.

He was of gentle demeanor and politely gave me his name. I asked him to wait while I conveyed his request to Krishnamurti, who was still in the kitchen. Krishnamurti seemed surprised by the man's unexpected appearance and hesitated a moment before going to meet him. While I continued to clear the table, I caught snippets of their conversation. Evidently, they had met before. Krishnamurti was emphasizing a point he was making, incongruously waving the bunch of flowers. The visitor, barely two steps inside the house, with the door still open behind him, seemed persistent. Krishnamurti stated emphatically, "Nobody even knows if Jesus ever existed...."

When I reentered the dining room a minute later, he was saying, "The Romans at that time kept meticulous records of all their court proceedings and executions. The name Jesus wasn't mentioned once on their lists of executions...."

Several moments later I saw both of them walking over to Pine Cottage. When I asked Krishnamurti about it the following day, he only commented, "We just had tea and a brief chat."

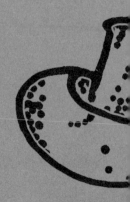

### Starters

*Baby limestone lettuce with
vinaigrette or Roquefort dressing.
Cherry tomatoes and alfalfa sprouts.
Red cabbage coleslaw, prepared with
cumin seeds, capers and chopped olives.
Grated zucchini, with a touch of lime.*

### Main Dishes

*Rice Provençal, with currants and
cashew nuts, accompanied by a
mushroom sauce with 'Marmite'(yeast extract).
Crustless spinach quiche à trois fromage
prepared with fresh goat cheese,
grated Gruyère and Parmesan cheeses.*

### Dessert

*Black mission figs preserved in honey
and lemon, served with vanilla-flavored
whipped cream.
Fresh, seasonal fruit.*

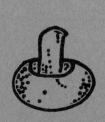

ON MAY 2 WE HAD AN EARLY LUNCH, SO THAT KRISHNAMURTI and Mary Z. could leave in time to get to Santa Barbara, from where they were to fly to San Francisco. A few hours after their departure, I also set out for the City on the Bay. Driving along Highway 101, I enjoyed the scenery of oak-studded, rounded hills, whose green was turning gold in the rays of the hot sun.

On Saturday and Sunday morning, Krishnamurti gave two talks at the Masonic Temple. I helped with the setting up of the book stalls and with the sale of books and tapes. During the second talk he spoke again of two friends walking along a shaded path through woods, talking about their serious concerns. It moved me, and I thought of myself as one of these friends. Right after the talk on Sunday I drove back south to Ojai, so that I would be back in time to prepare lunch the next day. It turned out that there were only four of us. It was great fun to talk with Krishnamurti at leisure about our common weekend in the Bay Area.

While visiting some friends on the East Bay, I had stopped near the university campus at Berkeley to browse through some of the enormous second-hand bookstores along Telegraph Avenue. To my delight, I chanced upon a copy of Theroux's *The Patagonian Express*. It was almost new, its dust-cover protected by a plastic covering. I bought it because I knew that Krishnamurti had developed a fondness for Theroux's ironic style of writing, and after reading *The Great Asian Railway Bazaar* had been looking for this second railway adventure, but without success.

Krishnamurti was on the point of leaving the kitchen to return to Pine Cottage, when it occurred to me that this might be a good moment to present the book to him. I called after him, "Please, Krishnaji, just a moment."

He turned around, an expression of equanimity and great patience on his face.

"What is it, Michael?" he asked mildly.

"I found the book," I eagerly sputtered, handing him the book, with a brief account of how I had located it.

His response was different from what I had expected. Instead of taking the book, which I held out to him, he looked at it apprehensively, as if it might harbor hidden danger. He hesitatingly stretched out a hand and briefly touched the plastic cover with one fingertip, swiftly withdrawing it. "Have you washed it?" he asked.

I felt perplexed. "Washed it?" I repeated.

"It's a used book, second-hand, isn't it? Many people might have touched it, sir, and it might be dirty."

It took me a second to follow his train of thought. For a brief moment I felt the urge to burst out laughing, since the image of myself standing over the sink, washing each single page of the book with soap and sponge, appeared quite ludicrous. "That's true, Krishnaji," I responded, still at a loss what to do about it.

"Just wash the cover and inside, and give it to me later," he said, before exiting the kitchen.

While I went about scrubbing the book with soap and water, I pondered his attitude toward hygiene and cleanliness. I had noticed his sensitivity to the physical—not only his appreciation of clean appearance and clean clothes, but also his aversion to casual contact with anything dirty, or touched by many hands. This was probably the reason he wore fine leather gloves when traveling in cars, trains and airplanes.

I started drying the laundered book with a clean dishtowel. Later that afternoon I took the book, together with some soup for dinner, over to Pine Cottage.

NINE OF US WERE PRESENT FOR LUNCH ON SATURDAY, MAY 12. In the course of the conversation Krishnamurti contrasted interest and attention, themes he later pursued during staff meetings and at the public talks. After two hours of lively conversation, we arrived at two statements which encapsulated the gist of our inquiry, 'Attention is learning; interest is non-attention'.

Three days later, Krishnamurti met the school staff in the sitting room of Arya Vihara at four o'clock in the afternoon. I recorded the session on a tape recorder. He started out by declaring that the true objective of education was the ending of the self. Since psychological knowledge *was* the self, it implied the ending of that kind of knowledge. He was very much against awakening the 'interest' of the child in a particular field, because interest was fragmentary, while attention was whole.

"The ending of self-interest is the beginning of intelligence," he pointed out.

We proceeded to revise a statement originally written by him in 1975 and known as 'The Intent of the Oak Grove School'. It aimed to provide a clear outline of the *raison d'être* of the school. Several of its formulations seemed somewhat vague or, in some instances, too radical. Since we all felt the need for a clear and precise statement, we went over it together, rewording it. Krishnamurti set the tone. We agreed that the school was to be 'an oasis...where one can learn a way of living that is whole, sane and intelligent'. And the purpose of our educational endeavors, both in regard to the students as well as to ourselves, was 'to bring about a profound change in the consciousness of mankind'. In subsequent years this statement was not only a guideline and inspiration, but also the focal point of much heated discussion among the staff.

ONLY A FEW MORE DAYS TO THE 1984 OJAI TALKS. THE WEATHER had been unseasonably hot, and the sun continued to scorch the hills and valleys.

There were eleven of us for lunch that day. Among the regular guests was one relative newcomer, who had come to Ojai for the first time. He was of small build, in his mid-fifties, balding, and he wore glasses. When we were introduced to one other, he told me that he was originally from Germany but had been living in Switzerland for many years. His discovery three years earlier of Krishnamurti's teachings had dramatically changed his life. Recently retired from the family business, he was now spending most of his time and energy exploring the deeper questions of life. The previous year, he had heard Krishnamurti speak at Saanen for the first time and had eventually met him in person. They soon struck up a friendship, which had affected him profoundly. After visiting Brockwood Park, he offered to support Krishnamurti's work with his considerable resources.

I was sitting opposite Krishnamurti at table, and Friedrich Grohe — which was the man's name — was to my right. Krishnamurti and a lady on his left were talking about a third person, who was not present, describing him as a real 'stick-in-the-mud'. I had been listening to their conversation and was puzzled by the expression. Since I didn't know its meaning, I said to Krishnamurti, "Excuse me, Krishnaji, what does it mean — stick-in-the-mud?"

He paused and, after a moment's deliberation, answered, "A dull person without any initiative."

Mr. Grohe was fluent in both German and French and normally conversed with Krishnamurti in French. Although he had a good understanding of English, he felt shy speaking it. A soft-spoken, modest person, he now asked me in a low voice what the phrase meant in German, since he had not quite heard Krishnamurti's explanation. I couldn't immediately think of an equivalent phrase in German and didn't even know if one existed, so I simply translated it word for word and said, "*Stock im Schlamm.*" Phonetically, it came across as *Shtok im Shlumm.*

Krishnamurti had observed the exchange between Mr. Grohe and myself. When I uttered the words, he burst into surprised laughter and exclaimed, "What? What is that, sir?"

"Well, Mr. Grohe didn't know what..."

"Yes, yes, I know that, but what did you just say?"

I felt a bit self-conscious and said, "Well, I translated the expression 'stick-in-the-mud' word for word into German, as there may not be an exact equivalent. It means, *Stock im Schlamm.*"

When I pronounced the German phrase, Krishnamurti again burst into exuberant laughter. The other people at the table, who had been listening to our conversation, joined in the merriment—perhaps because of the onomatopoeic quality of the words and their Teutonic ring. Mr. Grohe and myself, as the German contingent, needed a moment to get over our self-consciousness, before we also joined in the laughter. After it had died down a little, Krishnamurti looked at me with a twinkle in his eye and chortled, "Say it again, sir."

By this time I had started to appreciate my role as comic and intoned with increased volume, "*Stock im Schlamm!*"

There was another round of laughter. It was wonderful to see Krishnamurti in such a jolly mood, completely abandoning himself to the common cheer, laughing hard with his head thrown back and tears running down his cheeks. His whole being seemed to be shaking with physical waves of delight. When the amusement had calmed down, he tried to pronounce the phrase. But he couldn't quite form the Germanic sounds, blurring the consonants. Everyone joined in another round of joyous laughter, as I corrected him and slowly pronounced each syllable, "*Sh-tokk imm sh-lumm.*"

Interrupting himself with bursts of laughter, he tried again, voicing the words more accurately but still imperfectly.

"No, sir: *Sh-tokk imm sh-lumm.*"

He watched my lips as I shaped the sounds and tried again, to every-one's amusement. We went back and forth a few more times; then, without getting it quite right, we eventually stopped, exhausted from sheer laughter.

Moments later, when everyone had left, I still sensed the after-vibra-tions of our high spirits. Alone in the kitchen, I reflected on this whole laughing matter. It occurred to me that, from a higher point of view, most of us, including myself, could be described as stick-in-the-muds. I released a burst of laughter into the quiet, solitary kitchen. Yes, that probably was the real joke.

More than ever, I had come to appreciate Krishnamurti's wonderful sense of humor. His insightful words about humor, which rang so true, came to my mind: "Laughter is part of seriousness. Seriousness doesn't exclude joy, enjoyment. Humor means really to laugh at oneself, just to look at ourselves with laughter, to observe with clarity, with seriousness, and yet with laughter if one can."

He was ready to laugh, not only at the ironies and absurdities of other people's lives, but, more than anything, at himself and at the ridiculous situations in which he sometimes found himself.

ON TUESDAY, MAY 22, KRISHNAMURTI HAD JUST SAT DOWN ON the wooden folding chair for the question-and-answer meeting, when a young woman jumped onto the platform and quickly assumed the lotus posture at his feet, staring and smiling at him with frozen fascination. For a split second he seemed startled by the unexpected interruption, exclaiming, "What the…!"

Two volunteers in the front row sprang to their feet, intent on restraining the woman and removing her from the stage, but Krishna-murti had swiftly grasped the situation and waved back the two young men. Bending down to the woman, who had a slightly moronic grin on her face, he said, "She'll be quiet here, won't you? Then you can sit there." She happily nodded her head in silent agreement, remaining at his feet until the end of the dialogue. Then he bent down again and said to her, "It's over now, you can get up."

ON THE HOT, SUNNY AFTERNOON THAT SAME DAY, WE WERE going to commemorate the completion of the new High School buildings with a tree-planting ceremony. The complex, which included several classrooms and a library, adjoined the Oak Grove toward the north. There were close to two hundred people milling about—trustees, school staff, parents and students, volunteers and participants at the talks. Sipping juice and tea and nibbling on cookies, they were involved in lively conversations.

At last the grey Mercedes pulled up, and Krishnamurti shyly emerged on the passenger side. He was dressed with simple elegance, the only incongruity being the jogging shoes he was wearing for the occasion. He greeted those who came to shake his hand and to exchange a few words, smiling reservedly.

The tall director, who was in charge of organizing the talks, led him to where the trees were to be planted. Seven of us walked behind him, while the other guests gradually ambled over. He carefully studied the trees, listening to the director's explanation, "These here, Krishnaji, are liquid amber. In fall their leaves turn bright red and orange. And this is a peepul tree."

Throughout his life, Krishnamurti had been in love with the earth and all living things, reserving a special fondness for trees. Once he had said, "If you establish a relationship with the tree, then you have relationship with mankind." On another occasion he talked about listening to the 'silent sound of the roots'. Without further ado, he now picked up a shovel, while two of us lifted the heavy pot with the peepul (or bodhi) tree sapling and placed it in the hole, which had already been dug. He was watching closely what we were doing and immediately noticed what was wrong. "This isn't deep enough, sir," he said. "You have to take it out again, so that we can dig out more soil."

After lifting the pot out again, four of us, including Krishnamurti, scraped out more soil. Every so often, I used a pickaxe to loosen a rock at the bottom of the hole. Absorbed by the strenuous physical activity, one easily forgot that it was Krishnamurti, almost eighty-nine years old, who was there right next to us youngsters, wielding the shovel wholeheartedly. A circle of spectators had formed at a respectful distance, some of them taking snapshots of him digging the ground. Krishnamurti didn't mind the odd situation—performing manual labor in front of an audience: he happily gave his full attention and energy to the sacred task of planting trees.

"There is a big rock there, sir," he pointed out, startling me from a moment's idle contemplation.

"Oh, I'm sorry, sir," I said, and got to work, swinging the long, wooden-handled tool, bringing it down on the packed earth, loosening its hold around the rock. Finally the hole was deep enough and, once the sapling was properly leveled, we removed the plastic shelling of the pot and filled the gap with soil. Then all of us proceeded to compact the soil around the slender trunk of the sapling by stomping it tight. We left a slightly indented circle close to the trunk, so that the water which someone was now spraying from a hose would not immediately run off but collect close to the root system. We went on like this with several more trees, Krishnamurti showing no signs of fatigue. Some of the male onlookers got a taste of the action and, demanding shovels, joined the work force. Thus, it took less than an hour to plant fifteen to twenty new trees. When we were done, Krishnamurti looked with a tender and satisfied smile at the young plants dotting the lawn in front of the new school buildings.

THE AFTERNOON AFTER THE FOURTH AND FINAL TALK, Monday, May 28, Krishnamurti met with the trustees and staff at Pine Cottage to discuss the persisting difficulties at the school. After a long and lively discussion, a number of administrative changes were announced, including the appointment of a new principal of the High School.

The following day, several celebrities joined us for lunch. At table one of them, a film actor, sat facing Krishnamurti, while I found myself at the far end, unable to follow their conversation. After lunch, I noticed that Krishnamurti and the actor walked together to Pine Cottage.

The next morning around 8 a.m., there was a partial solar eclipse, which I was able to observe. When Krishnamurti entered the kitchen around 1:20 p.m., I still retained some curiosity about our guest from the preceding day.

"Excuse me, Krishnaji," I asked, "the gentleman with whom you talked yesterday—is he an interesting person, did he ask any good questions?"

He looked at me with an amused expression in his eyes and then answered diplomatically, "Ah, you know, sir, actors seldom know who they really are."

Initially, I took his answer to refer to actors only, until, upon reflection, it occurred to me that it held true for most us. Who really knew who he or she was? According to some, not even Krishnamurti fully knew who or what he was. He kept on questioning, inquiring and learning, and he never seemed to come to a definitive conclusion.

IN CONTRAST TO THE LUNCHES OF THE PAST FEW WEEKS, WE were a small group of only ten people that day. There were three former colleagues of ours, one of whom was earning his doctorate in philosophy at Oxford University; the second was employed in a construction business; while the third had joined a small, high-tech international company in a senior position. Toward the end of the luncheon, Krishnamurti recounted a joke, something he hadn't done for a while. For no particular reason, he started by asking, "Do you mind if I tell you a good joke, which I heard the other day?"

"Please, sir," I eagerly responded, and the others nodded in agreement.

"There are three monks, who have been sitting in deep meditation for many years amidst the Himalayan snow peaks, never speaking a word, in utter silence. One morning, one of the three suddenly speaks up and says, 'What a lovely morning this is.' And he falls silent again. Five years of silence pass, when all at once the second monk speaks up and says, 'But we could do with some rain.' There is deep silence among them for another five years, when suddenly the third monk says, 'Why can't you two stop chattering?'"

All of us cracked up and enjoyed a good round of laughter, before we rose from the table.

THE PAST WEEKS AND MONTHS HAD BEEN BUSY, BOTH AT THE Oak Grove and at Arya Vihara. A stream of visitors and celebrities came and went, in addition to the regular influx of trustees and teachers. The luncheons at A.V. had been well attended, often by over twenty guests at a time—which, of course, considerably increased my workload.

Krishnamurti continued faithfully to enter the kitchen through the patio door, and we had our brief, affectionate pre-lunch conversation. Even so, I experienced a sense of dissatisfaction, without being able to perceive its cause. Opportunities to present my news reports had recently diminished. Every so often Krishnamurti would approach me in the kitchen after lunch and ask, just between the two of us, "What's the news, sir?" And I would very briefly quote a headline or give a two-sentence summary of a noteworthy item. This, of course, wasn't quite the same as the leisurely presentation at table, which I had come to cherish.

Occasionally I thought I was experiencing pangs of jealousy, when I saw groups of guests trooping off for a walk with Krishnamurti while I had to drive into town to shop and run errands. More than anything, I wanted to see our friendship confirmed and flowering, less through any action of his—because I sensed his care and affection as strongly as ever—than through an action of mine. Out of some personal need, perhaps a sense of inadequacy, I had the urge to express my feelings to him: that I was his friend. It was slightly irrational, but I couldn't shake it off. I wanted to make sure he knew I was his friend.

On May 31, the day before his departure for England, he entered the kitchen in his usual manner. After we had exchanged greetings, I said boldly but hesitantly, "Krishnaji, there is something I would like to tell you—if you don't mind."

His easygoing demeanor swiftly changed, and a bright alertness came over him, "All right, sir, go ahead."

I started to feel extremely self-conscious, as he held me in his steady gaze.

"I...I wanted to tell you, I mean, I wanted to assure you..."

"Come to the point, sir," he said impatiently.

"I just want to tell you, Krishnaji, that I am your friend."

"All right, sir," he said, and the sharpness softened. "Very well, Michael. Now let's go and have lunch. I think the others are waiting."

I knew that he abhorred all sentimentality or any display of personal emotions, although he was a truly passionate person. He was wont to express his deep affection indirectly, such as during dialogues with the staff and trustees, when I had heard him say, "If I say I love you, will you listen to it? Or will you come up with all sorts of questions and objections: How much do you love me? How long will you love me, and so on? I love you—that's all."

Even then, the true measure of affection was in his action and in the care with which he encountered each person. At the moment, however, though he did not respond further and I hadn't expected anything but his quiet listening, I felt good and relieved about my simple confession of friendship.

The lunch that followed was a small, friendly affair. Apart from seven regulars, an old friend from Mount Shasta in Northern California was joining us for lunch. We talked about world affairs and mythology. I had recently read some of Joseph Campbell's books on world myths and asked Krishnamurti, "Sir, are you at all interested in the myths of ancient Greece and India? And do you think they have any significance?"

"Certainly, I like the stories themselves. But I'm not interested in all the analyzing, explaining what means what, and the endless interpretation of symbols, and all that other silly nonsense. They are wonderful old stories, nothing more."

The next day, Friday, June 1, we had an early lunch at 12:30 p.m., because Krishnamurti and Mary Z. were departing for England later that afternoon. Once again, we had occasion to say goodbye to them beneath the pepper tree.

# Part Four

# FLOWERING
# IN GOODNESS

## Chapter 21

# PEACE ON EARTH

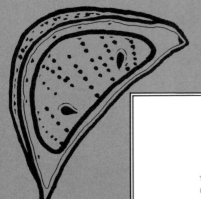

### Starters

*Tossed green salad with
vinaigrette or peanut dressing.
Celeriac salad in a dressing of
mustard & horse radish.
Cold green bean salad with onions,
parsley, olive oil and lemon,
garnished with toasted sunflower seeds.*

### Main Dishes

*Wild rice, with currants,
capers and pine nuts.
Greek lentils with onions,
tomatoes and celery.
Steamed broccoli served with
olive and caper sauce.*

### Dessert

*Mango cream, prepared with
mango pulp and a touch of cream.
Fresh, seasonal fruit.
Peanut butter cookies.*

WHILE KRISHNAMURTI WAS GIVING HIS TWENTY-FOURTH annual talks at Saanen, the XXIIIrd Summer Olympic Games were being held, sans the Soviet Union, at Los Angeles in July and August, 1984. Some of the Olympic action spilled over into the Ojai Valley, as the boating events were staged at nearby Lake Casitas.

In early September, as Krishnamurti was concluding the Brockwood Park Talks, we were having a heat wave of the first order, the mercury rising to 106° F (41° C) for days on end. There was also an extraordinary celestial event happening at the time, which was clearly visible in the western sky: a line-up of the major planets—Venus, Saturn, Mars and Jupiter. I was thrilled to observe the heavenly wanderers as white points of light against the color of the sunset sky.

On October 26, Krishnamurti and Mary Z. set out from England for New Delhi, India. A few days later, on October 31, Indira Gandhi, the Indian prime minister, who greatly honored Krishnamurti and often sought his advice, was assassinated at her residence by two of her bodyguards. Krishnamurti was staying at a house not too far from hers and soon left the city to avoid the political turmoil and the widespread riots, in which a thousand or more innocent civilians died. Except for slight modifications, he continued with his talking schedule, while Mary Z. who had fallen ill, returned to Ojai at the end of January.

Accompanied by Asit Chandmal, Krishnamurti arrived in Ojai on February 17, 1985. Exhausted from traveling and his busy schedule, he spent the next day in bed, resting and regaining his energy.

For his first lunch the following day, I prepared a corn and olive salad, guacamole, green bean soup, cumin potatoes with a three-cheese spinach quiche, broccoli with sauce olivos, and fruit salad and yogurt for dessert. There were eleven guests, and everyone was glad to see him again, inquiring after his time in India. He and Mary Z. gave us a vivid account of the tumultuous events surrounding Indira Gandhi's assassination.

Although he had a good appetite and was glad to be back in Ojai, he looked fatigued. While we were clearing the table, I commented on the enormous amount of traveling he had done recently. He looked at me with kind eyes and said, "You know, sir, all this traveling by air, ship and car is not very good for the organism. We have done it for seventy years, or more. It unsettles the body, upsets it. It always needs time to quieten down again and to adjust. If it wasn't constantly on the move, the body might live a lot longer—maybe a hundred years, or maybe even a hundred and twenty. So stay settled and lead a quiet life."

I understood what he was saying but was a bit skeptical, because I loved traveling and had a nomadic streak in me.

BY SUNDAY, FEBRUARY 24, KRISHNAMURTI HAD REGAINED his sparkling energy and was eager to learn more about the school. As the twelve of us were talking about the difficulties of the newly established boarding program, he began to reminisce about the Happy Valley School, which he and Aldous Huxley had helped to set up but from which he had disassociated himself after only a few years. "You see," he said, "first it happened at the old Happy Valley School, the same problems—smoking, drinking, drugs, sex, and so on. Now you have them here. The basic question is: 'What will you do with the students?' Will you give them leisure? Will you give them entertainment? Or will you have a rigorous program, keeping them busy, busy, busy, from morning to night? You see what it does to them. You will be fostering a division in them—work versus free time—which is the real fragmentation of life."

After discussing the boarding situation at some length and agreeing to the need for a balanced program, we started talking about unconventional approaches to health and disease. I mentioned the Bircher-Benner method of healing chronic diseases through a balanced diet of raw and cooked vegetarian food. I had been using some of their dietary principles in the meal preparations here.

"Ah, yes, Bircher-Benner," he said. "I stayed at their clinic near Zurich for some weeks."

"Did you go there for a specific purpose, Krishnaji?" I asked.

"It was in 1960, after a severe kidney infection in India; they tested me and put me on a strict diet."

"What type of food did they offer you, sir?"

"They mainly fed me zucchini—raw and cooked—in all sorts of forms and preparations. It cured me to some degree, but after a while it was a bore to eat the same thing over and over again."

We laughed at the funny face he pulled. Someone brought up healing of a different kind, and the name of Vimala Thakar was mentioned.

She was a fairly well-known Indian social activist. In one of her books she described how a severe ear ailment, that several medical specialists were unable to cure, had been healed by Krishnamurti through the touch of his hands. A teacher asked him about this incident, but he appeared rather reluctant to talk about it, because of the lady's subsequent claim that the laying on of his hands had done more than heal her ear ailment—it had also bestowed some sort of initiation on her.

He looked at his fine, long hands and mused, "Already my mother told me that I had the power of healing in my hands." Looking up at us, he said shyly, "I would like to tell you a story that happened recently, if I may. And, please, I'm not trying to cast myself as a healer or miracle worker. I really dislike that kind of publicity. So, please, don't go around promoting K as a healer, if you don't mind. It was in Madras, of an evening, and I was taking a walk along the beach at Adyar. There are a number of fishing huts there and some houses behind them. A young boy of about fourteen came running up to me from one of them and got hold of my hand and started to thank me profusely. 'Thank you, sir, thank you for what you've done,' he said. I didn't know what it was all about, so I asked him, 'What are you thanking me for?' And he said, 'I saw you just now walking here and recognized you. Don't you remember me, sir? You healed my mother a year ago. She was really ill, and we came to see you and carried her up to your room. And she is healthy now and can walk.' He kept thanking me profusely. Then I remembered that the previous year a car had driven up in front of Vasanta Vihar. The whole family got out of the car, several children among them, and they carried the mother on a stretcher upstairs to where I was staying. They implored me to help her. She was obviously on the threshold of death, couldn't move or talk, and the doctors seemed to be unable to diagnose her disease or do anything about it. So I told them to put the stretcher in front of my room and leave me alone with her. After a while she came to and could get up with some help."

The teacher was eager to know details of the actual healing process and asked, "What did you actually do, Krishnaji?"

At times, when questions became too personal or the demand for detailed information indiscreet, he could become a master of elegant side-stepping. He made a graceful gesture of 'hold it right there' and replied somewhat enigmatically, "We did what we could." Continuing his narration, he said, "They had to support her as she walked down the stairs, but she could walk. They all thanked me, and all that. The boy on the beach, her son, who was holding on to my hand, now invited me to come to their house and meet his family. I thanked him and excused myself. And that was that."

He fell silent, and the story stood before our mental eyes like a hologram, revealing the unusual magic of this compassionate man, whose existence was woven into the very fabric of our own lives like a thread of gold.

THE FOLLOWING WEEKEND, MARCH, 2 KRISHNAMURTI MET with the staff at Pine Cottage for the first time. We discussed the pervasive fragmentation in our lives and also the movement of specialization, that had divided life into work and leisure, thereby creating a source of conflict. We were caught in a vicious circle of unending problems. Although we did not fully understand our thinking process, we made constant, if improper, use of thought, our primary instrument of action and survival. This naturally resulted in all sorts of problems. The difficulty was compounded by the fact that we sought to solve them by the use of thought, the very tool that had caused them in the first place.

While we were on a journey of discovery into our minds, with their problems, a sudden downpour of hail produced an intense drumming on the roof and against the window panes. Looking out into the courtyard, I saw the ground covered with a thin layer of shining hailstones, glistening white pebbles that quickly melted away. For some reason, I took it as a good omen.

During lunch on the following Monday, Krishnamurti mentioned a book he had just started reading, *Breaking with Moscow*, by Arcady Shevchenko. The author had been the highest-ranking Soviet diplomat, an under-secretary general, at the United Nations in New York, until his recent defection to the United States. Having been debriefed and granted political asylum, he had begun to spill the beans to the public at large. Krishnamurti was fascinated by his firsthand account of the intrigues in the upper echelons of the Soviet political establishment. He eagerly discussed details of the book with Theo Lilliefelt, the former U.N. diplomat, who had recommended the book to him. He was appalled by the disclosures of cynicism among the top Communist leaders, their naked exploitation of power and privilege, and their irredeemable corruption. During the next few luncheons, he presented us with regular installments of his latest reading. He simply could not believe the depth of their depravity.

"Sir," he said to Theo, "it's incredible how they say one thing and do something entirely different. While the people are starving, these politicians pretend to be serving them, endlessly talking about the people—how good it is for the people, and so on. But they are only serving themselves. It's for the good old self—the luxury cars, houses, extravagant feasts and banquets—you know, all the corruption and deception they are involved in. And these are heads of state, with enormous power, in control of nuclear weapons. They determine the future course of humanity—it's appalling."

Generally, he was very skeptical of any of the socio-political systems devised by human thought, as they were invariably flawed by one basic component, human nature. To him, nationalism in any form was nothing but a glorified form of tribalism, the continuation of age-old divisions, prejudices, fears, hatreds, and wars. But he distinguished 'the false as the false, the true as the true, and the true in the false', as he put it. Without endorsing any particular form of government, he preferred democracy and clearly discerned the qualities of the totalitarian systems—intrinsically destructive and evil. In fact, he often said, "Power in any form is evil."

*Breaking with Moscow* appeared to provide him with the irrefutable, firsthand evidence that the Communist system was rotten to the core, deceiving its own people and the world at large, and posing a serious threat to the welfare of humanity. Shortly afterwards, I also read the book but felt somewhat skeptical about certain aspects of it. I voiced my reservations at table.

"Krishnaji," I asked, "don't you think that in many ways the author had ulterior motives, particularly in trying to whitewash himself by portraying his adversaries as more abominably corrupt? After all, he also had been a high-ranking party functionary for many years, fully participating in all this corruption?"

He didn't seem to be interested in pursuing my line of criticism and replied, "No, no, sir. Just see what he is saying." *Interesting*

It was around this time, in the middle of March, 1985, that the third leader of the Soviet Union in so many years had passed away while in office. Brezhnev had died in 1982, after many years at the top; his successor, Yuri Andropov, departed the world in 1984, after only fifteen months in power; and now Chernenko, ruling for barely a year, had died and was replaced by Mikhail Gorbachev, at fifty-four one of the youngest men to attain to power in the U.S.S.R. While we discussed these changes in the hierarchy of the Communist superpower, someone passed around a newsmagazine which contained a photo of the new party chairman. Krishnamurti did not say anything, but studied Gorbachev's face carefully for a long time.

After a while, he said, "I must tell you a joke that I heard recently. A man dies and goes to hell. As he approaches, he notices two large doors leading into inner hell. Both are guarded by devils. In front of one gate, there is a long queue of people waiting to enter, while the other one is without people. The man walks over to the gate without people and reads the sign on it, 'Capitalist Hell'. He asks the guarding devil, 'What exactly do you do here?' The devil answers, 'We drill holes in the condemned and fill them with boiling oil.' The man walks over to the other gate where thousands upon thousands of people are lined up. Here the sign says 'Socialist Hell'. The man turns to the guarding devil and asks, 'And what do you do here, in Socialist Hell?' The devil answers, 'We drill holes in the condemned and fill them with boiling oil.' The man is totally surprised and exclaims, 'But that is exactly what they are doing over there, in Capitalist Hell. So why is there nobody over there, while here thousands upon thousands are waiting in line?' The devil shrugs, 'Well, you know how in capitalism everything functions efficiently. Here in Socialist Hell we're still waiting for the drill bits, and we've also run out of oil.'"

Amidst the laughter, Krishnamurti chuckled, "That may be the only place where socialism and communism have the advantage—in hell."

THROUGHOUT MARCH KRISHNAMURTI MET WITH THE SCHOOL staff at Pine Cottage every Saturday morning at eleven o'clock, to discuss matters concerning our daily life and our educational activities—not as separate but as interrelated issues. He encapsulated the essence of one dialogue by saying, "The ending of self-interest is the beginning of intelligence." To grasp this not only intellectually but also, and more importantly, to realize it in one's daily life was a quantum leap beyond practically everyone's capacity. I found myself asking, 'Can I really end my self-interest? Why does it appear so difficult?' During the next dialogue we pursued the theme of self-interest at great depth, relating it to likes and dislikes, opinions and personal taste, and attachment.

The following Saturday, Krishnamurti started out by asking a deceptively simple question, "What does life mean to you?"

The conversation meandered through the fields of pleasure and pain, attachment, guilt and resistance. In the course of our inquiry, I felt I was being brought face to face with an actuality of daily living that I seldom perceived, the greater context. At the outset of working with Krishnamurti I had been deeply interested in enlightenment and transformation. Gradually I came to realize the elusiveness of these ideals, especially when conceived as goals to be reached through systems of becoming. When Krishnamurti started talking about the art of living, doing away with the concept of fixed points that one strives after, it was a wake-up call. Eminently practical and poetically wholesome, this approach related directly to one's actual day-to-day life and not to some fanciful ideal. Although not necessarily easy, it was clear and simple to see.

Krishnamurti explained it thus: "The art of living is the most important art, greater than any other, greater than writing a poem or composing a symphony, greater than all the temples and churches." He continued after a pause, "And nobody can teach you this art."

Eventually he made it clear that the art of living meant to have no fear, no sorrow, to live without any conflict or problem; and that it went together with the art of dying. *Unattainable, impractical nonsense.*

ON MONDAY, MARCH 25, THERE WERE ONLY SIX OF US for lunch. One guest from India had been a great friend of Krishnamurti's for more than thirty years. While we enjoyed a meal of wild rice, Greek lentils, steamed broccoli and olive & caper sauce, followed by persimmon cream, a feeling of friendship and openness developed. Krishnamurti was animatedly conversing with his old friend about the guru tradition and the Buddhist concept of bodhisattvas. Although he never stated unambiguously whether these beings existed or not, he was clearly fascinated by the topic. During public dialogues and private conversations he sometimes spoke of bodhisattvas and enlightened beings; he would also answer questions about the so-called Masters of Theosophy—but only either to dismiss or to explain, rather than confirm or deny the concept. He was quite sensitive about these matters and did not like the contents of his conversations to be repeated, since they could easily be misrepresented. None of it had anything to do with his teaching.

IN LATE APRIL, THE DIRECTOR OF DEVELOPMENT, WHO HAD recently returned from visiting several colleges and universities on the East Coast, joined us for lunch. During the meal he told Krishnamurti that his teachings formed part of philosophy courses at several universities. Krishnamurti's response was restrained but full of childlike fascination with the news from these institutes of higher learning. Producing sheets of paper, the director explained, "These, Krishnaji, are test questionnaires. The students who take your course have to pass this test."

Krishnamurti looked puzzled and intrigued and took the papers in his hands to study them more closely.

A lady trustee quipped, "Is it all true or false, or also multiple-choice?"

Everybody at the table, including Krishnamurti, broke out laughing, and the director answered, "Well, yes, there are true-false and multiple-choice questions, but the major part of the test consists of essays."

Krishnamurti, in the meantime, had perused the papers and placed them on the table next to his plate; he remarked with an appreciative laugh, "These are really quite good. Yes, they are really very good questions." Then he added whimsically, "I wonder if I would pass the test."

That totally unplugged the barrel of laughs. We were holding our sides with exuberant mirth. The director's response to Krishnamurti's remark added another jocular twist, "Of course, sir, I'm sure you'd pass with flying colors."

AT THE BEGINNING OF APRIL THE WEATHER SUDDENLY turned very hot. There were twelve for lunch on Monday, April 1. All of us, with one exception, were long-time members of the School and Foundation. I had prepared a marinated tofu salad, a potato-and-egg salad, gazpacho soup, couscous with vegetables Provençal, and chocolate brownies and ice cream for dessert.

Almost from the beginning, a strange, uncomfortable tension was prevalent among us. Suddenly, a chain reaction occurred, releasing pent-up feelings of animosity. The one 'outsider' among us, a visiting cook from Brockwood Park, had rather innocently marveled at what he thought were the expensive delicacies which we served for lunch, and one of the trustees promptly rebuked me for being too extravagant in the variety of food I served. This was followed by some of the trustees and directors having a go at one another. I was appalled—not only at being put on the spot, but also by this unexpected display of mutual resentment in front of Krishnamurti.

He clearly noticed the low-voiced altercation but didn't involve himself at all, keeping a shy, observant distance, not saying a thing. Eventually, without getting to the root of our controversy, we calmed down. The conversation turned to more remote conflicts—the global superpower situation and the threat of nuclear war. One person wondered, "After a nuclear war between the superpowers, there probably wouldn't be many places left on the planet where human beings could survive."

We started a guessing game, as to where we would want to be, should a deadly nuclear conflict occur. Someone suggested New Zealand as a safe place, another South America. A lady turned to Krishnamurti and asked him, "Where would you want to be during such a disaster, Krishnaji?"

Pondering the question for a moment, he answered with a playful smile, "I should think the Ojai Valley would be a fairly safe place, wouldn't it? It's protected by mountains all around, and one could sit under an orange tree and survive on the fruit."

"Live only on oranges?" I wondered.

The lady objected, "But it's so close to Los Angeles, which would be one of the first targets of an enemy attack. Certainly the nuclear radiation would affect the Valley."

"And Vandenburg Air Force Base would probably get a full hit by an intercontinental ballistic missile," the director remarked.

"All right, all right," Krishnamurti replied, laughing, "I'll find another safe place." He went through several other options, only to discard them. Finally, he said, "Ah, I've got it: the Dordogne in France would be a good place to live. Prehistoric man used to live there in caves, for tens of thousands of years. I've visited the region. It's quite beautiful and fertile, and it probably would be as safe a place as any."

THREE DAYS LATER, THURSDAY, THE DAY OF THE FULL MOON in April, there was no lunch. Mary Z. had to drive to Los Angeles in the morning, and Krishnamurti was going to stay in bed for the day. Therefore, we had all agreed to cancel regular lunch, while I was to prepare some food for Krishnamurti and take it over to him in Pine Cottage.

It was a hot, bright day, and the sunlight reflected brilliantly from the white-painted adobe brick walls of the house. Balancing the tray on my upraised right palm, I walked past the rosebushes, whose exuberant blooms were already beginning to wilt in the heat. Slowly ascending the stone steps to the crimson door, I steadied the tray with my left hand, in order to prevent the containers from knocking against one another. The previous day he had told me, "Come around one o'clock, sir, and ring the bell. I'll come to open the door for you. I'll keep the door locked, since I'm the only one in the house and I can't hear when somebody enters."

I carefully pressed the button and heard the bell's distant clang in the house. The seconds ticked away as I stood there waiting. There was no noise, only the heat of the day and the buzzing of many insects. I started to wonder if he had heard the bell and was on the point of ringing again, when the door was quietly opened, and he came in sight.

For me, Krishnamurti was always a remarkable sight to behold. But under certain, often unpredictable circumstances, he was even more remarkable than usual. This happened to be one of those rare occasions. Besides, we were meeting face to face, just the two of us. He was dressed in a snow-white, fluffy, terry-cotton bathrobe, that reached all the way to his sandalled feet. From wide, billowing sleeves his slender, dark-skinned hands protruded. His head was crowned by a halo of swirling silver hair.

The sheer abundance of light bowled me over. Everything was immensely white and bright: the strong light of the day flooding the interior of the house, reflected from white walls and white floor tiles; and Krishnamurti, white-haired, in a white bathrobe. It struck me like a powerful dream scene, where all elements merge into one flowing movement, vibrantly making and unmaking configurations and arabesques from a common background. He stepped forward from that vibrant background, like a medieval master of alchemy, who had attained to the highest good: not just to change lead and other base metals into gold, but to smelt and transform all things and beings into himself, and, through him, into clear emptiness.

"Hello, Michael," he said with a welcoming smile. He seemed to radiate, and his friendly eyes beamed with a gentle, mirroring fire.

"I've brought your lunch, Krishnaji," I explained. "Where would you like me to put it?"

"Put it over there on the kitchen counter," he said, and followed me as I went into the kitchen and placed the tray on the counter. As I usually did on these occasions, I pointed at the various dishes, naming them and reciting their ingredients. He listened attentively to my culinary discourse, inquiring into one or two details, before suddenly grabbing me by the arm in one of his characteristic gestures, and saying, "Thank you, sir. I'll take it into the bedroom on another tray."

Throughout our brief encounter, listening to the gentle resonance of his voice, I had a sensation of indescribable lightness. Worries, anxieties, and all mundane concerns had fallen by the wayside, and, as I now strode back to the front door, with Krishnamurti walking behind me, I sensed the seamless contours of an unknown immensity. Literally swimming out of the door and away from his encompassing presence, into the blinding brightness of the day, I turned, one foot already on the second step, to face Krishnamurti with a farewell greeting. He stood there, radiant in the enormous white bathrobe, very straight but fragile and diminutive, one hand on the knob of the half-opened crimson door, the other hanging relaxed by his side. He was looking at me in a sort of unfocused way, as if he was gazing at the space around my head and body, rather than at the body itself. I was on the point of uttering some words of gratitude, when he spoke first: he recited a sentence in a foreign language, which I could neither understand nor identify. There was a resonance of solemn dignity in the words, enhanced by his peculiar mode of enunciation. Tilting back his head and half-closing his eyelids, he pronounced the words like a magical mantra, full of sonorous profundity. Opening his eyes fully, he looked directly into my eyes, where he might have detected nothing but bewilderment.

I asked hesitantly, "I'm sorry, sir. What did you say?"

He intoned the words again, "*Anna dathu sukhi bhava*."

There was a rhythm to it, with several stresses and sustained consonants, creating a vibration in a low humming key. I tried to repeat the words, but failed. "What does it mean, Krishnaji?" I asked.

"It's an ancient Sanskrit saying. It means, 'May he who gives food be happy.'"

I felt an unexpected joy welling up within me, and I thanked him as if he had given me a precious gift, "Thank you, sir."

A resplendent smile passed between us, and I skipped back through the orange grove to the Arya Vihara kitchen.

THREE DAYS LATER, EARLY SATURDAY MORNING, KRISHNAMURTI and Mary Z. left for the airport to catch a flight to New York City, where he was scheduled to talk at the U.N. on April 11. On the weekend of April 20 and 21, he was going to give two talks at the Kennedy Center, Washington, D.C., and return to Ojai the following Monday. Thus, he would be gone for two weeks.

My colleague from Brockwood Park and I took the opportunity to drive up along the Pacific Coast through Big Sur to San Francisco for a week. After returning to Ojai, I caught a flight from LAX to Washington, D.C., to attend the talks there. It was my first visit to the nation's capital, and I was deeply impressed, not only by the enormous concentration of power, but also by the fabulous collections of art treasures, and the architectural design of the city.

What impressed me most, however, was to see Krishnamurti giving a talk at the renowned Center for the Performing Arts at 2:30 on Saturday afternoon. Dr.essed in a dark, double-breasted suit, with a burgundy-red tie and a small white handkerchief in his breast pocket, he sat on a simple chair in the center of the huge, dimly-lit stage. There was a microphone in front of him, and another clip-on microphone was attached to his lapel. It was hard to envision a more poignant contrast: one man alone on the large, empty stage, confronting an expectant, cosmopolitan audience of three thousand, gathered in a theater at the seat of power. It started out on a wrong note, because the speaker system temporarily malfunctioned. But, once it was adjusted, Krishnamurti embarked on one of the most compelling, compact summarizations of his teachings ever. He spoke most earnestly, with only spare gestures, upright and almost immobile in his chair. He talked about the human condition, about conflict and sorrow, about peace, about inquiry, about beauty and fear, about time and thought.

The following morning, at 11 a.m., he continued the panoramic journey into human consciousness with his listeners. As stern as on the previous day, he began by examining pleasure and the dominant role it played in our lives. At one point, he said, "We are frightened to look at ourselves. As we said—to look at ourselves very clearly, accurately, precisely is only possible in the mirror of relationship: that's the only mirror we have. When you look at yourself—whether you're combing your hair, or you're shaving, or whatever you're doing to your face..."

All at once and for a reason that wasn't immediately clear, he gave a short laugh and then said, "Sorry." There was a brief interval of silence as he attempted to regain his composure, but in the meantime some of the audience had started to titter at the humor implicit in the suggestion to look at oneself as one does in a bathroom mirror.

He continued, "You look in your mirror", but once again he was overcome by whatever hilarious image had been evoked in him. "Sorry," he said again with laughing eyes. There was more laughter from the audience in response to the sudden display of mirth, which contrasted sharply with his previous gravity. Regaining a straight face, he was on the point of continuing, when once again he was overpowered by an attack of laughter. Shaking his head with exasperation at his inability to shake off the impulse, he surrendered himself to the waves of laughter, which by now had engulfed the whole audience. After laughing without restraint for some moments, he gasped another apology, "I'm sorry."

His words were swallowed up by another round of laughter. This continued for a minute or two, while he looked at the thousands of laughing faces before him with an expression of sheer, undisguised delight. After the merriment had somewhat died down, he scratched his cheek with one finger and remarked, "I'm glad you approve."

At last, composed again, he went on, "That mirror reflects exactly what you are."

Although it might have been nothing but an outbreak of infectious merriment without rhyme or reason, there was a wonderfully telling quality about this incident, revealing Krishnamurti's free-flowing sense of humor. He continued the talk by going into order and disorder, learning, sorrow, love and death, religion and the sacred, and meditation. It was strangely moving, when, at the conclusion of this extraordinary talk, a little girl walked up to the stage with a bouquet of flowers and handed it to Krishnamurti, who leaned down to take it from her.

TWO DAYS LATER, WE WERE ALL IN OJAI AGAIN, SHARING LUNCH at A.V. Since five of the eight guests had not been to the East Coast, Krishnamurti, Mary Z., and I told them about the events in Washington, D.C. Curious about his time in New York City, I asked him, "And what about your talk at the United Nations, sir? How did that go?"

"I spoke at the 'Pacem-in-Terris Society', but I wonder whether any of the U.N. delegates are interested in peace at all. One chap came up to us afterwards and said, 'I've been with the United Nations for forty years, and after hearing you I've come to the conclusion that war is wrong.' Imagine that, sir; it took him forty years to come to that understanding! And those are the people who run the organization."

Mary Z. started laughing softly and explained, "Krishnaji was presented with a medal for peace. But then he forgot it on the table, and one man came after him with the medal."

We started to laugh at the unusual configuration of events, and Krishnamurti also joined our amusement.

The director asked him, more seriously, "Well, sir, what if you were nominated for the Nobel Peace Prize—would you accept it?"

Krishnamurti looked at him with a surprised look on his face, and then replied, "Sir, how could I accept an award like that? An award for what? The politicians have been awarding this peace prize to each other for years, but there isn't any peace in the world. It's all just a farce, some kind of game they are playing. No, sir, if you are doing the right thing, you won't accept any prizes or awards. Right action is an end in itself."

Suddenly, we were all talking excitedly at the same time, weighing the pros and cons of the Nobel Peace Prize, as if it were a real possibility. But Krishnamurti remained aloof, uninterested in any actual or potential prizes.

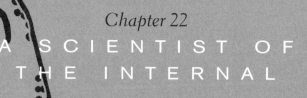
### Starters

*Tossed green salad with vinaigrette
or blue cheese dressing.
Marinated tofu salad, with grated carrots,
finely cubed celery, parsley and ginger.
Potato-and-egg salad flavored with dill weed
and finely cubed pickles.*

### Main Dishes

*Chilled gazpacho soup, prepared
with tomatoes, cucumbers and cilantro.
Couscous with parsley, raisins, and almonds.
Vegetable Provençal, dry stir-fried zucchini,
mushrooms, and green, red
and yellow bell peppers.*

### Dessert

*Super-rich chocolate brownies,
served with vanilla ice cream.
Fresh, seasonal fruit.*

AT THE END OF APRIL, THERE WAS A NEW HOUSE GUEST AT ARYA Vihara. Mr. Grohe, the retired businessman from Switzerland, moved into one of the rooms for the duration of the upcoming talks, since the house in Ojai which he had just acquired was being remodeled. He and his fiancée, a lady from Romania, regularly joined us for lunch.

As was usually the case, a number of Krishnamurti's friends came to have lunch with us during the last days of April. Among them was Ronald Eyre, a British television and theater producer, who had had a videotaped dialogue with him at Brockwood Park about playfulness in June, 1984. He was an exuberant, eloquent person, who seemed to enjoy laughter. Fairly soon into the meal, they were exchanging jokes with each other, to everyone's delight. Another, more regular guest, was Sydney Field, the Costa Rican consul in Los Angeles, and a Hollywood scriptwriter. He would come to see his old friend Krishnamurti and to have lunch with us a few times a year. They had first met sixty years before and had been good friends ever since. Sydney was a very warm-hearted, modest person, soft-spoken, but with an inquisitive mind. A third guest was Dr. Ravi Ravindra, a professor of religion, physics and philosophy, originally from India, who now lived and taught in Nova Scotia, Canada. He had visited Krishnamurti two or three times in the past few years, and they had established a good rapport with one another over a number of cordial conversations.

There really was no easy way to describe Krishnamurti and to cate-gorize his teaching. During the early theosophical days, he had been hailed as the Messiah and World Teacher, as the Christ, as an enlight-ened human being akin to the Buddha, and as the Vehicle of the Lord Maitreya. After rejecting the role designed for him, he was seen as a revolutionary, a spiritual rebel and iconoclast. More recently, he had been variously described as a spiritual teacher, an educator, a psychol-ogist, a mystic and a religious philosopher. Naturally, what defied con-ventional labeling was not only his holistic approach to living, but also the wholeness of his teaching, which went beyond specialization and academic strictures.

I often thought of him as a philosopher in the true, original sense of the word. He himself, on a number of occasions, defined philosophy as 'the love of truth', or 'the love of life'. Never a stickler for words, he read-ily concurred with our more literal translation of philosopher as 'friend, lover of wisdom'. Curiously, he frequently emphasized that he had never read any of the religious scriptures or philosophical writings. He denied that truth could be recorded, including the books published under his name. At one time he had told some close associates, "K's teachings are a living thing and the books, I'm afraid, are not. No book is."

Recently he had been watching a television program about Aristotle and Plato. It portrayed their inquiry into, and subsequent formulation of, philosophical concepts, such as beauty, justice, virtue, freedom, and happiness; and how, through the centuries, their thinking continued to exert considerable influence on the ethos of most modern-day societies. The program rekindled both his fascination with Aristotle and his critical attitude toward making Aristotle—or anyone else for that matter—a source of spiritual authority. Krishnamurti's style of dialogue, starting with not-knowing and relying on constant questioning, often reminded me of Socrates' method, practiced in the Athenian marketplace over two millennia ago.

DURING LUNCH ON THURSDAY, MAY 2, KRISHNAMURTI AND RAVI Ravindra engaged in an easygoing yet probing conversation, punctuated by friendly laughter, about the scientific mind and its method of observing and examining disinterestedly.

"Sir," Krishnamurti remarked earnestly, lightly touching the other man's arm, "you know the scientific approach—skeptical, doubting, questioning, always questioning, and impartial, right?"

"Well, Krishnaji," Ravi replied, "it's probably very much the way *you* inquire into an issue: objective, unbiased, and so on."

"Quite right, sir, up to that point we are of one mind. But why don't most of the scientists apply those same rational, disinterested standards of inquiry to their daily life—you know, without self-interest, and so on? You follow? Or even to examine the consequences of their work, which may be used for all sorts of destructive purposes?" He paused to allow the other to respond.

The professor seemed hesitant to explain or defend the scientist's moral dilemma. Typically, Krishnamurti asked questions which were descriptions of fact and which, therefore, did not have an immediate answer. They revealed a deeper meaning, if one quietly pondered them without hurrying to find a reply.

Ravi gave a dazzling bright smile and sidestepped the question by remarking with affection, "Krishnaji, you really are a scientist of the internal."

It wasn't meant as flattery, and though Krishnamurti didn't respond directly, he seemed quite pleased with this description.

The following day at lunch, Krishnamurti asked Ravi, who was staying at Arya Vihara, "Sir, you have studied the ancient Greek philosophers. You have read Aristotle and his work. Do you think he had an insight?"

He imparted a special meaning to the term 'insight'—it was the illumination of the total human activity. Ravi had a swift, bright mind and a fine sense of humor, so he answered with a smile, "Well, I don't know. Perhaps, yes, he probably had insight into some things..."

The conversation flowed on with much humor and affection, touching on Plato, St.Thomas Aquinas, Kant, Einstein, Bohm and others, and Krishnamurti was royally enjoying himself. Ravi told a joke and, to everyone's amusement, Krishnamurti, still laughing, responded in kind. "I heard this joke the other day," he said. "Two friends die and make it to heaven. They have wings and haloes and are above the clouds. One man says to the other, 'If we're dead and in heaven, why do I feel so awful?'"

When the laughter had subsided, Ravi mentioned two well-known Indian teachers of the past, Nagarjuna and Patanjali. He explained that there was no such thing as an Indian school of philosophy, in the strict Western academic sense. Krishnamurti responded, "Forget all that academic stuff for a moment—sorry—what does philosophy mean? It's the love of truth, the love of life, not the love of books. It's a living thing."

Ravi politely deferred to the older man by moving away from the academic standpoint, and the conversation flowed on to the Brahmanical tradition. Fundamentally, Krishnamurti rejected all organized beliefs, cults, religions, philosophies, gurus and spiritual authority. At the same time, however, he retained a fondness for some of the original aspects of world religions. He often expressed profound respect for the figure of the Buddha, and every once in a while he could be heard extolling the virtues of what he called the 'original' Brahmanical tradition.

Now he was telling Ravi, "Sir, the other day I was on an airplane, in the first-class section, and on the other side of the aisle there was an older gentleman, very cultured, apparently wealthy, fine clothes and all that. He was from a Muslim country, as he told me. At mealtime, the stewardess brought the food on a tray—mine was vegetarian. The gentleman noticed it and asked me about it. So I told him about the real Brahmanical tradition, the original one, which had been going on for centuries—you know sir, very strict, very austere, and without compromise: no meat, no alcohol, and so on, insisting on immaculate cleanliness—you know how fussy they can be...." He pulled a funny face, implying that he also cherished the cleanest in hygiene and sanitary conditions, but he clearly did not condone the extreme forms of Brahmanical conduct, which forbade a Brahmin to touch a person from a lower caste, or even to touch a physical object touched by a non-Brahmin. Nor did he practice any of the ritualistic cleansings and washings that orthodox Brahmins engaged in.

"So I described to him," he continued, "what was behind that austerity, that demand for purity—the real integrity of that way of life—not just empty words and dead tradition, but living—you know, sir—real." He clenched his fist emphatically, and his face became intense with the strength of inner passion, conveying what he meant by the word 'real' with a powerful burst of energy, which seemed to fill the room. "And the other man became very curious about the whole thing, so he asked the stewardess whether he could change his food and also have a vegetarian meal. And so he tried it."

We were all impressed. After a pause, Krishnamurti continued in an almost confidential tone, "But you know, sir, this original, true Brahmanical tradition—not to be corrupted by anything—hardly exists any more: not in India, nor anywhere else. Who nowadays lives that way? No, no," he answered his own question, "all that is gone." Another dramatic pause, then, as if to confirm that pure lifestyle through his own person and way of living, he exclaimed with a sense of affirmative joy, "But the strength and beauty that is in that; think of it, sir!"

After a brief interval of silence, Ravi quietly asked, "But how did it happen, Krishnaji? Why has the true, uncorrupted Brahmanical way of life become extinct?"

Krishnamurti gave him a surprised look. "You know how these things happen, sir; it becomes organized and institutionalized, with leaders and followers, the leaders seducing and exploiting the followers, and vice-versa. In that is already the seed of violence: because self-interest is the beginning of violence, and obedience is violence."

Ravi mentioned the famous chapter from the Indian epic, the

*Mahabharata*, which describes the dialogue between Krishna, the divine charioteer, and the warrior prince, Arjuna, as they are positioned between the two opposing fronts, preparing for the decisive battle. "Krishna tells him that it is the duty of the warrior, his right action, to fight for his cause, even if it involves killing. Because life and death are one", the scholar explained.

During public talks in India, Krishnamurti often took particular delight in pointing out that he had not read any of the sacred books, not even the *Bhagavad Gita*—the chapter that Ravi was referring to, often published as a book in its own right and considered sacred by many Hindus. Now he quickly moved away from scriptural theory to living actuality, responding, "But why kill? Why kill at all, sir? Nobody ever asks that question. Always one particular form is singled out and condemned— nuclear, laboratory animals—you follow? They never ask the total question. They keep saying it's for the national good, and so on. And you know the tricks the leaders come up with. Even Gandhi—I used to know him personally—with his so-called non-violence, attempting to force others to comply with his wishes and demands through fasting. That's not non-violence! Or think of it, sir," he turned to fully face Ravi, "Gandhi used to sleep with a young girl, I believe it was his niece—not sleep with, but sleep in the same bed, and then he would talk about not feeling any sexual desire, you know, not being aroused, being celibate. Can you imagine what must be going on in a man like that?"

I was puzzled to hear about the Indian national hero's strange behavior and asked, "But why did he do that?"

"To test himself, to prove his asceticism. But no concern for the girl, what she might feel...."

Ravi now addressed the question of teacher and student, guru and disciple, and asked Krishnamurti why he rejected the value of that relationship. "In a certain sense, Krishnaji," he pointed out, "all of us here are your disciples. We are listening to you, we are learning from you, and you are teaching us. Take Michael here," he said, pointing at me, "he is dedicated to you, and one can easily imagine him to be your disciple."

At the mention of my name, and the prospect of being cast as Krishnamurti's disciple, I felt a sudden emotional upsurge, which left me in two minds. On one hand, the notion of being his disciple appealed to me in a solemn, old-fashioned way, although I wasn't quite sure how to reconcile this with being his friend. (Was it possible to be someone's dis-

*Yes.*

ciple and friend at the same time?) On the other, I could see the inherent contradiction in discipleship, the old trick of power and knowledge.

Krishnamurti gave an amused laugh, shaking his finger at Ravi. "Ah, no, sir! That's the old game of 'I know' and 'you don't', of initiation, of the transmission of the secret knowledge, and all that traditional nonsense. We are saying something entirely different, sir. We are moving together, exploring together, discovering and learning together—otherwise, what's the point of it? Then we are back to methods, systems, and the stuff that's been going on in the name of religion for thousands of years. And you know what that has resulted in: conflict, sorrow, and war without end."

We didn't go any further into this question because Ravi had to leave for the airport to catch his flight home to Canada. He affectionately thanked us for our hospitality and bade us farewell.

*But K. is very much in charge. Treated with Seniority, no one can conceive of this, There is personal delusion here.*

SATURDAY, MAY 4, WAS THE DAY OF THE FULL MOON. WE WERE eight for lunch, including the newly wedded Grohes. The conversation was about cars. Krishnamurti liked excellence in all fields of human endeavor. He appreciated good clothes, good watches, and other manmade things that were of practical use in everyday life. He had a special fondness for good cars, and his favorite was the Mercedes. I took the opportunity to ask him, "Krishnaji, why don't you ever use a Rolls-Royce or a Bentley, which are famous for being the most exquisite cars? Why do you prefer a Mercedes?"

"Rolls-Royces are much too pretentious, too ostentatious. Mercedes cars are more subdued, and they have the best engineering. They were the first ever to build cars, so they have to be good."

As we talked about the latest automotive innovations, someone produced a brochure of the 1985 Mercedes models. Together we thumbed through the catalogue, admiring the sleek machines and their hefty prices. Krishnamurti admitted to liking the looks and other details of the 500 SEL coupe. Looking at the price list, he wondered, "How much would this car cost, if one bought it here?"

Erna turned toward me, "Can't we find out how much it costs?"

I remembered that the nearest Mercedes dealership was in Santa Barbara, so I jumped from my seat and said, "I'll find out, sir." A phone call confirmed that the basic sticker price was $58,000. I promptly relayed the data, and it became clear that one could save almost $10,000 if one bought the car from the factory in Germany and shipped it to the U.S. Krishnamurti looked impressed but seemed unwilling to commit himself, especially since there was already a 450 SLC dark-green sports coupe in the garage, less than ten years old with under 15,000 miles on the odometer, in mint condition, and, for all practical purposes, his.

TWO DAYS LATER, AS WE WERE CLEARING THE TABLE AFTER lunch, he took me aside confidentially.

"Michael, can you do me a favor?"

"Of course, sir."

"Do you know the author Leon Uris?"

I immediately assumed that he was on the point of telling me that the writer of several famous action yarns was going to join us for lunch. Then realizing that he asked whether I had heard his name before, I answered, "Well, yes. He wrote *Exodus* and several other adventure stories."

He grabbed my arm gently but with a sense of passionate urgency. "Yes, that's right, sir. Can you go into town — but please don't make an extra trip for it ... the next time you drive into town to shop, could you buy me some of his thrillers at the bookstore there? *Topaz* is one I haven't read. Mrs. Zimbalist is very busy with the correspondence — I don't want to ask her. She'll pay you the money for them."

"I'll be going into town this afternoon to do some shopping at the market. So I'll see if they have any of his books."

"Thank you, sir," he said and left the kitchen through the patio door.

Later that afternoon, I drove into town and, apart from running a few other errands, bought two paperbacks by Leon Uris at the local bookstore in the Arcade.

DURING MIDWEEK, BEFORE THE START OF THE TALKS, WE HAD a small luncheon with just seven of us. We talked about Hitler, Mussolini and Stalin, and their totalitarian regimes, which had perpetrated horrible crimes against humanity. Someone remarked, "The worst crime in the history of mankind must have been the Holocaust—millions of Jews and other innocent people systematically killed in the concentration camps of Nazi Germany."

Krishnamurti was seldom ready to make a scapegoat of anyone. He was rooted in the present moment and therefore seemed able to have a global outlook. He said, "Horrible things have happened in the past and are happening in the world today. The concentration camps are still going on. It wasn't only the Germans who committed the Holocaust; there are holocausts going on right now. You know what's happening in the world: Cambodia, Africa, Russia and China. Not only six million of a particular group of people, there are millions more now, tortured and killed for ideologies, and we are indifferent to it all. And you've had your own holocaust here in America: the extermination of the Red Indians—face it, sir!"

The conversation now turned to ongoing conflicts in the world: Iran and Iraq, Northern Ireland, the Lebanon. Someone criticized the Israeli government for excessively suppressing the Palestinian population. But Krishnamurti, as he usually did, staunchly defended Israel, "No, sir. What can Israel do? She's pushed against the wall. She's surrounded by wolves, with her back to the sea. Where is she to go? She has no choice but to defend herself. No, please, see the whole situation."

THE FIRST DAY OF THE 1985 OJAI TALKS WAS SATURDAY, MAY 12, which also happened to be Krishnamurti's ninetieth birthday. As I usually did on such days, I started lunch preparation early in the morning, so that everything was ready by eleven o'clock. Thus, I was able to drive to the Oak Grove, eight miles west of Arya Vihara and attend the talk at 11:30, which normally lasted between sixty and ninety minutes. Afterwards, I'd rush back to serve lunch on time between 1:30 and 2:00 p.m.

Krishnamurti never celebrated his birthday; far from allowing one to congratulate him, he did not really appreciate one's mentioning it. So, just before leaving for the Oak Grove, I went into the rose garden and picked a single rose, magnificent, dark crimson and fragrant, and placed it in a vase in front of his place at the table.

It was a curious day, cold, overcast and grayish. When I arrived at the

Oak Grove, I had difficulty locating my reserved seat amidst the thousands of people and finally sat on the periphery, where there was much coming and going. A man next to me kept making jerky movements and talking loudly to himself, while two army helicopters circled noisily overhead. I was rather distracted and had difficulty following what Krishnamurti was saying. But he was full of intensity and a few times resorted to paradoxical formulations to make his point. "Don't listen to the speaker," he said, "listen to yourself." Later he remarked ironically, "Therefore all the religions of the world ... say they're the divine revelation, directly from the horse's mouth..."

The next day the weather improved, the sun piercing and gradually dispersing the clouds. Krishnamurti addressed the complex question of guilt: how it was fueled by thought and memory, how utterly futile and destructive it was, and how it related to sensation, desire and fear. We were twelve for lunch that day, including Pupul Jayakar, who talked at length about her biography of Krishnamurti, which she was close to finishing.

IT WAS A BUSY WEEK, AND WE HAD A STEADY FLOW OF GUESTS from around the world, who came and had lunch with Krishnamurti.

During the second question-and-answer meeting on Thursday morning, he put aside the written questions which had been submitted in advance and started to interact directly with the audience, asking them what they really wanted to talk about. While conversing with several people, he emphasized, "Use K as a mirror to view yourself. The mirror, the person is not important. What he's saying may reflect what you are." After the meeting, fourteen of us, including Krishnamurti, went to the nearby Ranch House Restaurant for lunch, which was a delightful change.

By Saturday, the 18th, the weather had completely turned: it was sunny and clear, with a rare sharpness, that allowed each minute detail of the surrounding hillsides to stand out in pristine beauty. Krishnamurti began the talk by saying, "It's a beautiful morning, isn't it? I hope you are enjoying yourselves." He went on to talk about yoga and its commercialization, and about *raja* yoga, the king of yogas, which had no system or discipline but was about deeply ethical living. He added mysteriously, "And there is a yoga that cannot be taught to another."

He made a few other, rather startling pronouncements, quite contrary to conventional wisdom, such as, "Where there is fear, there is
God", "success is utter mediocrity", "the vanity of one's own cultivated
intelligence", and "we must be terribly honest to ourselves, otherwise
there is no fun in it." He repeated the joke about the two men in
heaven, which he had told at the lunch table a few days earlier, and
then commented on the social aspect of humor, "Humor is necessary.
To be able to laugh, to find a good joke. To be able to laugh together,
not when you are by yourself, but together." Later on, as he spoke about
pleasure, fear and desire, he said, "Having a good cigar, having a good
meal..." It was the first time I had heard him mention a good cigar.
Krishnamurti never ceased to surprise me with a new twist, a new
glimpse, something that one couldn't possibly foresee.

THE FOLLOWING DAY, SUNDAY, MAY 19, WAS THE FOURTH
and last talk. None of us knew then that this was to be his last talk ever
at the Oak Grove. Amidst birdsong in the dappled light among the trees,
he invoked the two friends who, without any barriers between them,
shared their intimate problems and together inquired into freedom,
continuity and death. He gravely declared, "There may be no other certainty, no other finality, but death."

When some of the audience laughed at a remark of his about death,
he advised them earnestly, "Please, don't laugh. This is much too serious. Not that we shouldn't have humor. It's good to laugh, but laughter
may be the means of avoiding facing facts. So one has to be aware of
that." After a moment, he lightened up and said, "Not that we should
not have humor. Laugh with all your being at a good joke." Amidst
increasing laughter from his listeners, he added whimsically, "The
speaker has collected a lot of jokes—not vulgar jokes, but good jokes.
But the speaker won't go into that."

Exploring disorder, the accumulation of knowledge, and attachment, he pointed out, "We are vast accumulations of memory; we are a
bundle of memories." His words struck me as a sudden revelation, even
though I had heard him say similar things before. They were so concrete, direct and logical, so obvious. I heard them and I could observe

the fact. He continued to inquire into death and ending, and laughingly recounted a story, "We used to know a man who had collected a lot of money, immensely rich. He was dying, and he kept a lot of it in his cupboard, literally—I happened to be there. He told his son to open the cupboard to look at all the diamonds, gold and banknotes. He was looking at it happily, and he was dying."

As the audience started laughing, he commented sadly, "I know." And, now laughing himself, "He never realized he was dying—because the money mattered enormously, not death." His passion intensified as he inquired into religion, which he viewed as something quite different from conventional church-going, rituals, and prayers. "Everything that man has put together as religion is not religion." He delved into the brain and the mind, into awareness and meditation, stating with utter humility, "The speaker has watched, not just his own petty little brain, but the brain of humanity." Finally he said, "There is something that is beyond time, when all time has stopped. That's the meditation that is the true religious mind."

I had seldom observed him empty his consciousness so completely as on this occasion. It seemed as if he had drained himself of every last ounce of energy. I hurried to my car and drove through town toward the east end. On Grand Avenue I passed the grey Mercedes sedan, driven by Mary Z., with Krishnamurti sitting motionless beside her.

THERE WERE ELEVEN OF US FOR LUNCH THAT DAY. I HAD prepared a carrot and ginger salad, a marinated artichoke and olive salad, freshly made spinach lasagna, asparagus, and a tropical fruit salad. Less than half an hour after my arrival, Krishnamurti entered the kitchen from the patio, carrying a few things in his hands.

"Good morning, Krishnaji," I said, although it was almost two o'clock in the afternoon.

"Good morning, Michael," he replied and walked over to the window, where he placed three paperbacks and a small, flat object in worn-out black leather on the counter. I noticed he had changed his clothes and was now wearing blue jeans, a navy-blue woolen cardigan and suede loafers. Only the green, raw-silk shirt had he been wearing earlier that morning. I looked into his face with some curiosity, as if to make sure that this was the same person who less than two hours ago had given one of the most complete, illuminating talks I had ever heard.

"So, that's that," he stated simply. I assumed he was referring to the conclusion of the talks. Leaning against the counter, he looked drained of energy, but self-possessed and quietly alert like a child. Out of the blue he remarked, "We saw you passing us in the car." I didn't quite know what to say, because my mind was still aglow from the talk. Usually we made no comment to Krishnamurti on the content or the quality of a talk—it simply would have been presumptuous—but I was still so overwhelmed by it that I felt compelled to stammer, "It, it was ... incredible, Krishnaji!"

He turned his head away from me to look out the window before saying simply, "It's over, sir."

So that was that. After a brief interval of silence, I took a deep breath and, gathering my wits about me, turned my attention to the objects on the counter. "What's this, sir?" I asked.

"Some thrillers, Michael," he replied. "See if you've read any of them. And this is an alarm clock. If it's any use to you, you can have it."

I picked it up carefully and was surprised at its weight. It took me several moments of guessing and fumbling before I managed to open it. Its square, gold-trimmed face bore the watchmaker's name. "Jaeger-Le Coultre," I exclaimed, remembering the name from The New Yorker ads of illustrious Swiss horologists. "Thank you very much, sir."

He brushed aside my exuberant gratitude, "I think it still runs fairly accurately."

Placing it back on the counter, I said, "We have quite a few guests today."

"Is everything ready?" he asked. "Shall I tell them?"

We proceeded to meet the other nine guests. The conversation was rather low-key: about Krishnamurti's forthcoming journey to Brockwood Park, England. Krishnamurti himself was quiet and withdrawn, empty of the demands of ordinary time, oblivious of ordinary human endeavors. We kept the lunch brief, since everyone knew he needed some rest.

*Chapter 23*

# THE LONG
# GOOD-BYE

*" Thought cannot hold this moment,*

*for this moment is not of time.*

*This moment is the ending of time;*

*time has stopped at that moment,*

*there is no movement at that moment*

*and so it is not related to another moment.*

*It has no cause*

*and so no beginning and no end.*

*Consciousness cannot contain it.*

*In that moment of nothingness*

*everything is. "*

–J. Krishnamurti
*Krishnamurti's Journal*

IT WAS THE MONDAY AFTER THE END OF THE TALKS, and in five days Krishnamurti was to leave Ojai for England. At table, the nine of us were eating rather pensively, and the conversation was monosyllabic. Everyone seemed to be absorbed in their own thoughts. I was beginning to feel self-conscious and nervous, and my brain was hectically scrambling for something to say. But I couldn't quite think of anything, not even a news item. In fact, I hardly knew where to look, since I was facing Krishnamurti, who looked like a monolith of stillness, stern yet at ease. While I concentrated on the food in front of me, I listened to the sounds of knives and forks against plates, and the few words exchanged between long intervals of silence.

Suddenly I looked up and encountered Krishnamurti's full gaze. I was looking directly into his eyes, which were quietly observing me. He didn't flinch or avert his gaze but kept on gazing at me with enormous quietude. For the instant that our eyes met, I thought I was gazing into stark blackness, into vast emptiness. There was no reaction on his part, no smile, no recognition, no judgment, only watching. I thought for a moment that the whole impersonal force of nature was contacting me, the limitless depth of space itself was watching my every move. I felt a tremendous shock, less of apprehension than of sudden alertness. My heart was beating strongly. Releasing a long breath, I relaxed, and only an unusual sensation remained, disquieting but vague and hard to define.

The man next to Krishnamurti, a radio journalist and old acquaintance of his from Australia, started to ask him a number of questions about the dissolution of the Order of the Star in 1929.

"Why did you choose to disband the organization, Krishnaji?"

"I didn't choose it, sir. I've never made a choice in my life. It simply became inevitable. When there is clarity, there is no choice."

The conversation between them continued, focusing on man's search for truth. "One cannot seek truth," Krishnamurti said after a while. "There is a beautiful story about this; I don't know if you've heard it before. A young man leaves home to seek truth, and he travels all over the world, studies with many teachers, acquiring knowledge and skills. But somehow truth always eludes him: he's never quite able to get a hold of it. When he's an old man, he returns home and opens the door, and there it is. Truth was there all the time; it was waiting for him all the time. Truth cannot be sought after," he concluded.

After a long interval of silence, the man went on with his questioning. "But why do you talk, Krishnaji?"

"I really don't know what else to do," Krishnamurti answered with humility. "I really wouldn't know what to do. I've done it all my life, you understand, sir? In the beginning, I was horribly shy, and it was a pain for me to speak in public. I tried all sorts of things: for a while I used to speak from behind a curtain, but then I gave it up—it was too silly."

We all laughed at the image of the young man speaking to an audience from behind a curtain. It was a relief to laugh.

A teacher asked him, "But what about all the worship and adoration you receive, sir, especially in India?"

"Not only in India," Krishnamurti replied, "here too." And he shot an ironical glance around the table. Everyone seemed to meet his gaze, as if to assert silently, 'Not me'. Suddenly he burst out in joyous laughter, exclaiming, "It's all so crazy, it's all so utterly absurd!"

Although I joined him in his uninhibited laughter, I was still puzzled by what he meant by 'it'. After our exhilaration died down, I asked, "Krishnaji, what do you mean by 'it'? You mean the talks and all this?" I gestured generally toward the other guests at the table, including the whole situation that we found ourselves in. There were still tears of laughter in his eyes, as he turned to look at me. "Yes, sir, all of that, and the whole circus around him," he replied with a puckish smile, pointing his slender index finger toward his chest. So, although all of us certainly were part of the circus, we joined his delight.

TWO DAYS LATER, THE FORMER GOVERNOR OF CALIFORNIA, Jerry Brown, and an aide of his, came to have lunch with Krishnamurti. I didn't have much of a chance to follow their conversation, since I was sitting at the far end of the table, but from the snippets I was able to gather, their approaches and concerns varied considerably.

Krishnamurti kept emphasizing the larger context, stressing the need for a transformation in consciousness. At one point he said to the governor, "Sir, if only five people get together and do the right thing, you know, really go into this, they could affect the consciousness of all humanity."

Mr. Brown, by contrast, seemed more concerned with ecological issues and talked about high automotive fuel consumption, the resulting pollution, and related statistical data. His approach was via outer, regulatory action. Although they agreed on a number of issues, they did not see eye to eye on the more fundamental questions.

ON SEVERAL OCCASIONS, I HAD SEEN KRISHNAMURTI enthusiastically wash his Mercedes, both here and at Brockwood Park, sometimes with the help of a staff member. Observing him polish the vehicle with the utmost care, I felt a curious desire to help him, to work together with him at a simple, menial task. At long last my wish was partially fulfilled when, after lunch with Governor Brown, he asked me, "Michael, can you do us a favor? Can you wash and wax the green Mercedes, the sports coupe?"

"Yes, sir, sure. When would you like me to do it?"

"If you have time, this afternoon. Mrs. Zimbalist will give you all the things you need. I'm sorry I can't help you—it's a bit too much for me."

I hastened to assure him that I could easily do it by myself, and, after finishing the clean-up in the kitchen, I phoned Mary Z. to tell her that I was coming over to wash the car.

It was a warm, sunny afternoon. The sleek green vehicle was parked on the turn-around in front of the garage beneath the pepper tree. Hundreds of bees were buzzing amidst an abundance of tiny white blossoms, which dangled from the arching branches. I went at it with chamois, soap and wax, buckets and drying cloths, and a long water hose. I wanted to clean the car as I had never cleaned a car before. Half-feverishly, I gathered my energy to scrub every square inch of the forest-green lacquer. After applying the wax, I polished it to a high, glossy sheen. The only problem was that fine, microscopic fibers from the polishing cloth adhered to the mirroring surface like magnetic filaments. There always seemed to be a final line that I had to struggle to get rid of. Finally, the car stood sparkling in the sunlight, ready for a drive to Lake Casitas.

The following day, when Krishnamurti entered the kitchen just before lunch, he commented on my car wash job, "You really went at it, sir, cleaning the car yesterday afternoon. I was watching you from the window."

He didn't mean it as praise, but I found it pleasing that he put it this way.

There were eighteen guests for lunch, and after we had cleared the table, Krishnamurti approached me in the kitchen and asked, "Are you going shopping this afternoon, sir?"

"Yes, Krishnaji: I have a couple of errands to run. Can I bring anything for you?"

"As we'll be leaving for England tomorrow, we still have a lot of packing to do. Mrs. Zimbalist has her hands full with all sorts of things—you know: emptying the larder, cleaning out the refrigerator, and so on." He produced a small white ceramic jar, which he handed to me. "Can you please go to the pharmacy, the one across from the post office, and buy one of these jars? It's skin cream. It's quite expensive, about twenty dollars. Mrs. Zimbalist will give you the money."

I took the small jar and studied the label. It was a skin cream made from almond oil. Assuming that it was meant for Krishnamurti himself, I thought it wouldn't last long and that it might be advisable to stock up for a nine-month absence. I asked him, "Are you sure, Krishnaji, that one is enough? Shouldn't I get two or three jars?"

He seemed irritated by my suggestion. He looked at me seriously and said emphatically, "I want one. Not two, not three, but one and only one. I want one and no more."

"All right, sir. I'll buy one and bring it over to Pine Cottage."

He grabbed my arm with a characteristic gesture and said, "Thank you, Michael."

"You are welcome, Krishnaji."

FRIDAY, MAY 24, 1985 WAS THE DAY OF DEPARTURE. WE WERE having an early lunch at 12:30 p.m., so that Krishnamurti, Mary Z. and Mr. and Mrs. Grohe, who were traveling with them, could leave at 2:00 p.m. for LAX. There were eleven of us at this luncheon, which, unbeknown to us, was to be the last lunch Krishnamurti ever had at Arya Vihara. Strangelyrangely, it was a rather solemn affair. Everyone, including Krishnamurti, was intensely and unusually taciturn and thoughtful. I was beginning to feel slightly depressed by the prevailing mood, and for some reason the Sanskrit saying which Krishnamurti had told me the previous month flashed through my mind. Impulsively, I intoned the sonorous phrase into the quietness, "*Anna dathu sukhi*

*bhava.*" As I recited the words, I looked at Krishnamurti and asked, "Excuse me, Krishnaji, is that the correct pronunciation?"

Quietly he said, "*Anna dathu sukhi bhava.*"

I repeated it after him, and he corrected me three times in a rather serious, dignified way, until I got reasonably close to pronouncing it accurately.

The other people at the table followed the exchange between us with polite interest, as if something larger and more significant were occupying their minds. Afterwards, the eleven of us resumed our silent pondering, punctuated by a few laconic remarks. Then Krishnamurti all at once collected himself and said something into the subdued air that I had never heard him say before. Raising his eyes and very deliberately surveying us, he addressed us individually and collectively, "Thank you, all of you, for having me here. Thank you for all that you have done for K. I have been, K has been a guest wherever he goes and stays."

It was a stunning announcement, delivered with a sense of deep seriousness, a royal dignity that couldn't be touched or questioned. At the same time, there was such humility about it, such guileless and simple innocence, that it touched me at the core of my being. Maybe the others, also, were startled by his unpretentiousness. At any rate, our normally quick and eager egos found themselves unable to react to his words. After an interval of alert silence, several people started to protest that the Foundation, the property, really were all his, bearing his name, and so on. Someone asked whether we weren't in fact all guests here on earth. While these animated exchanges were taking place, Krishnamurti remained silent. Listening and observing, he seemed far removed from the commotion. He sat as if clothed in dignity and an untouchable seriousness that rested in itself. He was a rock in the flood of our agitation.

Lunch over, everybody rose. Half an hour later, several of us were lined up beneath the pepper tree to say goodbye to him. As he shook hands with one of the directors, he said to him, "See you in India in December, sir", referring to an international educational conference at Rishi Valley that four of the Ojai staff, including myself, were going to attend.

Finally he came to shake my hand and said with a smile, "See you in Rougemont, Michael."

He was alluding to the village near Saanen in Switzerland, where he was going to be staying during the July Gatherings. He and Mary Z. had asked me earlier to do the cooking for them there, since the Italian lady who had prepared their meals for many years was too old to continue. I had gladly agreed to their request.

"Thank you, Krishnaji," I replied. "Have a good journey."

After we had secured the suitcases on the luggage rack of the new school van, Krishnamurti, Mary Z. and the Grohes got in, and we waved them goodbye as they drove off.

Did any of us have the slightest inkling that this was the last good-bye, the last time that we were to wave farewell to him beneath the pepper tree?

Less than two months later, in mid-July, 1985, a wildfire started at the west end of the valley, near the Maricopa Highway, and slowly advanced, fanned by strong winds and hot dry weather, toward the eastern part of the valley. Subsequently, flames flared up along the southern ridges, engulfing Sulphur Mountain and Black Mountain. The whole valley was at once encircled by a ring of fire, that raged for five days and nights. Dense smoke and fine white ash filled the air. The sun was only visible as a dim orange sphere, shedding an eerie reddish light over the valley. On two consecutive nights we had to evacuate Arya Vihara, because the conflagration had come within a few hundred yards of the buildings. It was the valiant effort of thousands of firefighters that contained the flames, combined with good fortune that made the winds change direction just in time.

When the flames finally died down and the smoke cleared, it seemed a miracle: there weren't any serious injuries; no one had died, nor had any homes been destroyed. But the surrounding mountains and wilderness trails were completely devastated. It was a wasteland of burned-out tree stumps, with black and grey ashes, and the cadavers of many small animals.

IT TURNED OUT THAT I COULD ONLY PARTIALLY FULFILL MY cooking assignment in Rougemont, as I arrived at the lush-green alpine valley a week after the talks had ended. Thankfully, I wasn't altogether too late, since Krishnamurti was staying for another two weeks.

It was a pleasant surprise to find that I was to live in the same chalet as Krishnamurti. Dr. Parchure and Raman Patel, the chef at Brockwood Park, had been sharing the downstairs apartment and didn't mind an additional roommate. Krishnamurti and Mary Z. had the upstairs apartment. Throughout the talks, Raman had been preparing the meals at the chalet, and for the remaining two weeks we agreed to share the kitchen duties.

Soon I learned the shocking news: Krishnamurti had decided that, after twenty-five years, the talks just concluded were to be the last Saanen Talks. In future years, only one annual Gathering would take place in Europe—at Brockwood Park. In this way, the need for extensive traveling and the resultant strain on his energies would be minimized.

These last days at Saanen with Krishnamurti were days of leisure, and they had an exquisite sense of culmination. The chalet had less space than one was accustomed to in California, and, consequently, my companions and I would encounter Krishnamurti many times throughout the day. To be in daily, physical proximity to him was an experience of heightened awareness for me. I became acutely aware, not only of my thoughts and emotions, but also of my shortcomings and limitations. It could be demanding, even distressing, to be so close to the flame. Since the nature of the flame was to be without a center, it tended to show up starkly the solidity of the selves within its range. More than ever, I came into contact with the ways in which I compared myself to others, with my desire to be appreciated, and with the resulting divisiveness, envy and jealousy.

Even so, the five of us enjoyed something akin to a family situation for these twelve days at the beginning of August. There were frequent guests, such as Vanda Scaravelli, who in the past had rented Chalet Tannegg for Krishnamurti; Mr. Grohe, who generously allowed us the use of his apartment, and Asit from India. They joined us for lunch and dinner almost every day.

FROM ROUGEMONT, KRISHNAMURTI AND MARY Z. TRAVELED TO Brockwood Park, while I went to visit my mother in Germany, before also going on to the residential school in Hampshire. The public talks at Brockwood Park were from August 24 through September 1. Colorful autumn was in the air and in the foliage of the many splendid trees, and Krishnamurti seemed once more to have gathered energy from sources beyond.

One sunny morning, I was surprised to see several workmen setting up a yellow crane next to the two large tents, where the talks were taking place. A platform connected to the crane was hoisted above the level of the tents, from where a cameraman filmed the scene of people filing in. An independent television company was producing a documentary on Krishnamurti, which was subsequently aired in the series *The Human Factor* in January, 1986. When I later watched the half-hour program, entitled *The Role of a Flower*, I was surprised by the liveliness and humor that Krishnamurti displayed during the interviews. At one point he responded to the question, how much longer he might carry on talking to thousands of people, "I've told my friends, the moment I'm 'gaga', stop me." Turning more serious, he added, "I've got plenty of energy...."

THOUGH SOMETIMES PUT IN THE SAME BASKET AS THE self-promoting, commercial gurus, Krishnamurti viewed the whole arena of spirituality with marvelous humor. A Monsieur Châtelain had recently written a brief satirical essay, entitled 'How to Become a Top Guru'. It humorously described how to become a successful guru: by practicing benevolent facial expressions in front of a mirror, by growing a long beard, and by giving one's disciples the illusion of spiritual progress. When the article was read out to Krishnamurti at Brockwood Park, he found it so hilarious that he recommended that it be translated and circulated. He even mentioned it during one talk, describing it as cleverly written and funny.

ALTHOUGH THE FOUR TALKS AND TWO QUESTION-AND-ANSWER meetings in the large tent showed him in excellent form, he looked frail and infirm on other days. It was clear that he was spending all his available energy on talking to the thousands who had come from near and far to hear him speak. I was helping in the school kitchen and would sometimes take his dinner up to the west wing. The evening after the end of the talks, I carried a tray with his meal into his bedroom, where he had been resting the whole day. After knocking on the door and hearing his response, I entered and was surprised to find the curtains drawn against the rays of the late sun. Suddenly I felt a curious shyness. He looked like a tiny child in the huge bed, his tousled head propped up against a large pillow, one hand on a paperback lying face down.

"Hello, sir," he smiled wanly, and I returned his greeting.

"Just put it there, Michael," he said, pointing to a low table next to the bed. I had seldom seen him looking so haggard, tired, old, and exhausted. It was heartbreaking. I stood next to the bed for a moment, sensing a great quiet but incapable of thinking of a pertinent remark. He looked at me with a warm smile and, raising one thin arm halfway, said, "Thank you, Michael."

"Thank you, Krishnaji," I said and quietly exited the room.

AFTER TALKING AT LENGTH WITH THE ARCHITECT OF THE large Centre building, that was to be constructed the following year at Brockwood Park, Krishnamurti departed for India in late October, accompanied by Mr. Grohe. Three weeks later, in November, 1985, I flew into Bombay and continued from there by train to Varanasi, arriving at the ancient city on the Ganges after a strenuous thirty-hour journey.

The Rajghat School and Educational Center is situated at the confluence of the Varuna and Ganges Rivers. It is a vast property, with many people milling about. Once I had my room, I went to look for Krishnamurti's house. Surrounded by lovely old trees, it was situated high on the river bank, in view of a vast sweep of the majestic stream.

Dusk was approaching, with its resplendent richness of colors. Suddenly I perceived a figure in loose, white clothes approaching through the dim, saffron-yellow light—it was Krishnamurti. He was accompanied by a group of eight people, all dressed in wide-flowing Indian clothes. My first impulse was to run toward him like a child, but I stopped myself, since I felt uncertain about the proper rules of conduct in a land where gurus were worshipped.

Evidently, he had also recognized me. He kept coming right at me, leaving his group of companions behind. It was like a strong wave sweeping toward me, and the only words I could muster from my blanked-out memory banks were, "Good evening, Krishnaji!"

Coming up to me, he exclaimed with undisguised surprise, "What the hell are you doing here, Michael?"

There was an overwhelming upsurge of affection within me, so that I could barely refrain from hugging him. At that moment he firmly grasped my arms, and I reciprocated by squeezing his thin elbows. There we were, arm to arm, in the evening light. Several of his companions were laughing at his choice of words of welcome.

"It's so good to see you, Krishnaji," I stammered.

"How come you are here, Michael?"

As I started to explain, he suddenly said, "Yes, I remember now, you told me in Rougemont. Where are you staying?"

After he had made sure that I was well taken care of, we wished each other good night and he proceeded with his companions into the house.

Four days later, at nine o'clock in the morning, the 1985 Varanasi Public Talks started in a shaded area beneath the trees. He began by telling the thousand or so people that he had no intention whatsoever of helping anyone. Moments later, he asked affectionately, "Am I saying something strange? You all look so damn serious."

From the moment he started speaking, I felt a peculiar joy bubbling up within me. It stayed with me throughout the talk and into the next day.

The following morning, during the second talk, he remarked, "Tears and laughter are part of sensation; humor is part of sensation", following it with, "Don't look at me as if I'm some crazy nut."

ON NOVEMBER 22, 1985, HE GAVE THE THIRD AND LAST PUBLIC talk at Rajghat. Almost from the outset, he was full of mirth and irony, asking invitingly, "Would anybody like to come and sit here? I really mean it, sir, you can come." And, before long, a bearded young man was sitting next to him on the platform. Talking about various practical skills, he said, "To learn a skill: to become an excellent carpenter, an excellent plumber, an excellent cook!" At that moment, he looked over to where I was sitting, and as our eyes met for a brief instant he murmured under his breath, "Hello, Michael." Then he turned to the audience and said, "There are several friends of mine, who are very good cooks. And also very good philosophers, and psychologists and psychiatrists—they are all here."

Commenting on the fact that life was a struggle for most of us, he presented his own abbreviated version of an evolutionary syllogism, "Monkeys struggle, so we are monkeys. A very famous author—we used to know him—wrote, 'Perhaps we should be behind the bars and not the monkeys.'"

Moments later he told his listeners with good-hearted laughter, "You are a crazy crowd." Then after talking about religion, he said," I must tell you a very good joke—may I? This happens to be hell, and the devil is there in the distance." Pointing straight ahead, he added, "I'm not pointing at anybody. The devil is away in the corner—you know, the Christian devil with two horns and a tail." And he put two fingers like horns to his head, for the benefit of those among the audience unfamiliar with the mythological beast. "There are two people talking together, and one says to the other, 'It's very hot here, isn't it?' And the other fellow says, 'Yes, it's very hot, but it's dry heat.'"

He started laughing quietly at his own joke, then noticed that the majority of the people did not respond. He had obviously neglected the crucial point that the two people in hell were a pessimist and an optimist. He looked around with a quixotic expression and asked, "No joke? You are funny people. I've got lots of jokes. I can't even begin with it."

Two days later, he left Varanasi for Madras and Rishi Valley.

By now, it had become apparent that he was not well: he was visibly losing weight, and his physical energy appeared to be diminishing dramatically. Even so, he went on with staff meetings, talks with the students, and interviews, without the momentum slacking off.

During one morning's talk with the students, he told the following story: "A religious teacher used to deliver a discourse to his disciples every morning. One morning he is on the point of starting his lecture and a bird comes flying in and sits on the windowsill. It sings with all its heart, and continues singing sweetly for some minutes. The teacher doesn't say a word, but only listens to the bird. And, after the bird flies away, he turns to his class and says, 'This morning's sermon is over.'"

He never seemed to run out of anecdotes and stories to tell, even when he was in physical distress. Later, during the third dialogue meeting with the Rishi Valley School teachers, he asked, "May I tell you a joke? The other day I was traveling by air, going somewhere or other. 'Where are you from?' somebody asked me. 'Oh,' I said, 'somewhere'. And he said, 'Actually, where are you from? Are you a Turk, are you a Persian, are you one of the Muslim World?' I said, 'No, no, no.' 'Where are you from?' I said, 'I'm from the Valley of the Rishies.' (It's rather a good name for this place.) He said, 'Where is that?' I said, 'You won't find it.'"

ON DECEMBER 14, THE INTERNATIONAL EDUCATION Conference began, attended by teachers from all the Krishnamurti schools. There were four of us from Ojai and five from Brockwood Park. Although Krishnamurti wanted to be just an observer, it didn't take long before he was participating fully, raising the deliberations to a higher level. To our delight, he also cheered us up with several of his jokes. One of them was a pun on Mysore in the neighboring state of Karnataka, which some of us had just visited. "I have traveled all over India and you should see my sore."

DURING HIS LAST FEW DAYS AT RISHI VALLEY, TEN TO TWELVE of us went with him for walks among the green paddy fields and fragrant mango groves in the powdery light of dusk. Although shaky, he strode ahead of us with long energetic strides. Walking with him among the ancient, rock-strewn hills was a great boon.

BEFORE DAWN ON DECEMBER 23, HE DEPARTED FOR MADRAS. A few days later several of us joined him at Vasanta Vihar. He certainly wasn't well: he felt frequent fatigue, had little or no appetite, and consequently lost weight and stamina. Although several physicians attended him, none of them was able to accurately diagnose the symptoms of what looked like a very serious condition. It was extremely worrying.

IT WAS CHRISTMAS DAY, AND I WAS INVITED TO COME ON Krishnamurti's evening walk on Adyar Beach. It was the same beach where, seventy-five years earlier, as a boy of fourteen, he had been 'discovered' by some of the theosophical elders: he had had a selfless, pure aura and, hence, was designated the Vehicle of the Lord. An hour and a half before sunset twelve of us were driven there in three Ambassador cars through the sprawling property of the headquarters of the Theosophical Society.

At the other end, we filed through a narrow gate in the wall that guarded the property and stepped into a scene of dramatic dimensions. Nature and the whole earth presented themselves with an exhilarating liveliness, with an enormous vitality, revealing beauty without end. A fresh wind was blowing from the blue horizon, and surf was crashing on the yellow sand beach. In the slanting rays of the setting sun, the colors of sky, earth and ocean were brilliantly clear.

The immensity of the moment overwhelmed my senses. For a split second I experienced myself as a minute dot, moving upright on the vast curved surface of the globe. And, as if to give my perception a global context, something huge and white emerged slowly from the depth of the sea on the eastern horizon: the full moon was rising over the mirroring waters. At the same moment, looking west, I saw the sun setting behind silhouettes of palms and banyan trees.

We were strolling in small groups of four along the narrow asphalt path that ran parallel to the beach. We reached the footbridge across the mouth of the Adyar River, of which only a fragment remained, and saw Krishnamurti standing there by himself at the broken edge above the river, his three companions a few feet behind him. He stood motionless, a monument of silence, alone with the beauty of the earth. The wind tore at his clothes, making them flap noisily like bright sails. He was watching several dark-skinned fishermen in loincloths, wading through the turbulent surf and hauling in their nets with a few wriggling fish. After a while, he turned to go back from where he came. When he passed me, his face seemed chiseled in gold, gaunt but luminous. His white hair was wildly tossing about, and he leaned into the sea breeze as he walked by. Sheer benevolence radiated from him.

*Chapter 24*

# L A S T   D A Y S

> "*As one looked at that dead leaf*
>
> *with all its beauty and color,*
>
> *maybe one would very deeply comprehend,*
>
> *be aware of, what one's own death must be,*
>
> *not at the very end*
>
> *but at the very beginning.*
>
> *Death isn't some horrific thing,*
>
> *something to be avoided,*
>
> *something to be postponed,*
>
> *but rather something to be with*
>
> *day in and day out.*
>
> *And out of that comes*
>
> *an extraordinary sense of immensity.*"

–J. Krishnamurti
*Krishnamurti to Himself*

THE NEXT DAY, KRISHNAMURTI UNEXPECTEDLY JOINED THE foreign guests and trustees for lunch in the guest dining room. To see him among us, talking and eating as he used to, nourished our hope and allayed our fear that he might be incapacitated by a serious illness. The Madras Public Talks were to start the following afternoon, December 28, 1985, and we were fairly confident that they would proceed according to schedule. But overnight a number of adverse symptoms indicated a precipitous worsening of his health. Most important, he had developed an extremely high fever. Listening closely to the doctors' advice, he expressed concern for the people who had made great efforts and come from afar to listen to him. Finally, a consensus was arrived at: despite his high fever, the first talk was going to happen as planned that same afternoon.

Almost from the outset of the talk it was abundantly clear that Krishnamurti was 'not himself'. His demeanor and delivery, and a great proportion of what he said, indicated beyond doubt that he was feverishly ill. After the talk he managed to climb down shakily from the platform and was promptly mobbed by crowds of devoted listeners. He still had to wade through a surging sea of humanity to reach the house, two hundred yards away. The two directors, from Ojai and Brockwood Park, quickly came to his rescue by taking him in hand and escorting him through the tumultuous throng. One of them, like a royal herald, shouted out loudly, "Make way, make way!" Watched from a distance, Krishnamurti appeared helpless and exhausted; he was shaking and stunned.

The following day it was decided to have only two more talks at Madras, on January 1 and 4, 1986. All other programs, including the Bombay Talks, were canceled.

Faced with the seriousness of his as yet undiagnosed condition, he made it clear that he wanted to return quickly to California via the Pacific route. Since he planned to arrive in Ojai within two weeks, I also needed to get back in a hurry, so that I could prepare the kitchen for this unexpected event. I, consequently, bought new airline tickets: I would depart from Madras in the late afternoon of December 30, 1985.

Before leaving, I went to say goodbye to Krishnamurti. He was in a large bed, looking quite lively. Genuinely glad to see me, he greeted me fondly. I was shocked to see him so haggard, almost emaciated, and noticed a large band-aid on his forehead. He immediately explained, "I was getting out of bed last night and slipped and fell." Noticing my shocked concern, he hastened to add with childlike innocence, "Don't worry. I only knocked my head against the edge of the bed—it's quite all right now." He moved a trembling hand to the injured spot. I told him I was leaving within a few hours and shook his gentle, sensitive hands. Always brief and unsentimental with good-byes, he was quietly confident as he said, "Have a good journey, sir. See you in California!"

FROM MADRAS I FLEW TO NEW DELHI AND ONWARD VIA EUROPE to California, arriving in Ojai on January 6, 1986. Five days later, January 11, we welcomed Krishnamurti once again beneath the pepper tree. But it was an event full of heartbreak: he was drained of energy and horribly thin, barely managing to walk by himself from the car to Pine Cottage. It turned out he was too weak to come to Arya Vihara for lunch, and instead he took all his minuscule meals at Pine Cottage. Three people attended him around the clock—Mary Z., Dr. Parchure, and Scott Forbes, the latter two of whom had accompanied him on his flight from Madras to Los Angeles.

Since I was busy preparing meals for the residents and visitors at A.V., I didn't see much of Krishnamurti but got the news about his current state of health primarily from Dr. P. Every so often there seemed to be a ray of hope and the promise of recuperation, such as when he took short walks up and down the driveway.

On Tuesday, January 21, I was carrying a tray with lunch over to Pine Cottage and coming out of the orange grove onto the turn-around, when a most unusual sight met my eye. Krishnamurti was sitting motionless on the low circular wall round the pepper tree, with Dr. P. and Scott just a few feet behind him, ready to come to his assistance if needed. He was looking at the contours of the blue hills in the sunlight, silently communicating with the earth, with something beyond the hills and valleys. I felt a sudden shyness overcome me, as if I were trespassing on sacred ground and witnessing the act of love, death and creation. At the same time I was appalled by his pallid complexion, his fatigue and emaciation. He didn't notice me, as I tiptoed past the group, but the other two quietly acknowledged my presence.

Because of intense pain, he was admitted next morning to the intensive care unit of Santa Paula Hospital. His three attendants went with him for the eight days he spent in hospital. While there, he underwent a number of tests, which eventually confirmed that he was suffering from a malignancy.

It was a time of high drama. While he was being subjected to X-rays, nose tubes, intravenous feeding, morphine injections, blood transfusions, CAT scans, and finally an attempted liver biopsy, more and more of his friends and associates from England, India and other parts of the world gathered at A.V. to hear the news that he had an incurable pancreatic cancer. By now, some public announcements had been made concerning the state of his health, and the upcoming Ojai Talks in May were officially canceled. Ironically, they would have been the first talks at Ojai with a fixed admission charge. Tickets had been printed, reservations made, and consequently the office was obliged to reimburse those who had sent in payments.

AT 10:00 A.M. ON THURSDAY, JANUARY 30, AN AMBULANCE PULLED up beneath the pepper tree, and Krishnamurti was carried on a stretcher by two paramedics into Pine Cottage. A hospital bed and an intravenous drip system had been set up, and nurses were to look after him around the clock. By now he was unable to take any food and was fed entirely by intravenous means.

CARRYING A TRAY INTO THE PINE COTTAGE KITCHEN AROUND 1:00 p.m. on February 1, I noticed in passing that the hospital bed had been set up in the living room. An angular metal stand next to the bed had several plastic bottles suspended from a chrome arm, feeding a clear liquid drop by drop through transparent tubes into the veins of the sleeping patient. A male nurse in an immaculate, white-starched uniform sat beside the bed, silently watching patient, monitor and drip system. On the way out, I briefly paused at a respectful distance to take a look at the rare sight. It was something I had never seen before: Krishnamurti asleep.

A frail and tiny child lost amidst billowing white linen, he was breathing gently and regularly, apparently without pain for the time being. His silver hair was disheveled and spread out like an aureole around his still beautiful features. It was an image of heart-breaking poignancy. I felt a sudden urge to shield and protect this precious life, at the same time realizing my utter helplessness. Clearly, nobody was exempt from the law of life, which dictated that old age, disease and death were our common lot. He himself had often talked about it, jokingly quoting an Italian saying: *"Tutti gli uomini debbeno morire, forse anch'io."* When I had asked him what it meant, he had translated it, "All men must die, perhaps I, too." Then we had all laughed. But now, contemplating the cessation of his life, laughter was far from my heart.

As I looked at him asleep on his sickbed, I realized that the mysterious protection, which he had enjoyed throughout his long life and which he himself had often marveled at, was still there—but only tenuously so. All we could do was watch with silent awe the unfolding of his life into its last dawn. I stood there spellbound, listening to his gentle breathing. A sudden, slight sigh escaped his lips, and the dark-skinned head framed in snowy-white stirred. Remembering the twenty-five guests in the A.V. dining room who needed my attention, I swiftly exited from Pine Cottage.

Entering the room full of people eating and talking, I experienced a sharp contrast: there, the gentle breathing of the dying man in the spaciousness of the quiet house; here, the conviviality of his friends. It seemed like two different scenes in a thrilling drama. But did any of us have any idea what was going on? Did we realize the immensity of the event we were witnessing, and that we were an integral part of it?

IN THE LATE AFTERNOON, WE GATHERED IN THE A.V. SITTING room to be briefed by Dr. P. on the current situation regarding Krishnamurti's health. None of us could be under any illusion as to the severity of his condition. The end was in sight. It might go on for days, weeks, or even months, but nothing would prevent the ineluctable decline. His condition was constantly shifting and resembled a roller-coaster ride, ranging from extreme pain, scarcely alleviated by the administration of morphine, to moments of pristine lucidity and clear awakenings in meditation. On a number of occasions, he assured those around him that the painkilling drugs had no detrimental effect on his brain and did not diminish his understanding.

Dr. P. reported that, during the preceding night, Krishnamurti had been able to sleep without a sleeping pill or any other drug, and that he had woken up refreshed and strong. The morning had passed without any of the fierce attacks of pain, to which he had been subject over the past few weeks. During the course of the day he had been seeing friends and trustees, who had come from overseas to receive his final instructions in regard to Schools and Foundations, and to pay him their last respects.

Throughout the night of Sunday to Monday strong winds rushed down from the mountains, whirling through the underbrush, shaking the trees, and whistling on the roofs and round the corners of the house like powerful spirits of the air. It was a night of fierce vitality, of the powers of nature unleashed.

ON THE AFTERNOON OF FEBRUARY 3, KRISHNAMURTI ASKED TO be taken outdoors in a wheelchair, so he could look at the hills and trees once more. Perhaps he wanted to say goodbye to the planet which he loved so much. It did, in fact, turn out to be the last time he was able to be out under the open sky, in the company of trees, communicating with nature.

We all at once harbored the irrational hope that he would be making a comeback—he appeared so fresh and strong.

That same evening I walked over to Pine Cottage, with some food for the people who were taking care of Krishnamurti. On my way through the darkened orange grove, I was wondering whether I would ever meet Krishnamurti again and have a chance to speak with him. I felt shy about requesting a meeting, since I didn't have any significant last questions or statements I wanted to put to him. Nor did I want to impose on him yet another ego with its petty needs and attachments. At the same time, though, he was such a splendid friend. How could I not want to say goodbye to him, even if it was only for a minute or two? These questions had been on my mind for several days now, and I had been pondering what to do about them.

After placing the tray with the food containers on the kitchen counter, I asked Mary Z. whether she felt it might be possible for me to see Krishnamurti for a moment. After brief reflection, she sent someone to check with him.

Some moments later I walked through the corridor that connected the new part of Pine Cottage with the older part where Krishnamurti had his rooms. Entering his bedroom, I was surprised to find it in almost total darkness: just a dim light illuminated the nocturnal room. It took me half a minute of breathless silence to orientate myself and to adjust my eyes to the contours of the room. It was an unusual scene. Krishnamurti was in his nightclothes, prone on his stomach on the hospital bed, his legs wrapped tightly in a blanket. Dr. P. was standing to his left, vigorously massaging his back and shoulders.

I couldn't think of anything to say. Even a simple greeting like 'How do you do?' would seem ambiguous and inappropriate. Neither of them said anything, either, as I approached through the shadows of the room. There was a large lump in my throat, and I was overcome by an immense wave of pain, compassion, and communion with the great man who had given so much—to all of us, to humanity, to myself. At the same time, I realized that any emotional display of pity, tears and grief would be anathema to him. All I managed to bring out was a gurgled "Oh, Krishnaji."

I stretched out my hand, which he took in his hand, as he raised himself slightly from his prone position. All the while Dr. P. continued with his massage, acknowledging my presence with a quiet, friendly smile. The touch of Krishnamurti's hand was the softest and most gentle I had ever felt. Like silk and velvet, it was smooth and pliable—not sweaty, moist or hot, nor brittle, dry, or cold.

He looked at me with wide-open eyes, "Ah, hello, Michael."

I perceived a most curious phenomenon, which neither startled nor surprised me, but rather filled me with awe. I could see light in Krishnamurti. Actual light was shining from that organism, now almost a century old and terminally diseased. A subtle light visibly shone through him, and it was as if he were shining it on me as I stood there, holding his hand. While Dr. P. went on with his massage, Krishnamurti and I silently held hands—friends without barriers. There was a sense of newness and great freedom, of an untouchable innocence that communicated itself.

By the watch, our wordless hand-holding didn't last longer than a few minutes. But it wasn't within the parameters of ordinary time. It was in between time, in the interval from one moment to the next. Emotionally, I felt completely choked up. And very quietly he said, "I'm sorry you have to cook for so many people."

For a moment I was completely dumbstruck. He really meant it. Even more than before, I was at a loss how to respond. I mumbled, embarrassed and close to tears, "Oh, please, sir, it's really no problem at all."

As our hands let go of one another, I could still perceive the subtle light emanating from him, while Dr. P. went on with his skillful manipulation to relieve the physical discomfort. I felt an enormous wave of gratitude rising within me. Before turning to leave the room, I said, "Thank you, Krishnaji, thank you, sir!"

He responded by saying, "Goodbye, sir."

THE FOLLOWING DAY HE FELT UNUSUALLY WELL, CONSIDERING the advanced condition of his illness. The attending physician from Santa Paula, Dr. Deutsch, indicated the possibility of a remission. Krishnamurti even asked if he might travel and speak again. For one last time, hope rose among us, the ardent wish for a miracle, a foolish expectation against all the odds. This gives an idea of the kind of sentiment that prevailed during Krishnamurti's last days on earth. The roller-coaster ride continued.

By February 5, most of the friends and associates, to whom he wanted to communicate final urgent matters, had arrived in Ojai. We numbered thirty people, who were put up at Arya Vihara and at the homes of local trustees and friends. In addition to teaching the Current World Affairs class at the Oak Grove High School, I was preparing both lunch and dinner for all the guests every day of the week—which kept me busy. Maybe it was this high rate of activity that created a protective buffer for me against the full painful impact of what was happening just a hundred yards away on the other side of the orange grove. I felt strangely numbed and quite removed from the hectic deliberations of most of the guests. Every so often, word filtered through about his current state of health, and from time to time I caught sight of him in the living room of Pine Cottage when I was carrying food over. Oddly, I was incapable of thinking about him. At a deeper level I was aware that my knowledge and imagination could not fathom the depth of suffering that he was enduring.

LATER THAT DAY, FEBRUARY 5, THE BY NOW CUSTOMARY deterioration set in again. He had called together the leading figures from the Foundations, and in the course of talking to them, pain and discomfort had so overwhelmed him, that he broke down several times, weeping from pain and weakness. He beseeched them to leave Ojai and not to hang around waiting for his death. Most, but not all, honored his request. Of course, it was a profound dilemma. Not all of those present loved one another, but all of us, doubtlessly, were united in our all-too-imperfect love of K.

TWO DAYS LATER, ONE OF THE ENGLISH TRUSTEES PUT HIM A question: "What *really* happens to that extraordinary focus of under-standing and energy that is K after his death?" His answer was immedi-ate, short and unambiguous, "It is gone." Almost as an afterthought, poignant and poetical, and not without an enigmatic touch, he added, "If you only knew what you had missed—that vast emptiness."

When I was told about this comment, I thought it a most intriguing remark. But I never felt entirely certain whether he meant that most of us, while alive, had simply missed out on the beautiful splendor of life, its vast emptiness in that sense; or whether he was specifically referring to the fact that we had missed the opportunity of perceiving the empti-ness which he had been showing us through his teachings and his pres-ence. Or both.

Several hours later, on his own initiative, he made his last recorded statement. In it, he spoke of the energy and intelligence that had passed through and used his body. He also made it clear that, in his eyes, nobody had any inkling of the immensity of what had happened, stress-ing repeatedly that no one around him, nor in the world at large, had understood what he had been talking about. It was a shocking pro-nouncement, especially for those who had been very close to him. When I was told of it, it reminded me vividly of a story he had recounted on a number of occasions: only two of the Buddha's disciples had really understood the Awakened One, and both had died well before their master's ultimate nirvana.

IT WAS THE SECOND WEEK OF FEBRUARY, AND A SUBSTANTIAL number of guests had started to depart in compliance with his request. But a few of the trustees from overseas simply could not bring themselves to leave at this juncture; they stayed on to observe his slow decline from a distance. Thus, the number of guests who had lunch and dinner at A.V. shrank from thirty to between fifteen and twenty.

IN THE EARLY AFTERNOON OF FEBRUARY 10, I TOOK A TRAY OF food to Pine Cottage. If it hadn't been that Krishnamurti was gravely ill, the scene in the living room would have been one of leisure. A few people were sitting quietly in armchairs and on sofas, while a blazing fire roared in the fireplace, although it wasn't especially cold. The sofa had been placed lengthwise directly in front of it. On my way out I noticed that Krishnamurti, who had been lying on the sofa, was being helped by the male nurse to sit upright. It gave me a shock to see him thus: throughout his life he had maintained the independence, not only of his mind but also of his body, and now he was reduced to dependence on another for the simple act of sitting up. It brought tears to my eyes. It was pitiful.

I felt impelled to move closer to the frail figure wrapped in blankets, and I knelt down beside him. He could hardly move his head; instead, he turned his large eyes toward me. They were like mirrors, with a measureless depth to them, balanced as they were between life and death. Carefully entering his visual field, I said out loud, above the crackling of the fire, "Good afternoon, Krishnaji." I couldn't think of anything else to say.

In response, he lifted his right hand a few inches and dropped it again from utter exhaustion. There was no strength left in him. He slowly opened his mouth, mumbling something, croaking like a person dying from thirst in the desert. His voice sounded weak, and his words were drowned out by the crackling of the fire. I touched his hand very lightly with the tips of my fingers, hardly sensing the pulse beneath the silken skin. Swallowing hard to overcome the upsurge of pity and pain within me, I murmured, "Thank you, sir. Goodbye."

He rolled his eyes in acknowledgment and heaved a heavy sigh. It was the last time we met. Having seen him in this pitiful state, I wished only that his suffering would end.

Dr. P. kept us informed about the progress of his illness, giving regular briefings in the sitting room. Besides, he composed daily news bulletins, which described his current condition. These notices were posted next to the telephone in the kitchen, so that anyone answering an inquiry could read out the printed statement. There were a great many calls from the media and from people around the world, who wanted to know his state of health.

BULLETIN #1, February 13, 1986: 'Krishnaji slept well. He had no pain or any other physical discomfort. He feels weak. He does not wish to talk much. His temperature, pulse, and respiration and blood pressure are within normal limits. Intravenous nourishment adequate. He likes to watch TV and listen to the news.'

BULLETIN #2, same day (Medical Bulletin for people who ask about Krishnaji's condition as of Feb. 13, 1986): 'Krishnaji had a good night's rest. His temperature went up twice for short periods. He sat propped up before the fireplace enjoying the sight of the dancing flames. He wanted the world news read out to him. Sat for 5 or 6 hours like this, then rested. Nutrition is maintained through intravenous means. He makes up his sleep with short naps during the day. He watched television in the evening. Signed Dr. P.'

BULLETIN #3, February 14, 1986 (Medical report on Krishnaji for friends who ask about him [not for the press] as of Feb. 14, 1986):

'Krishnaji did not have a good morning. He did not have a good night, either, even though he had no pain. In the forenoon he had two small attacks of pain that quickly passed. He preferred to stay in bed, rather than go to the sitting room. He had a low grade fever for a short while. Dr. Deutsch visited him in the afternoon and they had some interesting conversations about movies, golf, skiing. Krishnaji slept well. Dr. P.'

BULLETIN #4, February 15, 1986: 'Krishnaji slept well, continuously for 8 hours, and woke up fresh and alert. He felt weak and tired and was inclined to doze off. There was not much of a fever but perspiration continued. He watched a movie in the afternoon and exchanged some jokes with the people around. He went to sleep at 8:30 p.m.'

BULLETIN #5, February 17, 1986: 'Krishnamurti slept fairly well until 3 a.m., Feb. 16th. From then on it was rather a rough day. The whole day he had pain with varying intensity at irregular intervals. By evening he was completely exhausted and wanted to sleep. His usual sleeping dose was given at 7:00 p.m. He could not sleep for an hour due to the pain, but later, as the pain started diminishing, he became unconscious and passed away at 12:10 a.m. on Monday, Feb. 17, 1986. Dr. Parchure.'

We as a group visited on Feb. 17/12
26 years later to the day.

# EPILOGUE

TEN YEARS HAVE GONE BY SINCE KRISHNAMURTI DIED, shortly after midnight on February 17, 1986. During these years, the greatest change has been to live without Krishnamurti, the friend of wisdom, the friend of life and truth. The Schools and Foundations, of course, go on—even though quite a few trustees, directors and staff came and went. Many other changes have occurred, within ourselves and worldwide. There were constant challenges. Most important of all was the question: What would we, together and individually, do with this jewel that we had been given?

He left behind an enormous legacy—if measured only in terms of quantity: over twenty-five hundred audio recordings, over five hundred videotapes, close to one hundred thousand pages of printed material (books and transcripts), thousands of pages of letters and handwritten manuscripts, numerous photographs, and a considerable amount of film footage—in short, a literal mountain of archive material, much of it unpublished. Clearly, the preservation and publication of this material is important, both from a historical and a practical point of view. But Krishnamurti himself emphasized that his teachings are a living thing, and that books and other records are not.

So that's what we are left with—the living thing, our own lives. How ready are we to take on the challenge that Krishnamurti put to all of us: that of being completely free? Not only free from fear and conflict—although that is obviously of vital importance—but free, simply free, unconditionally free.

# ENDNOTES

1. The original version of this joke was told by Krishnamurti at the very beginning of his famous 'Truth is a pathless land' speech, in which he dissolved the 'Order of the star', at Ommen, The Netherlands, August 1929 (reprinted in the September 1929 issue of the 'International Star Bulletin').

   A highly modified version of it can be found in the book *Krishnamurti to Himself* (London & New York, 1988), entry of Saturday, April 23, 1983 (pp.86–87).

   A 'final' version of it was recounted by Krishnamurti during the 1st Question-and-Answer Meeting at Brockwood Park, England, August 28, 1984. On this occasion, he revealed that he 'thought out' this story.

2. Alan Hooker, *Vegetarian Gourmet Cookery*, Santa Rosa: 101 Productions, 1970.

3. *Mind in the Waters*, Joan McIntyre, ed., Charles Scribner's Sons, New York & Sierra Club Books, San Francisco, 1974

4. *Things of the Mind—Dialogues with J. Krishnamurti*, composed & arranged by Brij Khare, Philosophical Library, New York, 1985

5. Richard Feynman (1918–1988), U.S. theoretical physicist, worked at Los Alamos, NM on the atomic bomb project from 1942–45. Author of *Surely You're Joking, Mr Feynman*, 1985.